Sustainability Assessment

Criteria and Processes

Robert B. Gibson
with
Selma Hassan, Susan Holtz, James Tansey and
Graham Whitelaw

D1369022

London • Sterling, VA

First published by Earthscan in the UK and USA in 2005

ISBN-13: 978-1-84407-050-3   hardback
ISBN-10:   1-84407-050-6   hardback
ISBN-13: 978-1-84407-051-0   paperback
ISBN-10:   1-84407-051-4   paperback

Typesetting by JS Typesetting Ltd, Porthcawl, Mid Glamorgan
Printed and bound in the UK by Bath Press, Bath
Cover design by Ruth Bateson

For a full list of publications please contact:

Earthscan
8–12 Camden High Street
London, NW1 0JH, UK
Tel: +44 (0)20 7387 8558
Fax: +44 (0)20 7387 8998
Email: earthinfo@earthscan.co.uk
Web: **www.earthscan.co.uk**

22883 Quicksilver Drive, Sterling, VA 20166-2012, USA

Earthscan is an imprint of James and James (Science Publishers) Ltd and publishes in
association with the International Institute for Environment and Development

A catalogue record for this book is available from the British Library

Library of Congress Cataloging-in-Publication Data

Gibson, Robert B., 1950–
    Sustainability assessment : making the world better, one undertaking at a time /
Robert B. Gibson ; with Selma Hassan ... [et al.].
        p. cm.
    Includes bibliographical references and index.
    ISBN 1-84407-050-6 – ISBN 1-84407-051-4
  1. Sustainable development. I. Hassan, Selma.   II. Title.
    HC79.E5G513 2005
    338.9'27–dc22

                                            2005018172

Contents

List of Figures, Tables and Boxes

Figures

Tables

Boxes

Preface

Matchmaking·

For the past decade or so a couple of good ideas have been circling each other in what may be a semi-conscious mating ritual. On the surface at least, they seem well matched. But so far there have been only a few amicable meetings and the occasional tentative embrace. Our task here is to propose a union, perhaps even sketch out the pre-nuptial contract.

The marriageable pair are environmental assessment and the pursuit of sustainability – two of the major concepts introduced over the past few decades to improve the odds of continued human survival on this planet. While both are of age and have had some experience in the world, neither can claim to be fully developed. For that, arguably, each needs the other.

Something old, something new

The sustainability idea is both very ancient and quite recent. Before the modern era, most cultures, excepting those with elites devoted to conquest, aimed for stability and continuity. Their gods encouraged humility and their elders stressed respect for tradition. Change still happened, of course. But it was not sought. People saw that innovation was more likely to bring peril than progress, and even mere curiosity could open a Pandora's box of trouble. Vestiges of this inclination to stick with the tried and true are still evident in aspects of most people's lives today. But as a dominant concern it was gradually abandoned over the last few hundred years in favour of progress through technological and economic advance. The expectation, or at least the hope, for progress has now spread almost everywhere. For many people, in many places, the benefits have been huge. But there have also always been costs, some of them also huge, and in the latter part of the 20th century this led to the resurgence, in a new form, of the old sustainability idea.

The story of how this happened is complicated and there is far from universal agreement on how it should be interpreted. The basics, however, were quite clearly centred on a simple tension. On one side were the major political and economic powers, promoting progress through faster and greater economic growth. These included subscribers to the cheerful belief that a self-adjusting positive market mechanism would ensure progress in perpetuity if barriers to economic and technological advance were properly eliminated. On the other side was a widening circle of other organizations inclined to question the agenda of progress through growth, at least as it was ordinarily practised. The critics pointed to the persistence of desperate poverty, the deepening of dangerous inequities, the proliferation of risky technologies and the degradation of essential ecological systems. The overwhelming evidence, they said, was that economic growth had failed to deliver benefits where they were most needed, that it was destroying its own foundations and that things could not possibly go on this way.

The resolution, most influentially proposed in 1987 by the World Commission on Environment and Development (the Brundtland Commission), was 'sustainable development' – a concept that promised to bridge the gulf between the advocates and critics of progress through growth. As terminology, 'sustainable development' was wildly successful. Within a few years, governance bodies in a host of jurisdictions had officially embraced the idea. Within a decade, governments had written it into a wide range of pronouncements, policies and even laws. Just what it meant was less certain. Scholars, activists and competing powerful interests debated whether sustainable development was an oxymoron or a redundancy, whether the noun prevailed over the adjective and whether interpretative flexibility was its chief merit or its fatal flaw. Some key essentials, however, were soon evident.

If nothing else, 'sustainable development' stood as a critique of the status quo. No one would have bothered with the idea; certainly no governments would have rushed to embrace it, if the old faith in growth as an automatic path to well-being had still been plausible. The Brundtland Commission, which had been assigned to address the problems of poverty and environmental degradation, saw that many present conditions and practices were not sustainable, that the trend was towards disaster, and that serious reforms were needed to reverse this. Conventional growth was not just an unreliable route to real progress; it was a path in the wrong direction. Governments that claimed commitment to sustainability mostly failed to accompany their words with any substantial shifts in behaviour. But at least as a matter of public image, they found it wise to wrap themselves in the shroud of sustainability and this put them, at least officially, with the critics.

No doubt some authorities adopted sustainability as form rather than substance and were happy to hide behind the uncertainties of interpretation. Some fundamentals were, however, clear from the outset. Perhaps the most important insight was that long-term gains depend on intricate combinations of social, economic and ecological factors that intertwine in different ways depending on local and regional conditions. The Brundtland report documented this in the interplay of poverty reduction and environmental rehabilitation. But complex interrelationships and context dependencies were evident everywhere and these have remained the biggest challenge for sustainability implementation. Over the past decade and a half, continuing analysis and implementation efforts have gradually clarified the basic requirements of sustainability. But there has been no easy solution to the complexity and contextuality problems.

A suitable partner

Environmental assessment is thirty-some but still just approaching maturity. Its official birthplace was the US *National Environmental Policy Act* of 1969, which included a few brief clauses requiring proponents of environmentally significant undertakings to consider the environmental implications before US government approval could be granted. The rationale was simple: because environmental damages were too costly to tolerate and too costly to repair, prevention had to be encouraged. And because existing incentives were evidently insufficient, new obligations had to be imposed. The US law was one version. Over the following three decades, environmental assessment requirements were adopted in one form or another by most capable governments and by other governance bodies ranging from multilateral aid institutions to small municipalities.

Always there were debates about how mandatory, comprehensive, open, broadly applied, forceful and subversive of convention environmental assessment requirements should be. In most jurisdictions these matters are still contested today. Implementation also remains highly imperfect almost everywhere. But gradually and unevenly assessment has evolved towards greater scope and ambition. Attention to cumulative effects and application to strategic level policies, plans and programmes as well as specific projects have been the best recognized recent developments. In addition, there has been more critical examination of the purposes of proposed undertakings and alternatives that might serve these purposes better, plus more inclusive and better integrated attention to social, economic and cultural as well as ecological effects, greater willingness to respect local knowledge, and deeper appreciation of the limits of science, the roles of values and the inevitability of surprise.

The culmination of these changes is now just emerging in the form of a more demanding set of decision criteria. Environmental assessment processes – and similar planning, evaluation and decision making processes under other names – are being pushed to apply a higher test in deliberations about what kinds of undertakings should be assessed, what concerns should be given most attention, what proposals merit approval and what considerations should be imposed. In the past the main objective was to predict and avoid, or at least mitigate, the potentially significant negative effects of major undertakings. The new and higher objective is to plan and implement the best responses to publicly examined problems and opportunities, and to ensure overall long-term gains.

This is where the pursuit of sustainability enters as a marriageable partner. With the higher test, the key challenge for proponents is, as a recent Canadian assessment panel put it, to show 'the extent to which the Undertaking may make a positive overall contribution towards the attainment of ecological and community sustainability, both at the local and regional levels'.

On the surface there is nothing very novel here. Overall long-term gain is what proponents and approval authorities have conventionally promised, though often just implicitly as an assumed result of more heavily emphasized short-term economic benefits. The difference when environmental assessment processes impose the 'contribution to sustainability' test is that claims about long-term gains must be made and defended directly. There is no assumption that immediate economic growth will bring lasting benefits. Moreover, in properly open and independent assessment processes, the claims and evaluations are subject to more effective public scrutiny than is typical in conventional approval processes. Finally, with the sustainability test environmental assessments must attempt integrated consideration of the relevant social, economic and ecological factors. This is, as we have seen, a basic requirement of the pursuit of sustainability.

Environmental assessment thus seems to be a particularly suitable mate for sustainability efforts. In many jurisdictions, it is the main open process for the planning and evaluation of new projects and, increasingly, new policies, plans and programmes. It is both established and adaptable. It is designed to force neglected considerations into conventional decision making. Well conceived assessment processes include critical examination of purposes and alternatives, and cover the full suite of social, economic and ecological factors in a single process. And environmental assessment is meant for case specific, context sensitive application.

Many environmental assessment processes, especially newer ones, are officially committed to furthering sustainability. Unfortunately, there is rarely much evidence that anyone has given much serious thought to the implications. While the potential fit between environmental assessment and the pursuit of sustainability is good, few existing assessment processes manage to serve environmental objectives as well as they should. Even fewer are designed to serve sustainability purposes and, so far, most efforts to pursue sustainability through environmental assessments have been weak, though there have been a few exemplary exceptions. The partnership, mostly, has great potential.

Drafting the terms of union

If there is to be a successful union of environmental assessment and the pursuit of sustainability, we will need to be clearer about how to translate a general commitment to sustainability into a workable set of practical assessment criteria, process design characteristics and implementation methods.

We will have to clarify what sustainability requires, and identify well integrated means of ensuring that these requirements are addressed. The predominant current approaches encourage separate attention to social, economic and biophysical matters – the three 'pillars' on which most descriptions of sustainability are constructed. For effectively integrated sustainability assessment, the pillar boundaries will have to be overcome and some other way found to manage the multitudes of considerations without obscuring their intercon-nections.

We will also have to provide guidance on how to deal with trade-offs. In a world as imperfect as this one, most proposed undertakings will bring sustain-ability losses as well as sustainability gains. It will, therefore, be necessary to determine when certain sustainability objectives may have priority over others, which compromises and sacrifices may be acceptable, and how overall con-tributions to sustainability may be identified.

We will have to set out the practical means – the essential characteristics of deliberative and decision making processes, the necessary and useful tools, and the openings for adjustment – by which the considerable challenges of sustainability assessment can be met by ordinary officials, proponents and citizens with limited resources and plenty of other obligations.

And all of this we will have to accomplish with due respect for the particulars of context. Only so much can be set out in general rules, generic guidance and standard procedures.

The book you have now opened will not satisfy any of these needs finally or completely. While some of the basics are easy enough, sustainability assess-ment faces a world that is difficult and complicated. It must deal not only with uncertainties but whole vast areas of mystery. Such is the nature of the social, economic and ecological realities in which we live and in which all assessable undertakings intervene. No doubt we will learn a great deal from further experience and more careful analysis. Perhaps the initial steps taken here in the very early days of sustainability assessment will soon seem hope-lessly primitive. We can live with that. This is only the stage of matchmaking and honeymoon advice. Marriage counselling will come soon enough.

Acknowledgements

Much of the initial research and thinking behind this book began with a monograph (Gibson, 2002) and background papers prepared under a research contribution agreement with the Canadian Environmental Assessment Agency. This was followed by more particular studies on sustainability assessment options for the Canadian International Development Agency. Neither agency bears responsibility for the contents of this book, and neither should be presumed to agree with the positions taken or the recommendations made. Nevertheless, both provided important support and have been admirably quick to recognize that sustainability-based assessment is worthy of careful examination.

In addition to the contributors recognized on the title page, a long list of excellent scholars and practitioners assisted our research on sustainability assessment and the preparation of this book. We would like especially to thank Jennifer Agnolin, Petr Cizek, Peter Croal, Theo Hacking, David Hirsh, Tony Hodge, René Kemp, Lorri Krebs, David Lawrence, Tamara Levine, Angus Morrison-Saunders, Saeed Parto, Doris Pokorny, Jenny Pope, John Robinson, Erin Rogozinski, Hendrik Rosenthal, Jack Santa-Barbara, Lindsay Staples, Jenna Watson, Bob Weir and Susan Wismer. Thanks also to the wonderfully patient and helpful folks at Earthscan, especially Rob West, Ruth Mayo, Victoria Brown and Camille Adamson.

List of Acronyms and Abbreviations

Cdn$	Canadian dollars
CFC	chlorofluorocarbon
DDT	dichlorodiphenyltrichloroethane
EIS	environmental impact statement
GDP	gross domestic product
GIS	geographic information systems
GNP	gross national product
IUCN	World Conservation Union (*formerly* International Union for the Conservation of Nature and Natural Resources)
LA21	Local Agenda 21
MMSD	Mining, Minerals and Sustainable Development project
NEPA	National Environmental Policy Act
NGO	non-governmental organization
OECD	Organisation for Economic Co-operation and Development
t/d	tonnes per day
UK	United Kingdom
UN	United Nations
UNCED	United Nations Conference on Environment and Development
UNDP	United Nations Development Programme
UNESCO	United Nations Educational, Scientific and Cultural Organization
US	United States

1

Beginnings

Stumbling Towards Sustainability Assessment

Beginning in Labrador

They say that on the seventh day, God hurled stones at Labrador. Perhaps it is true – even by Canadian standards, Labrador is a hard land. The north coast is all rocky islands and headlands swept by Arctic waters flowing out into the North Atlantic. The interior is more rock, rivers, barrens and boreal forest. And yet for millennia Inuit and Innu people have lived there successfully – the Inuit on the coast, harvesting seal and fish, the Innu in the interior, relying on the caribou. European contact and the arrival of new residents led to changes in economy and culture, and more recent decades have brought more outside influences. But for most people in northern Labrador the hard land is home; it has been so since time beyond memory and will continue to be in any desirable future.

Whether the future of northern Labrador will be desirable for people who consider it a permanent home is a question of sustainability. It is a matter of how to ensure viable and fulfilling livelihoods over the long haul from one generation to the next. Essentially, the same concerns apply to communities everywhere, since the basic challenges of sustainability face all of them. But so far only a few places have chosen, or been permitted, to confront these matters explicitly. Northern Labrador has been the site of one such attempt.

Between 1997 and 2002, a proposed major mining project beside Voisey's Bay, a deep inlet on Labrador's north coast, was the subject of an environmental assessment and a set of associated and consequential deliberations that wrestled directly, often openly, and by some interim measures successfully, with the project's potential contribution to local and regional sustainability.

Serious application of sustainability-based evaluation criteria is not yet common in environmental assessments or other decision making on important undertakings. 'Contribution to sustainability' is frequently presented as an official objective of environmental assessment. In a host of related practical circumstances – urban neighbourhood planning, corporate responsibility reporting, regional growth management initiatives, new versions of progress indicators and so on – reasonably comprehensive lists of sustainability considerations have been adopted. But true sustainability assessments, carefully designed and intentionally influential, are still rare. The Voisey's Bay case in Labrador is just one example of an emerging practice and, inevitably, it has some unique characteristics. Nonetheless, it captures well the basic needs and challenges involved in sustainability assessment.

On Voisey's Bay

The Voisey's Bay mining project began in a moment of extraordinary good fortune. In 1993, prospectors Albert Chislett and Chris Verbiski, returning home from work further north, flew over the Voisey's Bay area just as sunlight from a particular angle reflected off a mineralized outcrop. They landed to investigate and discovered rich deposits of nickel with associated copper and cobalt. The most spectacular part of their discovery, a body of exceptionally high grade ore called 'the ovoid', was later found to contain about 31 million tonnes of reserves – 2.9 per cent nickel, 1.69 per cent copper and 0.14 per cent cobalt (Inco, 2002a). Moreover, it was right at the surface, mineable by open pit methods and conveniently near tidewater. Subsequent drilling delineated over 100 million tonnes of additional ore underground in less rich but still commercially extractable deposits.

In 1996, Inco Ltd paid Cdn$4.3 billion for the claims and associated drilling information. Though the company later announced a Cdn$2 billion write-down of that investment, the Voisey's Bay deposits continued to be seen as the foundation for an economically important development for the province of Newfoundland and Labrador, as well as for the northern Labrador region. Deliberations on the nature of the development and conditions for approval had to overcome a variety of difficulties, including court challenges and high-stake negotiating positions, but in June 2002 the five key parties – Inco, the federal and provincial governments, the Innu Nation and the Labrador Inuit Association – announced an agreement. It covered the mine, mill and concentrator operation at Voisey's Bay, plus a closely linked metal processing/refining operation to be established at Argentia in Newfoundland.[1] The announced overall capital cost of mine and smelter components was Cdn$2.9 billion.

During the negotiations, Inco was understandably most interested in recouping its investment and maximizing its financial returns. For the provincial and local interests, however, durable longer-term gains were more important.

Expecting long-term gains from a mining undertaking may seem futile. Non-renewable resource extraction projects are generally poor candidates as contributors to sustainability. Mine project life is limited by orebody geology and made uncertain by market fluctuations. Often the boom is closely followed by a bust, and the lasting local effects – economic, social and ecological – are largely negative.[2] This has frequently been accepted as the nature of the industry, though the busts usually inspire some last ditch efforts by local residents and relevant governments to encourage further exploration in hopes of life-extending discoveries, or to attract some other employer to the area.

Options beyond that have been limited, though some jurisdictions have taken anticipatory steps to build 'heritage funds' while the resource income is flowing, to diversify mining centre economies or to foster downstream processing – additional ore milling, refining and smelting, perhaps even manufacturing using the product – that might continue after the initial orebody is exhausted.

Provincial authorities in the Voisey's Bay case took the latter route. Long dependent on the fishery and often frustrated by failed development ventures in other sectors, the province of Newfoundland and Labrador insisted that the Voisey's Bay ore be smelted in Newfoundland. This, in the provincial view, would make the Voisey's Bay mine a stepping stone to a technologically advanced and globally competitive smelting industry in the province and an accordingly longer stream of economic benefits. After an extended campaign fought partly in the business media and partly in private negotiations, the province did get Inco to agree to process the ore in Newfoundland (Newfoundland and Labrador, 2002a). This may not be enough to win the province a lasting role in the industry. However, the province has certainly shown commitment to more durable gains.

While the difficult contest over the processing question attracted the bulk of press reporting on the Voisey's Bay project, more innovative steps, from a sustainability perspective, were taken in the deliberations about the mine itself. In the processing negotiations, the province's longer-term concerns centred on conventional economic development considerations – creating more jobs, capturing value added benefits from provincial resources, enhancing provincial revenues, fostering economic diversification. Environmental issues received some attention and sustainability may have been an implicit objective, but it was not pursued in a comprehensive or well integrated manner.

The mining part of the package was treated differently. At Voisey's Bay, sustainability effects were the central issue. This was in part because the mining was to be in aboriginal homelands and in part because the proposed undertaking was reviewed through an extraordinary environmental assessment process.

Homelands

The lands in question were traditionally shared by the Innu and the Inuit (perhaps not often simultaneously or always amicably) and remain part of their traditional territories. Emish is the old Innu name for the area where the nickel deposits were found. Tasiujatsoak is the Inuit name for the nearby deep inlet, which they used long before Amos Voisey, a fur trader and merchant, settled there in the 1800s. Although the usual name now is Voisey's Bay, the area remains Innu and Inuit land, at least in as much as aboriginal title is recognized, since neither people ever signed away title to these lands. As a consequence, the Innu Nation and the Labrador Inuit Association, as bodies representing the Inuit and Innu, became participating government authorities in the evaluations, negotiations and decisions on the Voisey's Bay mining proposal.

The Labrador Inuit Association represents most residents of five communities on the Labrador north coast including Nain (population 1200), which is located 35km north-east of the mine site. While the Inuit have been subject to European colonial, evangelical and commercial influence since the 18th century, they signed no treaties. Their land claim was accepted for negotiation by the federal government in 1977 and has since moved gradually towards resolution.[3] Among the people included are descendants of Amos Voisey and other settlers whose families are now assumed to have partial Inuit ancestry.[4]

The Innu Nation represents the roughly 600 Mushaua Innu who now live in Natuashish, about 80km south-east of Voisey's Bay. The Mushaua Innu were nomadic hunter-gatherers in the Labrador interior until 1967 when they were moved to Davis Inlet (which the Innu call Utshimassits: the place of the boss). The coastal island site was inconvenient for access to mainland hunting and other culturally familiar activities and, not surprisingly, the social, cultural and economic effects were largely tragic.[5] Whether things will be better in Natuashish, the new mainland community established in 2002, remains uncertain, but that move symbolizes Innu determination to make a better future. The Innu have also been negatively affected by low level military test flights over their lands and this led to lengthy and bitter conflicts with the federal government. The government has, however, recognized the Innu land claim, which was submitted in 1977. Negotiations began in 1991 and a Canada/Newfoundland/Innu framework agreement was signed in 1996 (INAC, 1996b).

In their different ways, the Innu and Inuit communities of northern Labrador are hybrids of the traditional and the modern. The people have been, to varying degrees, separated from many of their old ways. But they are not far in time or place from the traditional understandings and practices that over countless generations made it possible to sustain themselves. They are still close enough to the land to feel the interdependence of the social, ecological, economic and cultural aspects of their lives. Perhaps their traditional lives were rarely easy. Probably the customary practices of the Innu and Inuit were in other respects as flawed as those of other cultures. Nonetheless, their ways of getting along with each other and being part of the land worked well enough – were sufficiently respectful, flexible and sensitive – to demonstrate the possibility, nature and importance of durable livelihoods.

For both Innu and Inuit the prospect of a nearby mining project raised hopes and fears. It brought the promise of new economic opportunities and associated improvements in regional infrastructure and services. But it also meant less control over traditional lands, more disturbance of wildlife and damage to local ecosystems, and further disruption of already fragile social conditions. Moreover, the gains could be brief and the negative effects permanent.

In the northern Labrador communities, the mine became the focus for discussions about future relations between traditional renewable resource harvesting activities and the modern, globalized market economy. While the traditional activities had long been the foundation for survival and identity, they no longer seemed to offer a sufficient basis for community livelihoods. Unfortunately the mine, like many other modern economy options for places like northern Labrador, offered only a transitory economic alternative. That might be good enough for people willing to move from one such opportunity to the next. But for people with deep roots and a long-term commitment to their home place, the mine would not be acceptable unless it built the short-term opportunity into something both desirable and lasting.

That test of acceptability – grounds for confidence that there will be desirable and lasting gains – might seem obviously reasonable. But it is not commonly applied in major project decision making. As a rule, proposed undertakings gain approval if they have devoted and apparently capable proponents, however narrowly motivated, and if there is no persuasive evidence of likely undue harm to any interests deemed worthy of attention. While that is a simplified version of the general rule, it is the essence of processes centred on limited restriction of enterprise. In the Voisey's Bay case this general rule was replaced. How this was accomplished and what it entailed is worthy of attention.

A landmark assessment

From the outset of the Voisey's Bay project deliberations, the Inuit and the Innu made it clear that they had long-term rights and interests to be respected.[6] On the strength of their claims to aboriginal title, both groups were recognized as relevant authorities for key project evaluations and decisions especially in two processes that were to play particularly important roles in forcing attention to sustainability considerations. These were the Voisey's Bay mine and mill environmental assessment review and the subsequent negotiation of impact and benefit agreements.

The Voisey's Bay environmental assessment was a landmark in Canadian and global assessment practice because it introduced 'contribution to sustainability' as the basic test of acceptability.

As a major project with inevitable environmental significance, the proposed Voisey's Bay mine-mill was subject to assessment requirements as well as Inuit and Innu approval. To consolidate the review, the four government bodies signed a memorandum of understanding and drafted terms of reference for a single review by a five member environmental assessment panel. The panel, with appointees recommended by the four parties, then prepared guidelines for the proponent to follow in preparing an environmental impact statement that would be reviewed through a set of public hearings in the relevant communities, including Nain and Utshimassits.

Aside from the willing agreement among four parties with a considerable history of tension and conflict, none of this was particularly remarkable. Consolidation of hearings where two or more jurisdictions are involved is a common means of avoiding duplication and inefficiency. The panel's terms of reference were broad and progressive – covering the full range of 'social, economic, recreational, cultural, spiritual and aesthetic conditions that influence the life of humans and communities', as well as the biophysical aspects of the 'environment' – and including attention to traditional ecological knowledge, cumulative effects and the precautionary principle.[7] But all of these elements had been included before in environmental assessment practice.

The panel took a further interpretive step. It concluded that its obligations, taken together, imposed a requirement to consider the sustainability effects of the proposed undertaking. 'Promotion of sustainable development', the panel observed, 'is a fundamental purpose of environmental impact assessment'. Accordingly, the panel, established 'contribution to sustainability' as the key evaluative test. In its *Environmental Impact Statement Guidelines for the Review of the Voisey's Bay Mine and Mill Undertaking,* the panel stated:

> *It is the Panel's interpretation that progress towards sustainable development will require the following:*
>
> * *the preservation of ecosystem integrity, including the capability of natural systems to maintain their structure and functions and to support biological diversity;*
> * *respect for the right of future generations to the sustainable use of renewable resources; and*
> * *the attainment of durable and equitable social and economic benefits.*
>
> *Therefore, in reviewing the EIS [environmental impact statement] and other submissions, the Panel will consider:*
>
> * *the extent to which the Undertaking may make a positive overall contribution towards the attainment of ecological and community sustainability, both at the local and regional levels;*
> * *how the planning and design of the Undertaking have addressed the three objectives of sustainable development stated above;*
> * *how monitoring, management and reporting systems will attempt to ensure continuous progress towards sustainability; and*
> * *appropriate indicators to determine whether this progress is being maintained (Voisey's Bay Panel, 1997, s3.3).*[8]

The guidelines set a national precedent by setting out sustainability-based decision criteria. These obliged the proponent to meet a considerably higher test than is usual in environmental assessments. In most assessment practice the focus is on avoidance or mitigation of significant negative environmental effects. Sometimes 'environmental effects' are defined broadly to include aspects of the human as well as biophysical environment. Sometimes the need for and purposes of the undertaking are to be addressed. And sometimes, comparative evaluation of alternatives is required. But typically, the working objective is just to recognize and reduce any potentially severe adverse effects, to ensure the project damages are acceptably minimal. Demanding 'a positive overall contribution' is very different.

Especially for a mining project, making a case for the project as 'a positive overall contribution towards the attainment of ecological and community sustainability, both at the local and regional levels' is quite clearly more difficult than merely showing that any significant adverse effects will be mitigated to an acceptable level. The panel made it clear that it expected Inco to show that it would create or enhance beneficial effects as well as mitigate the negative ones. The panel also clearly saw the sustainability test as reason for attention to the project's legacy – how closure would be managed and what would be left behind. In other words, an overall positive contribution to ecological and community sustainability would have to be demonstrated for an undertaking with a limited anticipated economic life and no prospect for ecological improvement given that the area was essentially pristine at the outset.

Inco was not visibly distressed by the challenge. Less than six months after the guidelines were finalized, the company submitted its proposal and impact assessment statement. Not everyone was persuaded that the submission passed the assigned test. A consultant for the Innu Nation prepared a detailed report arguing that the proponent had failed on many grounds to meet the panel's requirements and to establish that the project would make a positive overall contribution to sustainability (Green, 1998). Additional concerns were raised in the public hearings. While these covered a variety of specifics, a common theme centred on how to avoid the boom and bust effects of a short mine life.

In March 1999, the panel issued its report. The panel concluded that the project could be acceptable if specified conditions were met and offered 107 recommendations on a wide range of project related matters. Of these, the most significant focused on steps to address concerns about the durability of project benefits and to ensure avoidance of negative effects. The panel urged the decision making authorities to ensure:

- that the lifespan of the project was sufficient to permit establishment of lasting benefits;
- that land claim negotiations were completed before the project was allowed to proceed;
- that specific agreements were reached with the Inuit and Innu on project impacts and benefits, and on co-management of environmental reviews during project implementation (Voisey's Bay Panel, 1999).

Building a bridge

The life span issue raised the most substantial implications for project design and implementation. As initially proposed, the mining operations would feed a 20,000 tonnes per day (t/d) concentrator. If sufficiently rich underground resources were confirmed as expected, the project life with the 20,000 t/d mill would be 20–25 years. But if only the very rich 'ovoid' deposit were mined and the less attractive underground deposits judged economically questionable, the project life could be as short as seven years. The panel referred to this as the 'scoop and run scenario' (Voisey's Bay Panel, 1999) and recommended means of ensuring a longer project life to avoid negative boom and bust effects, ensure more lasting gains, and permit better preparation for local economic viability after the mine closed.

Chief among the possible means of extending project life was reducing the annual production rate by allowing only a smaller mill. Inco argued in its assessment submission that a significantly smaller capacity mill (anything below 15,000 t/d) would not be economically viable. The Innu and Inuit, however, insisted that if the sustainability test were to mean anything at all in this case, then durable contributions to community livelihoods would have to be provided, and for this a reasonable project life span had to be ensured. Mill capacity therefore remained a central issue during the post-assessment negotiations. In the end, Inco agreed to use a 6000 t/d mill, at least initially, and with further delineation of the Voisey's Bay deposits it confidently predicted a project life span greater than 30 years (Inco, 2002a).

Ensuring a 30-year mine life is not the achievement of sustainability. For the mine it is just a longer period of boom before the bust. For the communities it is just an extended but still limited period of income and opportunity. The key issue for sustainability is whether the longer run of revenues and opportunities strengthens the foundations for viable and durable livelihoods after the mine closes. Like other necessarily temporary undertakings, the Voisey's Bay nickel mine can make a contribution to sustainability only if the limited period of economic viability serves as a bridge to a more sustainable future.

While the panel did not use the bridging concept explicitly, it recognized the link between a longer project life span and the potential for constructing a more lasting economic base. A longer period of mine operation, the panel observed, would:

> ...enable workers to earn pensions and accumulate savings beyond one generation, and to develop industrial and business skills that could support new economic activities. At the same time, communities could use the increased flow of income over a long period to diversify their local economies. A long duration would also reduce the risk of negative effects associated with the community boom-and-bust effect (Voisey's Bay Panel, 1999, p8).

By itself, however, an extended mine life would not ensure successful bridging to a more sustainable long-term future for the communities near the mine. Two additional requirements would have to be met: first, sufficient resources and opportunities would have to flow from the mine to the communities and second, these would have to be used effectively to build a more durable base for the decades following mine closure.

Some of this extended beyond the ambit of the panel's review. But the panel did emphasize measures to ensure that the local communities gained the economic and political wherewithal to pursue a more sustainable future. This was addressed in the second set of key panel recommendations, which concerned relations between the project and the aboriginal title holders, in particular relations that would be established through land claim agreements and impact and benefit agreements.

In Canada, negotiation of land claim agreements is the conventional, though usually very slow, means of addressing the claims of aboriginal groups that retain title to traditional territories and rights to continue traditional activities. Land claim agreements vary but typically involve recognition of ownership over some portion of the traditional lands, certain rights to use larger areas (e.g. for hunting and trapping), defined roles in land management decision making (e.g. on wildlife management and in environmental assessments), other self-government provisions, financial compensation and shares in resource royalties (INAC, 1996a).

In northern Labrador, both the Inuit and Innu had submitted claims in 1977, and neither had been resolved despite some years of negotiation with federal and provincial government authorities. The panel urged that claim agreements be reached prior to project approval to solidify and specify the communities' foundation of authority, to establish basic arrangements for sharing mine royalties and other benefits, and to provide a firm foundation for participation in co-management bodies that would monitor and guide mine development. Failing that, the panel recommended negotiation of similar packages of provisions specific to the mine. Either way the idea was to give the local people the capacity to capture significant overall gains from the mine and to use these in ways that would enhance their communities' long-term prospects.

The panel saw negotiation of impact and benefit agreements between the Innu and Inuit and the mining company in the same light. Impact and benefit agreements are case specific documents that set out, for example, commitments for training and employment of local people, for provision of opportunities for local businesses, and for environmental monitoring and protection. While their scope and influence are generally smaller than those of land claim agreement provisions, they too can be important means of maximizing local gains and minimizing damages.

In August 1999, five months after the panel's report was submitted, the federal and provincial governments announced their general acceptance of most of the panel's recommendations. The governments refused to commit to reaching agreement on land claims prior to project approval (DFO, 1999; Newfoundland and Labrador, 1999) – a decision the Innu and Inuit challenged in court (Robinson, 1999) – but did proceed, more or less as the panel had recommended, to ensure equivalent case-specific arrangements.

Making a difference

The June 2002 project approval in principle for the Voisey's Bay mine and mill covers a variety of substantive conditions and continuing processes to minimize negative effects and enhance local benefits and participation over the whole project life. These include, in addition to the applicable regulatory obligations:

- an environmental co-management agreement that establishes a joint body (with two representatives from each of the four governance parties) to

> monitor project effects, review new and to-be specified project-related actions including tailings and waste rock disposal options, and recommend necessary adjustments;
> - impact and benefit agreements – one between the company and the Innu Nation and a separate one between the company and the Labrador Inuit Association – that allow the project to proceed on traditional lands in return for certain special arrangements for revenue sharing, local employment and contracting, training programmes and community roles in ongoing review of project implementation (Newfoundland and Labrador, 2002b);
> - commitments to address additional details in special Voisey's Bay chapters in land claim final agreements with the Inuit and Innu (Newfoundland and Labrador, 2002b).

Together, the key elements of the Voisey's Bay project agreement represent a significant effort to meet the sustainability test. The major concession by Inco to use a 6000 t/d instead of 20,000 t/d mill to extend project life, and the set of arrangements dealing with community participation in benefits and impacts, address a broad range of sustainability-related concerns – social, economic and ecological – in a reasonably well integrated package. The agreement also provides for reviews and adjustments intended to increase prospects for a continuing flow of benefits.

Adoption of sustainability-based decision criteria in the Voisey's Bay case clearly made a difference. It changed how the main issues in the case were addressed, how the project was designed and what was approved. The higher test of 'contribution to sustainability' shifted the focus from the mitigation of negative environmental effects during the life of the mine to net gains over the long term. The net gains requirement meant attention to trade-offs and compensations. Because there would be at least some lasting ecological damage, a plausible 'contribution to sustainability' could be provided only if strong environmental stewardship were combined with steps to lengthen and strengthen socio-economic benefits. To establish grounds for claiming the project would have a positive legacy, the proponent and government decision makers had to find ways of enhancing the communities' long-term prospects. The two most obvious practical effects were the influence on project design, especially concerning the size of the mill, and the negotiation of impact and benefit agreements centred on engaging local people in environmental protection and enhancing the flow of resources and opportunities. Both should help the communities prepare for life after mining.

Whether the end results will actually be net gains for sustainability is far from certain. At the mine site, there will inevitably be at least some residual ecological damage after remediation and closure. The mine's products and revenues may also contribute to increases in consumption and waste generation in ways that lead away from sustainability. There may well be compensating positives. Tax and other revenues from the mine may be used to improve community infrastructure in ways that enhance long-term economic prospects and reduce negative ecological effects. Longer-term social and economic gains are also possible, especially with the extended project life and other efforts to strengthen local training and capacity-building. But these steps mostly enhance the *potential* for positive bridging to an economically and ecologically viable future. Successful delivery is not assured and much still depends on implementation.

This is no criticism of the efforts by the Voisey's Bay panel and others who played key roles in the assessment and the associated deliberations on approval conditions and the impact and benefit agreements. Even the best planning can only go so far. Moreover, the Voisey's Bay participants were pioneers in sustainability-centred assessment. They had no established path to follow and no assembled collection of previous case experiences to go by. None of the agencies involved had anticipated such an assessment and none had prepared relevant sustainability-centred guidance documents. No special criteria or process rules for sustainability assessment had been established.

Specifying the higher test

At the time of the Voisey's Bay assessment, there had been plenty of other serious efforts to apply sustainability criteria in practical decision making. Sustainability objectives had underpinned a variety of initiatives in regional and community planning, in building and neighbourhood design, and in the implementation of poverty reduction projects. There had even been a few other environmental assessments using the rough equivalent of a sustainability-centred approach. But, like the Voisey's Bay effort, these had been more or less ad hoc, exploratory and primitive.

The situation is not much different today. The last few years have seen a continued proliferation of official commitments to sustainability, some of them directly embedded in environmental assessment law. There have also been increasing numbers of new sustainability-centred initiatives, led by actors ranging from neighbourhood organizations and municipalities to corporate sectors and multilateral agencies in jurisdictions around the world. Many of these initiatives have been exemplary and most have offered important lessons of some sort. But there has been little consistency of concept or approach. The 'contribution to sustainability' test is just as vaguely and variously defined today as it was when the Voisey's Bay panel went to work. The practical implications for deliberations and decisions – in policy and project planning, the evaluation of competing options, the design of review and approval processes, post-approval monitoring and adjustment – have not been carefully delineated. We are still stumbling towards sustainability assessment.

Some stumbling is unavoidable. Different circumstances demand different approaches and uncertainty demands flexibility. One of the key lessons to be drawn from the unsustainable results of conventionally guided development decision making is that context matters. Any useful guidance for future sustainability assessments must incorporate adaptive flexibility and respect the specifics of context. But some elements of context are universal. While the pursuit of durable and desirable futures may take a host of different forms, it always faces intertwined ecological, social and economic factors. There are always complexities and uncertainties to respect and good reasons to anticipate surprise. We may debate how far to go with generic criteria and standard processes, but we certainly have the wherewithal for some basic shared understanding of what is required for sustainability gains, and we have enough experience to consolidate into a useful basic package of overall guidance.

That, at least, is the presumption of this book. The agenda here is to consider what we have learned from environmental assessment experience and from sustainability thought and practice so far, to identify the key requirements for sustainability and sustainability-oriented assessments, and to outline the essential steps for implementation.

Notes

1   Under the *Statement of Principles* signed in June 2002, Inco agreed to construct a pilot hydrometallurgical processing plant and either to expand it to a commercial scale operation or to build instead a conventional refinery for the Voisey's ore. Initially, the Voisey's ore would be shipped to Inco processing facilities elsewhere, but the company agreed to treat this as a loan, with an equivalent amount of ore from elsewhere later brought to Argentia in compensation (Newfoundland and Labrador, 2002a).

2   Even while they are operating, mining projects can have negative effects on local communities and economies. Uneven distribution of new incomes can lead to tensions and conflicts. Sudden addition of new revenues for community programmes can lead to dependency on a transitory activity while reducing incentives to pursue other opportunities. And inflationary effects can undermine traditional non-mining economic activities, leaving the community with fewer viable alternatives after the mine closes. These problems, considered more broadly, may help explain why the economies of resource rich developing countries tend to grow more slowly than the median for developing countries (Östensson and Uwizeye-Mapendano, 2000; MMSD, 2002).

3   A Canada/Newfoundland/Inuit framework agreement was ratified in 1990, and an agreement-in-principle signed in June 2001 (INAC, 2001).

4   At the formation of the Labrador Inuit Association, the rule of thumb was that members of all families that had been on the coast before the establishment of the airbase at Goose Bay in 1942 probably had at least some Inuit ancestry, and could be considered legitimate participants in the Association and its claim.

5   Reports of this transition to sedentary life with a money economy disagree on whether it was encouraged or forced. But the island site seems clearly to have been chosen for servicing convenience.

6   In February 1995, for example, the Innu occupied the site and issued an eviction order to Diamond Fields Resources, the exploration company

then holding the Voisey's Bay claims, for failure to obtain Innu permission and failure to prepare an environmental and cultural protection plan before starting exploration on aboriginal lands (Innu Nation, 1996).

7 The *Memorandum of Understanding and the Panel Terms of Reference* are included as appendices to the panel's final report (Voisey's Bay Panel, 1999).

8 For a discussion of the broader significance of these guidelines, see Gibson (2000).

2

Assessment

Thirty-some Years of Environmental Assessment

Growing up in a difficult world

The Voisey's Bay assessment was atypical when it was initiated in 1997 and remains so today.[1] As we will see in later chapters, there have been plenty of other efforts to define and use sustainability principles and criteria in practical decision making – in a host of applications from urban growth management to corporate responsibility reporting. There have also been many official statements of devotion to sustainability in environmental assessment work. Many recent assessment laws list contribution to sustainability among their statutory purposes. Nevertheless, serious efforts to use sustainability gains as a guiding objective and central criterion in actual assessments are still rare. Even for the most progressive jurisdictions, the idea remains in the experimental fringe of innovation in assessment law and practice.

This may not change soon, but there are reasons to expect, as well as to hope for, an eventual effective union between environmental assessment and the pursuit of sustainability. We can expect necessity to be the mother of assessment innovation. Researchers, policy makers and affected interests disagree on how worried we should be about the worsening of ecological degradation, economic inequity and other threats to long-term well-being. They also disagree on the causes and solutions. But only the most wildly optimistic and the profoundly ill-informed claim that the present practices can continue indefinitely without wrecking the biophysical foundations for survival. If the extraordinary popularity of sustainability language reveals only one thing, it is widespread recognition that what prevails today is not sustainable and that changes of some sort are needed. As important conditions get worse, and the costs of unsustainable behaviour become more evident, mother necessity will spur more determined responses. Almost certainly these will include efforts to impose a 'contribution to sustainability' test in the planning and approval of new or renewed undertakings.

Environmental assessment is not the only, or necessarily the best, vehicle for applying a 'contribution to sustainability' test. Land use planning for towns and cities, urbanizing regions and rural and resource areas, is also a good candidate. So are, for other applications, government priority setting processes, neighbourhood and building design charettes, ethical investment analyses, and programme development procedures for international aid projects. Indeed, almost any existing decision making process could and should be used, if it deals with matters that may have long-term effects on factors influencing the prospects for sustainability. The chief advantages of environmental assessment are that it has for over 30 years been maturing in the direction of sustainability assessment, and that it can be adjusted for application, under any convenient label, to decision making on almost any sustainability related undertaking – not just to the familiar sorts of new physical projects but also to ongoing activities and renovations, plans and programmes, government and corporate policies, fiscal or regulatory initiatives, trade regimes, communication strategies, product designs, even lobbying campaigns by environmental organizations.

The maturing of environmental assessment, since its birth in the 1969 United States (US) *National Environmental Policy Act* (NEPA), has been a global phenomenon, influenced by experiences in the hundreds of jurisdictions – nations, provinces and states, municipalities, corporations, national and multilateral agencies, and aboriginal governance bodies – that have adopted, applied and revised environmental assessment processes in various ways over the years. It has, accordingly, reflected many of the same insights and influences responsible for the inception and elaboration of sustainability. The two grew up in the same large neighbourhood, facing similar challenges and learning similar lessons. It is hardly surprising that they should fit well together.

Basic and more advanced approaches

Environmental assessment is one of several names for processes designed to encourage, if not force, better attention to environmental considerations in the planning and implementation of particular undertakings. Sometimes it is called environmental impact assessment or environmental appraisal or social and ecological assessment, and sometimes the use of different names reflects differences in approach. Certainly there are and have been great variations – in the range of undertakings subject to assessment, the procedural steps, the scope of considerations, the nature and roles of participants, the flexibility of application, and even, as we have seen in the Voisey's Bay case, the criteria to be satisfied. But the essential purpose has remained: environmental assessment is meant to change the nature of decision making. Under ordinary circumstances, decision makers can be relied upon to consider economic and technical matters. Governments also have reliable incentives to pay attention to political concerns. Environmental assessment was introduced as an incentive as well as a means to take environmental factors just as seriously.

The aim of ensuring due attention to environmental considerations in decision making determines the necessary basic structure of assessment processes. Box 2.1 lists the basic components of potentially effective processes, and identifies a core set of additional components that are included in more advanced and ambitious processes.[2] The main difference is that the basic list processes are designed only to avoid or mitigate serious negative effects and ensure that approved undertakings are 'acceptable'. The additional components give more attention to difficult environmental realities – especially scientific uncertainty and cumulative effects – and encourage planners and decision makers to identify the best responses to carefully considered needs and purposes. The importance of this distinction, for environmental decision making and for a union with sustainability objectives, we will discuss a little later.

Note that even in basic processes, environmental assessment involves a series of deliberations and decisions through the full life of an undertaking from initial conception to final decommissioning. A formal assessment review may happen at a particular point in the process, usually timed to provide or contribute to an approval decision. But assessment activities (and due attention to environmental factors) are meant to continue.

Given the purpose of ensuring serious attention to environmental considerations, even in environmental assessment processes with modest 'acceptability' aims, the specifics of process design are important. It matters a great deal whether environmental assessment is introduced through voluntary encouragement or legal mandate and whether 'environment' is defined narrowly to cover only biophysical and ecological matters or broadly to cover socio-economic and cultural concerns. It matters whether proponents of new projects begin their deliberations knowing they will have to satisfy environmental assessment requirements or have these requirements imposed only after they have decided what they wish to do. It matters whether the process is efficient or cumbersome, whether the joint roles of science and preference are understood, and whether those with the most to lose can get a fair hearing. On all these topics and more the theoreticians and practitioners of environmental assessment have now struggled for more than 30 years. Considerable diversity remains, in thinking as well as in practice. But it is now possible to look back on the birth and growth of environmental assessment, to identify the key stages and most significant areas of maturation and to appreciate how these have led us to sustainability assessment.

Origins

The general origins of environmental assessment lie in the wave of public environmental concerns and demands that rose in the wealthy nations of the world in the mid- to late 1960s. Among the underlying factors were comfort, confidence, distrust and dread – the odd legacies of World War II and the post-war boom in industry and consumption. The boom had brought ever rising material ambitions, from kitchen appliances and synthetic fabrics to private vehicles and detached homes with weed-free lawns. But these came with rising

Box 2.1 The structure and key components of potentially effective assessment processes

Basic components

1 Application rules that specify what sorts of undertakings are subject to assessment requirements (so planners and proponents know from the outset that they will have to address environmental considerations).

2 Guidance and procedures for determining more specifically the level of assessment and review required in particular cases.

3 Definition of the range of 'environmental' considerations to be addressed, preferably including socio-economic and cultural as well as biophysical factors.

4 Requirements to identify and evaluate the potentially significant effects of proposed undertakings, in light of existing environmental conditions, pressures and trends.

5 Provisions for scoping (setting reasonable boundaries and focusing assessment work on the most important issues).

6 Requirements to identify and evaluate means of mitigating predicted negative effects.

7 Overall evaluation of the effects of the proposed undertaking, with chosen mitigation measures.

8 Provisions for public as well as technical review of the proposed undertaking and the assessment work (to evaluate both the proposed undertaking and the adequacy of efforts to incorporate attention to environmental considerations in developing the proposal), including review through public hearings in especially significant cases.

9 Means of ensuring that the assessment and review findings are incorporated effectively in approvals and permitting.

10 Requirements and provisions for monitoring and enforcing compliance with approval conditions.

Additional components of more advanced processes

1 Application rules that ensure assessment of all undertakings, including policies and programmes and plans as well as capital projects, that might have significant environmental effects.

2 Requirements to establish the need and/or justify the purpose to be served.

3 Requirements to identify the reasonable alternatives, including different general approaches as well as different designs, for serving the purpose.

4 Requirements for integrated consideration of related undertakings and of cumulative effects of existing, proposed and reasonably anticipated undertakings.

5 Requirements to identify means of enhancing positive effects.

6 Requirements for comparative evaluation of the reasonable alternatives with justification for selection of the preferred alternative as the proposed undertaking.

7 Requirements to identify and evaluate the significance of uncertainties (about effect predictions, mitigation and enhancement effectiveness) and associated risks.

8 Provisions, including funding support, to ensure effective public as well as technical notification and consultation at significant points throughout the proposal development and assessment process.

9 Requirements and provisions for monitoring of actual effects and comparison of these with predicted effects (to allow adaptive management and enhance learning from experience) through the full life-cycle of the undertaking.

10 Provisions for linking assessment work, including monitoring, into a broader regime for setting, pursuing and re-evaluating public objectives.

expectations for health and security, and a gradually strengthening willingness to challenge authority. The spectacular advances in technology – living better with chemistry and electricity while watching the Americans and Soviets race into space – were accompanied by gnawing fears about where it was all leading, especially as the Cold War powers persisted in adding to stocks of atomic weapons that were already sufficient to annihilate life on Earth.

Rachel Carson's exposé of global scale chemical contamination came in 1962, the same year as the Cuban Missile Crisis. It was quickly followed by a succession of books presenting frightening statistics about population, pollution and depletion trends (later compiled in the Club of Rome's 1972 *Limits to Growth* computer projections), further undermining confidence in economic and technological 'progress' as a universally Good Thing. Such ambivalence about industrial progress was nothing new and the driving concerns were as much conservative as radical. But in the 1960s it was accompanied by a rising disaffection with authority and a proliferation of public interest groups that, often with surprising media support, raised public awareness and pushed governments to address matters such as environmental stewardship in which they had previously shown little interest.

The first steps were in basic environmental protection and resource management – stronger efforts to control air pollutants, improvements to waste management and sewage treatment facilities, additional efforts to protect natural and heritage areas. Environmental assessment came a little later. While it is now broadly recognized as an approach to planning and decision making, environmental assessment emerged in most jurisdictions from environmental regulation. It was an outgrowth of pollution abatement law. Or, more precisely, it was a response to the failures of environmental laws that focused on responding to particular, identified abuses.

By the late 1960s most industrial countries had put in place a suite of laws, and some enforcement staff, to deal with noxious and costly pollution problems. Most of these laws addressed air, water and land as separate areas of concern. Most were reactive, more concerned with correction than prevention. And most assumed simple cause–effect, source–receptor relationships. Accordingly, enforcement was typically seen as a technical matter, not just in the confirmation of offences but also in the determination of appropriate resolutions. Sometimes there were prosecutions and legal penalties, but more often the regulators and the regulatees sat down together to determine what abatement action would be suitable and sufficient (Schrecker, 1984).

This approach had some successes. Where the problems faced were quite simple, the abatement responses could be suitable and sufficient. But three inadequacies became increasingly apparent.

First, the problems to be addressed became more complicated. The kinds of pollution commonly recognized in the 1960s were a cartoonist's delight – billowing black smoke, dead fish floating upside down, cesspools stinking enough to create odour waves. Soon, however, a host of more insidious problems emerged. There were invisible and odourless trace contaminants that moved through air, water and soil and acted in combination, often with delayed and nasty effects. In ecosystems this could mean acidification, species loss or nutrient-driven system collapse. In humans the rising threats were cancer, birth defects or immune system disruption. The sources were multiple, the effects no longer just local and the prospects for scientific certainty dim.

Second, the approach was highly inefficient. Damages proved often to be impossible or too costly to repair. Poisoned aquifers could not be decontaminated; paved wetlands could not be resurrected; asthmatic children could not be cured. Even where significant correction was feasible, reactive mitigation was much more expensive than proper initial design. Interests that preferred to avoid environmental expenditures of any kind might be happy with acting only after problems had emerged and were undeniably serious. For the wider public, especially those living downstream and downwind, the reactive approach meant responses that were too little and too late. As industrial activities expanded, the public costs grew larger and less tolerable. Eventually the political costs were also unbearable.

Third, the credibility of the authorities crumbled. Treating environmental protection as a matter of reactive technical analysis and response could only work if technical monitoring revealed all the serious problems, if good information were available on causes and solutions, and if this information were used impartially in decision making. In practice, these conditions were rarely met. Most actual problems were complex and ill-understood. Authorities everywhere tended to mistake limited evidence of harm for limited prospects for damage. They offered assurances that problems were small or well in hand. Sometimes they withheld evidence to forestall public panic. But inevitably the information would leak out, or further research would confirm suspicions – revealing contaminant health effects at ever lower concentrations, ecological losses over ever wider areas, and multiple risks from an ever lengthening list of products and activities. As this record continued, the assurances brought more suspicion than comfort.

When corrective actions were taken, often belatedly and minimally, further suspicions grew around the processes for deciding what to do. Despite the technical emphasis, most actual responses involved value laden choices among more or less imperfect options and the choices were made behind closed doors in negotiations between the regulators and the polluters. When the results were disappointing, affected citizens and public interest advocates saw unsavoury collusion and demanded more rigour and openness. In truth, the frequently observed phenomenon of regulator capture by regulatee was not often due to any overt corruption. Usually it was just that the regulatory officials and the managers of regulated facilities spent a lot of time together. Perhaps they had also gone to engineering school together. In any event they quite naturally found it easy to develop shared sympathies. To forestall this, citizens increasingly called for greater public scrutiny with more rigorous requirements and more players at the table when decisions were made.

In response, governments began to introduce more integrated, anticipatory and open processes. They placed more emphasis on the permitting and licensing of new facilities and activities, hoping to prevent or minimize later problems, and they began to coordinate attention to water, air and land effects. Initially these approvals processes still centred on technical and economic considerations with little public involvement, were still limited to the usual air, water and land issues, and were applied mostly to a limited range of known pollution sources. Typically they were also centred on determinations of 'acceptability' – whether undertakings would meet established environmental criteria or standards – rather than on promotion of the most desirable or even least negative options. But gradually the anticipatory controls were expanded and strengthened, and in this the introduction of environmental assessment processes played a large role.

Resistance, adoption and proliferation

Many early environmental assessment processes were quite narrowly focused on biophysical concerns, technically oriented and discretionary. But an ambitious initial standard was set by the first process – the environmental impact assessment obligations introduced in the US *National Environmental Policy Act* (NEPA) of 1969 – and assessment processes ever since have been gradually expanding their scope and coverage and becoming more demanding. NEPA section 102 (2) required US federal agencies to prepare 'statements' to accompany proposals for all new legislation or other activities that might have significant environmental effects. The statements had to consider alternatives to the proposed action, address long-term as well as immediate concerns, and be taken seriously in overall decision making. This was an 'action forcing' requirement. The required actions were meant to change the nature of the proposal development process so that environmental factors were habitually integrated with the usual economic and technical considerations. And the law made such action mandatory.

Not surprisingly, the new obligations were resisted. Passage of the NEPA requirements was followed by a flood of court cases and, later, by an outpouring of regulatory specifications that clarified what 'significant' meant, what kinds of undertakings were covered, what the statements had to include, and what constituted adequate attention to the findings. Other jurisdictions hesitated before this path. Many claimed to fear the prospect of interminable litigation, though the US reliance on court decisions was due mostly to the early absence of regulations, administrative oversight and other good means of clarifying the law's requirements (Wood, 2003). In most places, the main reason for resistance was that the new assessment obligations fell on government agencies that were not eager to think differently, to accept the new burdens or to face additional scrutiny.

Experienced practitioners of environmental assessment today can point to a long list of cases demonstrating that serious assessment efforts bring important direct benefits for project proponents. Arguably, environmental assessments often provide *net* benefits for proponents. Nevertheless, like other measures initiated to serve the public good in the face of the prevailing government and corporate motivations, effective environmental assessment processes have had to be imposed on proponents. Most proponents have at least initially resisted subjection to effective assessment requirements, and have tended to appreciate the benefits of assessment only through imposed experience.

Certainly it was not proponent enthusiasm that drove the adoption and strengthening of environmental assessment. It was mostly public pressure plus fear of political damage from more environmental disasters. And as more and more jurisdictions adopted assessment requirements, slower moving governments also risked being labelled as environmental dinosaurs.

By 1998, environmental assessment processes were reportedly in place in over 100 countries (Donnelly et al, 1998) and more have been adopted since. In many countries, national level initiatives are accompanied by separate processes applied by provinces or states, regional and municipal authorities and aboriginal governments, often with provisions for process combination or cooperation. Some specialized sectoral agencies – for example, those responsible for managing energy, mining or fisheries activities – have their own processes, as do most major international aid bodies, including multilateral ones such as the World Bank. And a host of private sector corporations have integrated environmental assessment processes, formal and informal, into their planning and decision making structures.

Development stages and growth trends

The substantive and procedural variations among these processes are great. Even at the national level, among countries with roughly similar capabilities and governance traditions, process specifics differ in important ways. Moreover, most processes have been in a more or less constant state of adjustment and elaboration in light of experience and in response to new pressures. There are, nevertheless, some common essentials – fundamental design considerations that each process must address in one way or another. While commentators have listed these in different ways as basic assessment process components or as criteria for evaluating process design and implementation (see, for example, Sadler, 1996; Senécal et al, 1999; Wood, 2003), there is broad agreement on the main elements. And in these matters it is possible to trace a general path of environmental assessment maturation, in theory and practice, over the past three decades.

Box 2.2 presents a four stage account of how environmental assessment has grown since the 1960s from its regulatory roots. The stages are a considerable simplification of what has been a messy, uneven and still incomplete global process, but they illustrate the basic character and direction of change involved. A more specific list of the major trends is provided in Box 2.3. They represent, broadly, a shift towards adoption of the more advanced and ambitious components listed some pages ago in Box 2.1.

In the list of trends, too, a good deal of simplification is involved. The identified trends are not universally shared nor are they all at the same level of achievement. Many assessment processes are largely untouched and remain

Box 2.2 Four stages in the development from environmental regulations to advanced environmental assessment

Stage 1: reactive pollution control through measures responding to identified, local problems (usually air, water or soil pollution), with solutions considered technical matters to be addressed through closed negotiation of abatement requirements between government officials and the polluters.

Stage 2: proactive impact identification and mitigation through impact assessment and project approval/licensing, still focused on biophysical concerns (though now integrating consideration of various receptors) and still treated as a largely technical issue with no serious public role (but perhaps expert review).

Stage 3: integration of broader environmental considerations in project selection and planning through environmental assessment processes with:

*   consideration of socio-economic as well as biophysical effects;
*   obligatory examination of alternatives, aiming to identify the best options environmentally as well as economically;
*   public reviews (that reveal expert conflicts and uncertainties, and consequently the significance of public choice).

Stage 4: integrated planning and decision making for sustainability, addressing policies and programmes as well as projects, cumulative and global effects, with review and decision processes:

*   devoted to empowering the public;
*   recognizing uncertainties and favouring precaution, diversity, reversibility, adaptability;
*   expecting positive steps towards sustainability.

little more than regulatory procedures under a misleading title. Some initially strong processes have been weakened. Many processes that have incorporated some advanced components listed in Box 2.1 still lack some of the items from the basic list. In several areas implementation still lags far behind thought and policy. Overall, however, these trends are clearly evident not just in the advocacy of environmental assessment practitioners but also in the nascent practices of leading jurisdictions.

Arguably each of these trends is important on its own grounds. Our interest here, however, is in their significance in building a base for sustainability assessment. For this, the key differences between primitive and advanced environmental assessment are perhaps best considered under the categories of ends and means.

Box 2.3 Twelve major trends in the growth of environmental assessment

Over the past three decades, environmental assessment in concept and practice has moved or is moving towards being:

1 more mandatory and codified (increased adoption of law-based processes, further specification of requirements, reduction of discretionary provisions);

2 more widely applied (covering small as well as large capital projects, continuing as well as new initiatives, sectoral and area developments as well as single proposals, strategic as well as project level undertakings);

3 more often initiated early in planning (beginning with purposes and broad alternatives, sometimes beginning with the driving policies, programmes and plans);

4 more open and participatory (not just proponents, government officials and technical experts);

5 more comprehensive of environmental concerns (socio-economic, cultural and community effects as well as biophysical and ecological effects, regional and global as well as local effects);

6 more integrative (considering cumulative and systemic effects rather than just individual impacts);

7 more accepting of different kinds of knowledge and analysis (informal and traditional knowledge as well as conventional science, preferences as well as 'facts');

8 more closely monitored (by the courts, informed civil society bodies and government auditors watching responses to assessment obligations, and by stakeholders watching actual effects of approved undertakings);

9 more humble (recognizing and addressing uncertainties, applying precaution);

10 more sensitive to efficiency concerns (questions about process emphases, costs and relations with other evaluation and decision making processes);

11 more often adopted beyond formal environmental assessment processes (through sectoral law at various levels, but also in land use planning, through voluntary corporate initiatives, etc.);

12 more ambitious (aiming for overall biophysical and socio-economic gains rather than just individually 'acceptable' undertakings).

Ends

The goals of environment assessment processes can be modest or ambitious. In many jurisdictions, environmental assessment as an outgrowth of environmental regulation has aimed only to prevent or mitigate serious problems. Projects and other undertakings under review are generally assumed to be desirable and assessment decisions merely identify needed adjustments and suitable conditions of approval. As with regulatory decision making, the preferred emphasis is on ensuring compliance with established standards, testable 'objectively'. Proponents typically want to know what the tests of acceptability are, so they can design accordingly. In practice, even basic assessment processes recognize that there are important categories of potentially negative effects for which no general standards have been set. Moreover, one strength of environmental assessment as a process applied to individual undertakings is that it takes into account the particular environmental context (with its more or less unique set of ecological and social conditions, stresses, sensitivities, etc.) and the particular characteristics of the proposed initiative. Nevertheless, assessment processes that have remained close to their regulatory origins continue to centre on testing the acceptability of undertakings and considering needs for additional mitigation measures.

Proponents doing the required assessment work are expected to adjust their project planning and design to minimize environmental problems. As well, the findings from assessment reviews at the project decision stage may be incorporated more or less directly into project permitting and have some influence in overall approvals. But in most cases this remains at the periphery of decision making and in almost all cases the assessment conclusions are delivered as advice to the core decision makers.

At the higher level of most comprehensive and advanced environmental assessment processes, the goals are to identify and favour best responses to carefully considered needs and opportunities. Such assessments require critical consideration of the purposes involved, comparative evaluation of the reasonable alternatives in light of their openly assessed socio-economic and biophysical effects and risks, and attention to the broader context including cumulative effects of other activities, existing and anticipated. The resulting proposals are expected to be the best options (or the least bad ones) over the long term. Assessments of this kind are typically more sensitive to uncertainties and place more emphasis on making explicitly value-laden choices.

Assessment processes with these more ambitious objectives have a much greater potential for changing thinking and practice. Certainly they have had major effects on the subject and results of planning and decision making in particular cases. For example, ordinary acceptability-oriented assessments of new solid waste landfill proposals consider alternative design components (clay or engineered fabric liners, competing options for leachate collection and treatment, etc.) and might also evaluate alternative sites. If done well, the assessment and associated planning and decision making ensure a well designed and suitably sited dump. In contrast, the more ambitious form of assessment questions the simple waste disposal purpose, requires attention to a broader range of waste management options, and engages more stakeholders in the deliberations. The alternative approaches assessed normally include waste reduction options (waste minimization incentives, initiatives to encourage re-use, recycling and composting programmes) in combination with options for disposal of the residuals. The results therefore include not only well-designed recycling, composting and landfill facilities but also important shifts in waste management policies and programmes, in commercial and industrial practices, even in citizen behaviour – all with a greater potential for positive ripple effects than the 'better dump' approach.

The more ambitious approach is not new. The original 1969 NEPA law in the US had high aims – it defined 'environment' broadly, required evaluation of alternatives and addressed long-term effects. Many other early processes also started with stated commitments to substantial change in the nature of planning and decision making. Often, however, the specific provisions and their implementation fell short. Just having admirable ends was never enough – assessment processes also needed the means of delivery and these have been the main areas of attention, frustration and improvement in environmental assessment over the years.

Means

While some changes in environmental assessment processes have centred on matters of high principle, most have resulted from much more directly practical adjustments. Of the 12 trends listed in Box 2.3, only the final one is entirely about ends. Many of the others facilitate more ambitious assessments, but in most cases these changes have been driven by needs to address apparent political and ecological realities, including pressures from citizens and other stakeholders who found that existing processes were not working well enough.

Mandatory and codified

Assessment expectations were gradually specified and codified because experience taught that discretionary openings would be abused, and because proponents demanded clearer delineation of what they had to do to obtain approvals. Some countries, including Canada and New Zealand had introduced environmental assessment through non-legislated policy pronouncements. But these processes suffered from discretionary avoidance and substantive inconsistency. Requirements for Canada's first major project assessment review, which considered the Point Lepreau nuclear power station in New Brunswick, were watered down to avoid conflict with a financing and construction schedule. The second review, which considered the Wreck Cove hydroelectric power project in Nova Scotia, was not initiated until after the project had been approved and the findings that should have affected project design were not available until after much of project work had been completed (Emond, 1978). Performance improved over time. Nevertheless, many government agencies gave little more than lip-service to assessment expectations until the requirements became legally binding. The Canadian experience was far from unusual and the gradual shift to legally mandated, obligatory and reasonably well specified requirements stands globally as a common feature of environmental assessment maturation.

In jurisdictions that began with or later adopted assessment law, there was a parallel administrative transition from procedural and substantive guidelines to more firmly applicable regulations (e.g. on categories of undertakings subject to assessment requirements, notice provisions, report contents, and procedures for more and less detailed assessments). Here too the objective was to limit discretion and clarify obligations, without constraining the needed flexibility of a case and situation based process.

Widely applied

The initial focus of most environmental assessment regimes was on major new capital projects that could have significant negative effects. Such projects were familiar subjects of regulatory permitting and the required impact assessments would provide bases for various licensing approvals. The US NEPA process also applied from the outset to environmentally significant policies, plans, programmes and legislative initiatives, as well as to small projects though through a less demanding and more streamlined version of the process for major undertakings. There was, however, considerable early uncertainty about just what was and was not subject to the full and streamlined NEPA requirements. Clarification came only after some years of court rulings.

Most other jurisdictions relied on regulatory or administrative specification of the application rules. Some chose to make decisions on assessment requirements only after projects had been proposed and seemed worrisome, but this reactive approach conflicted with the objective of encouraging proponents to assess potential effects and incorporate the findings during proposal development. Better regimes tried to pre-identify and list all categories of undertakings that would be subject to assessment at some level. In most cases the lists were gradually expanded, despite opposition from proponent interests.

The main expansions reflected three lessons from experience. The first came from the evident inconsistency of requiring quite rigorous assessments of new undertakings, while neglecting existing activities that were serious sources of environmental abuse. Sometimes the response was simply to tighten regulatory controls on existing operations. But some jurisdictions also moved to extend assessments requirements to ongoing activities such as timber cutting operations, major changes to existing facilities such as airports, and decommissioning of potentially dangerous sites such as hazardous waste treatment facilities.

The second lesson was that while assessments focused on case by case examination of individual projects, actual environmental effects usually came from combinations of activities, existing and new. Some jurisdictions responded with requirements to consider cumulative effects in individual assessments. But it was soon apparent that broader assessment of the set of relevant activities – through assessments of undertakings, alternatives and cumulative effects in a particular sector or area – would be more efficient and would allow fairer assignment of the costs.

The third lesson was that many individual project assessments raised larger policy issues that needed attention but could not be addressed effectively in project-centred decisions. The acceptability of a major new highway cutting through an ancient forest or an amiable neighbourhood might depend heavily on whether the proposed road would fit sensibly into a broader transportation plan that was itself defensible. And the same issue might well arise in assessments of other individual transportation projects in that jurisdiction. Here too, individual assessments proved to be an inadequate and inefficient mechanism used only because no better option was available. It made more sense to assign assessment resources directly to the strategic level and introduce assessments of policies, plans and programmes.

The latter have become the most lively area of environmental assessment innovation in the past decade. Most jurisdictions with serious environmental assessment processes for the project level now also apply assessment requirements of some sort at the strategic level (Wood, 2003). Some, California for instance, have extensive experience and well developed means of application, including specified implications for project level work. Malawi and some other countries with very limited administrative capacity have chosen to focus on strategic level assessments to gain more widespread benefits from resources that would be stretched too thinly at the project level.

Earlier in planning

As more jurisdictions introduced and applied requirements to consider purposes and alternatives, effective consideration of environmental factors was pushed into earlier stages of proposal development. Eventually this trend led environmental assessment further upstream – into the realm of policies, plans and other strategic level activities that set the context for proposal development. When assessment adopts the regulatory tradition and focuses only on already preferred and perhaps largely designed undertakings, all that is practically feasible is marginal adjustment for mitigation. The only other possibility is a denial of approval that would force the proponent to give up or at least to go back to an earlier stage and begin again. When comparative evaluation of alternatives is required, assessment begins before there is a preferred option. And when purposes must be justified, the starting point is the conceptual beginning where many proponents may be pushed to consider issues and options they had previously left unexamined.

Requirements to assess alternative options have often posed difficulties, especially for private sector proponents and public sector agencies with narrowly focused interests, capacities and mandates. A company that makes its money building natural gas pipelines and supplying residential and industrial customers, for example, is likely to be disinclined to consider energy demand reduction options and may be ill-equipped to act on such options if they emerge as the preferred alternative. This problem can be exaggerated. Narrowly interested proponents can still be required to establish that their proposed undertaking is the best option available, whether or not they consider themselves able to pursue the alternatives. But the immediate concern points to a deeper one about the context for consideration and the pursuit of alternatives.

Attractive but unconventional options can often be most effectively facilitated and favoured through initiatives at the strategic level. For example, many jurisdictions have chosen to encourage energy demand reduction through changes in pricing regimes, certificate trading, product standards and labelling, or new tax provisions (van der Laar and Vreuls, 2004; Nilsson, 2005). Sometimes these can spur rapid shifts in proponent attitudes and abilities to pursue alternatives. But the more important implication is that careful attention to alternatives may be at least as beneficial at this strategic level as at the project level. And strategic level assessments may be more efficient, especially if they address issues that would otherwise be left to repeated coverage in a succession of project assessments (Stinchcombe and Gibson, 2001). Not surprisingly, greatly expanded application at the strategic level has been one of the most dramatic developments in environmental assessment in the past decade.

Open and participatory

Increased public involvement has been a common feature of many governments' environmental initiatives over the past three decades. Along with environmental assessment processes, resource management regimes, permitting procedures, standard-setting exercises, even international convention negotiations have come to include a public role and to accept much greater public scrutiny. Commitment and performance vary greatly among and within jurisdictions. But relative openness is now common and still increasing almost everywhere. Certainly there has been resistance. Approval delays and other embarrassments have led some proponents and government authorities to seek restrictions on the public role (usually under the cover of demands for process efficiency). Some jurisdictions have responded by limiting the number and scope of public participation opportunities. Nevertheless, the general trend has been to greater openness, despite proponent preference.

Pressures for more open and participatory processes originated in general distrust of regulatory authorities and dissatisfaction with the results of conventionally closed regulatory decision making. But these pressures grew as public participants gained experience in assessment deliberations and learned more about the limits of technical expertise. Well publicized, more or less adversarial public hearings on major assessment cases have invariably featured disagreements among technical experts who are supposed to be presenting the best scientific information and the most rigorous analyses. In each case, highly credentialled experts appearing on behalf of the proponents present technical evidence favouring the proposal, and similarly expert witnesses speaking in support of the critics present technical evidence opposing the proposal. Sometimes the contesting experts have taken opposing positions while relying on exactly the same body of information (see, for example, Brunk et al, 1991).

These displays, repeated in environmental law proceedings, judicial inquiries, planning controversies, resource management debates and other deliberations on apparently technical matters, have thoroughly undermined claims that technical experts can be relied upon to make the necessary decisions based on objective science. Values and preferences, clearly, play a major role. Assessment decisions are therefore increasingly seen as matters of public choice. In these circumstances, denial or restriction of public scrutiny and involvement in the decision making raises questions about hidden motives and significant political costs can be involved.

The more positive side of the story is that in environmental assessment practice, affected citizens and public intervenors have repeatedly proved to be the most powerfully motivated and the most capable critical reviewers of submitted assessment documents and associated proposals. Better planning and better projects have resulted.

Participative experience has also had a self-feeding effect. Involving the public in assessment deliberations fosters an expectation that the decision making will be transparent and will reflect the participants' expressed judgements and preferences. It also encourages those involved to expect similar engagement and transparency in other similarly weighty matters.

Advocates of greater public involvement argue that it brings long-term educational benefits as well as immediate improvements in project planning (Sinclair and Diduck, 1995). Citizen participants focus on learning about the contested proposal and its effects, but in the course of this they typically also learn a great deal about their community and environment, about how to evaluate evidence and defend a deeply held position, and about the complexities of decision making in the public interest. Assessment deliberations can also exhaust participants, disrupt family lives and split communities. Overall, however, the experience tends to build the capacities of participants to be effective contributors to civic life (Jackson, 1993).

Comprehensive

The NEPA process in the US began with a broad definition of 'environmental' considerations that included socio-economic and biophysical aspects. Many other jurisdictions followed this lead, some sooner than others. The European Union and most of its member countries have chosen to focus on biophysical concerns only, perhaps to compensate for the greater conventional attention paid to social and economic concerns. The more comprehensive approach is common, though not universal, in Canadian processes, in Australia and New Zealand, in developing countries and in international aid agencies such as the World Bank, perhaps because of the more obvious and pressing links between socio-economic and ecological concerns. The broader scope is also widely adopted for assessments at the strategic level.

There is a possible trade-off here. The greater emphasis on biophysical concerns seems likely to be compromised by inclusion of socio-economic concerns. In Canadian experience, no substantial loss of ecological concern is evident in broader assessments. Indeed, in major cases – from the Mackenzie Valley natural gas pipeline inquiry in the mid-1970s to the Voisey's Bay case a quarter of a century later – the combination of biophysical and socio-economic concerns has been mutually supporting. This has been especially true where protection of aboriginal cultures has been a major consideration. But in urban and suburban cases too, ecological and community protection have often been closely associated. Indeed, the common public reaction, in city neighbourhoods as much as in remote villages, is that separating the social and the ecological is arbitrary and inappropriate, especially if the core concerns are about such things as health, security, community culture, ambience and lasting quality of life.

In practice, many public concerns do not fit tidily in the ecological, social or economic categories. This is true at the regional and global as well as local levels. The big advantage of broader assessments is that the full range of significant possible effects can be considered together and the trade-offs examined openly and explicitly. Because environmental assessments often provide the only public forum for case specific deliberations, they are often the one opportunity to address the full set of concerns, linkages and compromises through public governance. Where assessments do not address socio-economic matters, narrowly biophysical assessment recommendations that have been developed with some public involvement are fed into a closed process where the relevant authorities decide among themselves what priorities will prevail and what trade-offs will be made. While the conclusions are announced, the actual reasoning typically remains hidden.

Integrative

Early environmental assessment work suffered from motivational and methodological weaknesses. Proponents tended to treat assessment requirements as a paper obligation best addressed by submitting voluminous reports. These typically covered all possible concerns, but without much attention to priorities, interrelationships or synthesis. The work also tended to mirror the fragmentation of scientific and technical expertise. In reports on the biophysical environment, individual factors were documented in detail. Great long lists of identified species were provided. But little light was shed on the nature of the biophysical and ecological systems, their response to current human interventions, and the possible systemic implications of proposed new activities.[3] Social impact assessments suffered from similar weaknesses and capable integration of the biophysical and social work was rare.[4]

Environmental assessment practitioners soon recognized the need for more systemic and better integrated understanding of existing environments, and more effective emphasis on how these systems, not just individual components of them, might be affected by new undertakings (Beanlands and Duinker, 1983). Similar conclusions were also being drawn in other fields. Experience, including failures, in the management of forests, fisheries, protected areas, watersheds and, most recently, atmospheric chemistry and global climate, has led to new appreciation and understanding of complex systems (Gunderson et al, 1995). The results, in research design, study methodologies and approaches to management are just beginning to be adopted in environmental assessment practice. But they fit well with the growing emphasis on assessment of regional and cumulative effects, and the broader implications of policies, programmes and plans.

Accepting of different kinds of knowledge and analysis

The general undermining of faith in technical expertise has been accompanied by a growing acceptance of other kinds of knowledge – not as a replacement for conventionally specialized expertise, or with any expectation of greater reliability, but as a complementary source and a route to greater overall understanding. The acceptance of traditional ecological knowledge, as in the Voisey's Bay assessment, is one example. In that case, like many others involving Aboriginal people with long traditions of living close to the land, there was good reason to anticipate that they had knowledge that was practically unavailable to scientists able to spend only a few field seasons in part of the area. And it was not just a matter of facts and data. The Inuit and Innu knowledge and ways of knowing combined ecological information with cultural practice and commitment to a future in that area, all of which were relevant to the assessment, difficult as it may have been to fit into the usual categories of assessment review.

Much the same has been recognized about the deeply rooted, experiential knowledge of other long-term residents and land users. Consequently, when the Canadian government amended its environmental assessment legislation in 2003, it chose to recognize that both 'community knowledge and aboriginal traditional knowledge' were worthy of consideration in environmental assessments (Canada, 2003b, s8(16.1)). Environmental assessment practices have also increasingly embraced new methodologies that combine explicit social choice with technical analysis of scenarios, options, effects and risks. The underlying factor here is our still just dawning appreciation of ecological and socio-ecological system complexity, the consequently unavoidable role of values and preferences, and the enormous challenge of assembling a reasonable basis for competent decision making.

Monitored

Critics of environmental assessment practice have long harboured two suspicions – that assessment obligations would be avoided and that the actual effects of assessed projects would be worse than predicted. Both have had important influences on the maturation of environmental assessment.

Fears about tendencies to avoid assessment obligations were quickly confirmed. Many project proponents openly resisted assessment requirements or, where enforcement was weak, simply failed to comply. The flood of litigation following the introduction of NEPA assessment requirements in the US was driven at least as much by avoidance as by desire for clarification. In Canada, extensive non-compliance by government agencies was repeatedly confirmed by internal audits until the country's policy-based process was replaced by a law (Gibson and Hanna, 2005). Pressure for the legislation and codification discussed above was one response, but these, by themselves, were generally insufficient. Certainly there are jurisdictions whose legislated requirements are not effectively applied.

Clear obligations, committed senior authorities and capable administrators all help. But in many jurisdictions the key to effective implementation has been the critical vigilance of independent auditors (including those within governments) and informed civil society organizations (including public interest environmental law groups) with public credibility and the capacity to initiate court actions were necessary. Such bodies play important roles on many issues of public concern, operate differently in different political cultures, and do not everywhere include groups particularly focused on environmental assessment. Generally, however, they have been an increasingly significant force for strengthening the substance as well as the implementation of environmental assessment.

Some of the major implementation concerns have centred not on whether assessments are done as required, but on what happens after assessed projects are allowed to proceed (Wood, 2003). Here there are two monitoring questions. First, are the assessment commitments and approval conditions met in implementation? And second, how do the actual effects compare with what was predicted? Both of these matters have attracted more attention with the maturing of environmental assessment, though there is still plenty of room for improvement. Compliance monitoring has often been undermined by vagueness in approval statements, failure to assign enforcement responsibilities and resources, and unimpressive penalties for non-compliance. Assessment authorities have only gradually begun to correct these problems, and costs remain the biggest barrier. The most promising responses may come from the few jurisdictions that are now empowering and supporting citizen monitors and local stakeholder monitoring committees as complements to conventional enforcement officials.

Citizen and stakeholder mobilization has also been part of the answer to the traditional neglect of effects monitoring. Advancement in the science and art of impact prediction has been hampered by the widespread failure to check impact predictions against actual effects. Budgetary constraints are usually blamed, though passing up such learning opportunities is likely to be a false economy. Some jurisdictions have begun to introduce mandatory follow-up requirements, which are probably necessary if effects monitoring is to be done commonly and well. Further involvement of motivated local stakeholders may make this more affordable and more broadly educational but it is also recognized that good monitoring will require technical expertise, consistent research protocols for reporting, and widely shared access to the results (Hunsberger et al, 2004). While few of these are yet in place, the necessary technical and organizational capacity for the work is probably now possible.

Humble

In environmental assessment, as in other fields of biophysical and socio-cultural study, advances in methodology and comprehension have been accompanied by a deepening awareness of how little we know. The phenomenon of conflicting credentialled experts, noted above, is only part of the story. Experts increasingly agree that the key reality faced in environmental work, and in most other policy fields, is the functioning of intersecting, interdependent, dynamic and perhaps inconceivably complex systems. These systems may be quite resilient but also appear to be normally in processes of change. They can, if overly stressed, change dramatically into systems with very different characteristics (Kay et al, 1999; Gunderson and Holling, 2002). This is the big risk in global climate change from the greenhouse effect – not that temperatures will simply continue to edge upwards, but that the climate system will begin to fluctuate wildly and then flip into a new form that is much different (hotter, colder, drier, wetter, windier, etc.) from what we have and depend on now. Unfortunately, we do not and probably cannot know where the threshold is.

Not all systems are as complex as the global climate system (though few have been as energetically studied). And not many will bring equivalent catastrophe if they are not maintained more or less in their current form. But all are dynamic and connected with others with complexities beyond full understanding.

The upshot is that we have a limited basis for confidence in system descriptions, much less impact predictions beyond the individual component level. That does not mean that predictions of system response are impossible. In many circumstances, quite reliable predictions can be made on the basis of experiential data, assisted by sophisticated modelling. But even where we have good information and capable assessments, surprises are possible, if not likely. For environmental policy generally, this means precautionary approaches should be adopted. For environmental assessment particularly, it means putting greater emphasis on identifying impact uncertainties and associated risks, avoiding potential problems and favouring low risk alternatives. It also means attention to adaptive design and preparation for adaptive management. Adaptive design includes preference for diversity, reversibility and substitutability, safe-fail rather than fail-safe technologies,[5] preparation of fall-back options and plans for careful monitoring. Adaptive management uses these design features to make adjustments as implementation proceeds and surprises emerge (Holling, 1978, 1986; Gunderson et al, 1995; Dearden and Mitchell, 1998).

Precautionary language is now appearing more often in environmental assessment laws and guidelines (Lawrence, 2003a), as it is in other environmental policies and processes. Delineation of the implications is not yet well advanced, but progress in this area seems likely (granting the limits of confident prediction).

Sensitive to efficiency concerns

In most jurisdictions the imposition of environmental assessment obligations has been resisted, often energetically. Not surprisingly, much of the opposition has come from development interests – in both the public and private sectors – whose undertakings would have to be assessed. But resistance has also come from government approval authorities with mandates to promote economic growth. It is likely, though difficult to prove, that a good deal of their discomfort centres on being pushed into unfamiliar territory, where the old methods of decision making and the usually preferred project options no longer prevail. Most often, however, the open criticisms have focused on the costs of implementation, approval delays and process inefficiencies.

The continued expansion of environmental assessment applications despite these concerns suggests widespread confidence that the benefits generally exceed the costs – that better and more acceptable decisions result and that prevention of damage is cheaper than repair. Nevertheless, there have certainly been legitimate concerns about assessment inefficiencies. Critics in many jurisdictions have pointed to questionable resource allocation (assessment of minimally significant projects and effects while the implications of major undertakings are unexamined), the proliferation of overlapping and divergent assessment regimes, tolerance of poor quality work (assessment reports that are huge in volume but weak in analytical quality), unnecessarily lengthy reviews and hearings, and weak efforts to learn from experience (general failure to undertake monitoring of actual effects and compliance with commitments).

A few governments, usually ones that are closely aligned with economic development interests, have chosen to weaken core assessment provisions or exempt more undertakings from them. Most have responded more directly to specific inefficiency problems. As we have seen, many jurisdictions are codifying expectations (to reduce process confusion), putting more emphasis on strategic level assessments (to resolve or simplify project level issues), streamlining application to less worrisome projects, and strengthening post-approval monitoring. Other common efficiency initiatives include negotiating arrangements for process harmonization where obligations overlap, facilitating issue scoping (focusing assessment attention on the major concerns), and introducing review timelines.

Despite these efforts, efficiency challenges will no doubt continue to increase. Part of this will simply reflect the expansion of assessment obligations to cover more issues and undertakings. An additional emerging factor centres on process integration. As assessment spreads into the strategic level and begins more commonly to address cumulative effects across the full socio-economic, cultural and biophysical range, its role in overall decision making inevitably shifts. Initially, assessment work produced findings that were to be integrated into conventional decision making. Gradually, especially with critical attention to purposes and alternatives, it assumed more importance as an influence on basic planning assumptions and options. Now assessment is itself becoming a vehicle for more integrated deliberations and is closer to the core of decision making. This raises new questions about how assessment processes should cooperate, link or merge with other more traditional planning, evaluation and approval processes.

Adopted beyond assessment regimes

Experience has taught that serious attention to environmental considerations does not happen reliably without some powerful incentive. But that incentive does not have to be environmental assessment legislation. Assessment requirements can and have been incorporated in a wide variety of other statutes to cover undertakings not otherwise subject to assessment obligations, or to add environmental components to existing processes. Examples in Canada include sector-based laws governing federal decisions on export subsidies, provincial licensing of mines and sand and gravel pits, and municipal approval of subdivision developments adjacent to environmentally sensitive areas.

Some additional applications have been driven largely by non-legislative factors. Urban planning and mining project development provide illustrative cases. In North America, especially in urban and urbanizing regions subject to substantial growth pressures, planning authorities face increasingly costly urban sprawl and persistent political pressures for more healthy, green and liveable communities. The planners have responded in part by adopting versions of biophysical and socio-economic assessment to assist decision making at many levels – from evaluations of broad development scenarios to preparation of renewal plans for particular properties and neighbourhoods. The mining industry globally too has concluded that it needs to give much more careful and better integrated attention to biophysical and socio-economic concerns. Its motivation is essentially economic. A series of major environmental catastrophes, mostly resulting from tailings dam failures, and widely reported cases of local communities rejecting proposed mining operations, or sabotaging existing ones, has increased mining costs, added to the difficulties of raising project financing, and damaged the industry's reputation enough to make it harder for mining companies to recruit new talent.[6]

The rising importance of such motivations may not reduce needs for legislated assessment processes. But it does indicate wider recognition of the practical value of greater environmental awareness, and the usefulness of environmental assessment approaches as means to this end.

Ambitious

In the Voisey's Bay case, environmental assessment decision making centred on demonstration of 'a positive overall contribution' to long-term community and ecological gains. Such an objective is a long step from the mitigation of significant negative effects – the prevailing aim of most early assessment processes and of many still today. Arguably, the more ambitious target was at least discernable in the initial NEPA language. It is also implied in assessment processes that require critical comparative evaluation of purposes and alternatives. These should, in theory, lead to the selection of options that are not merely acceptable but, relative to the alternatives, most in accord with broad public interests.

In practice, the expansion of assessment ambitions from acceptability to sustainability has been slow and fitful. It also remains far from complete. Consideration of alternatives has not always been required and when it has, authorities have often retained the acceptability test, seeking to identify and approve a clearly acceptable option but not necessarily the best one. This is understandable when assessments look only at the environmental factors. But as the interdependence of factors becomes more fully appreciated, and as citizens demand more scope in the process most open to them, environmental assessment has gradually become a vehicle for more comprehensive and better integrated analyses. In many places it has been extended to cover the strategic and project levels, cumulative as well as individual effects, socio-economic and cultural as well as the biophysical considerations, traditional knowledge and community preferences as well as technical calculations, and post-approval adaptations as well as pre-approval planning. Together these give assessment a bigger role and move it closer to the centre of decision making.

High ambitions come with this territory. But they also come with the larger world of challenge and change in which concerns about sustainability have emerged. The trends observed in the maturation of environmental assessment have not been pushed only by the immediate lessons from experience in assessment applications. They also reflect broader influences such as those arising from greater understanding of complex systems and precautionary needs, and from new political pressures for more openness and efficiency. Concerns about sustainability may be the most significant of these broader influences, in part because sustainability has become a sort of organizing framework for thinking about the full set of major factors that seem likely to affect prospects for a desirable future.

Maturing assessment and emerging sustainability

The 12 trends discussed above are leading environmental assessment into a bigger range of applications (from the project to the strategic level), with a broader agenda (attention to purposes, alternatives and a full suite of inter-related effects, individual and cumulative), more sophisticated understanding (systemic and precautionary), more players (civil society organizations and traditional knowledge holders), and higher ambitions.

None of this movement has been accidental. Each of the shifts has been the product of concerted effort, in the face of often stiff resistance and with continuing tensions. In some areas, progress along the trend line has been modest and tentative. And there have been some retreats accompanying the overall advances. However, the story here has not just been one of struggles among competing interests. The trends also reflect response to realities that have become more evident or more pressing in recent decades, and that decision makers ignore at their peril. As noted above, these realities include the rise and persistence of sustainability as a fundamental concern and objective.

We can see the Voisey's Bay environmental assessment equally well as an early experiment with sustainability-based assessment or as a late example of environmental assessment reaching maturity. Sustainability is a difficult concept, not yet well elaborated for assessment purposes. But it clearly in-volves a combination of aspects that overlap closely with the 12 trends in environmental assessment maturation outlined above. Any planning, decision and follow-up process that aims for contributions to sustainability must surely be comprehensive and integrative, critically attentive to purposes and alter-natives, appreciative of uncertainties, and applied firmly, widely, openly and efficiently.

It does not follow that assessment processes with these characteristics will necessarily serve well as vehicles for the pursuit of sustainability. It is one thing to be sufficiently broad and ambitious, and to have suitable participation and humility. It is quite another to be clear about what is needed for reasonable progress towards sustainability, what improvements are crucial, and what compromises can be tolerated, generally and in specific circumstances. For that, we need to look much more closely at what sustainability is and what its pursuit might entail.

Notes

1   The sustainability-centred higher test of the Voisey's Bay assessment review has, however, been adopted and elaborated by some subsequent hearing panels under the *Canadian Environmental Assessment Act*. The most recent is in the case of a quarry and marine terminal project that is subject to a joint assessment under the Canadian federal law and the provincial law in Nova Scotia. See WPQP (2005).
2   This breakdown of the key design features for environmental assessment processes is an elaboration from an initial list in Gibson (1993), with additional insights from Sadler (1996), Senécal et al (1999), CSA (1999), IAIA (2002) and Wood (2003).
3   These weaknesses, and appropriate solutions, were identified in the landmark study by Gordon Beanlands and Peter Duinker (1983).
4   Important exceptions were in assessments and assessment reviews involving impacts on aboriginal people, of which the model was, and remains, the Mackenzie Valley pipeline inquiry. See Berger (1977).
5   Safe-fail technologies such as home insulation can fail without serious consequence. Fail-safe technologies such as nuclear power plants with multiple containment and safety systems are necessarily designed to be heavily protected against failure because failure would be catastrophic.
6   Examples of planning and mining adoptions are discussed further in Chapter 4.

3

Sustainability

The Essentials of the Concept

A necessary and difficult idea

Over the last decade and a half, the concept of 'sustainability' (or 'sustainable development'[1]) has been widely, if vaguely, embraced by government bodies and other influential organizations around the world. Its meaning and implications have been much disputed, and the actual behaviour of institutions that have claimed devotion to sustainability has been much criticized. The idea, however, has persisted and spread.

This is a more extraordinary phenomenon than is commonly recognized. However we may choose to define it, sustainability stands as a critique; it is a challenge to prevailing assumptions, institutions and practices. The concept of sustainability would spur no interest in a world generally confident that its current approaches will resolve looming problems and ensure a viable future. Critique is not the whole story, of course. The appeal of sustainable alternatives may be as much hopeful as critical – offering a response to doubts about the viability of current trends while accommodating optimism about our ability to turn things around without much pain. But the notion quite clearly rests on rejection of things as they are. Its adoption by governments and other prevailing authorities, who are generally the embodiments of established thinking and practice, is a remarkable, if implicit, admission of broad failure and the need for substantial change.

Predictably, most authorities have proven slow to act on their commitments to more sustainable practices. Also predictably, authoritative acceptance of a serious critical concept has led to lively debates about definitions, implications and obligations – debates in which the authorities have usually been inclined to favour the least demanding options. It is, nonetheless, clear that the door to serious deliberation and experimentation is wedged open and that expectations for demonstrable improvements have been raised.

The desirable next step, logically, would be a broadly accepted clarification of sustainability's practical implications. Certainly if environmental assessment is to be transformed into sustainability assessment, it would help to have some shared agreement on the fundamentals of what sustainability is, or at least what the pursuit of sustainability requires. Because the specifics depend on context and must vary between one circumstance and the next, all that is possible is general agreement on the basics and how to proceed from there. But even that is a tall order.

Of all the notions, buzzwords and catchphrases circulating in the academic and policy worlds, sustainability may be the most slippery. Researchers have devoted years to pursuing the Holy Grail of the robust definition, with diverse and often conflicting results. Hundreds of definitions have been proposed and thousands of variations have been applied in practical initiatives. Some participants have argued against seeking a common foundation. Constructive ambiguity, they say, has been valuable. It has helped to ease concerns about a new and unfamiliar concept. It has allowed incompatible interests to embrace the idea and wildly diverse advocates to attempt application. In the process there has been learning and a gradual spread of confidence that substantial gains can be achieved under the banner of sustainability.

There is much to be said for this argument. An unambiguous and clearly subversive concept would have received a much more limited welcome. And the lively debates and great diversity of applications have indeed promoted creative thinking and experimentation in a way that firm specification would not have inspired. But after a decade and a half of wrestling with the ambiguities, of deliberating and testing the options, we seem to have reached a stage where more comprehensive and consistent approaches to sustainability are both possible and necessary for serious applications, including sustainability assessment.

The first waves of official commitments in rhetoric have gradually been expressed in law and policy, and increasingly entrenched in public expectations, to the point where we now must begin to spell out more clearly the meaning and implications for practical use. As we saw in the preceding chapter, the need for greater clarity about sustainability requirements is evident in environmental assessment, which has evolved to demand better integrated and more anticipatory decision making. As we shall see, the same can be said about urban planning, corporate responsibility, development assistance programming and a host of other areas where pressures to deal with intersecting forces and objectives, and to provide plausible long-term assurances, amount to expectations for sustainability.

These developments coincide happily with the emerging possibility of agreement on the basics of sustainability. Out of the great diversity of theoretical formulations and applications, an essential commonality of shared concerns and principles is increasingly visible. That, at least, is the argument here.

We begin with a quick review of the history of the idea.

Old sustainability

Sustainability is an old wisdom, perhaps *the* old wisdom. For most people in most human communities since the dawn of time, the main earthly objective was to continue. And the core strategy was to stick with what worked, which meant maintaining the traditional practices that ensured viable relations with nature and other people and the realm of spirits, gods or God. It was a view apparently shared by virtually all hunters and gatherers, by almost everyone in the early agricultural societies, in the ancient civilizations and in feudal arrangements.

It is easy enough to see why. These were customary societies. Respected elders might give direction and powerful military or religious authorities might give orders. On most everyday matters, however, the ways of doing things – how to till the soil, educate the children, deal with the in-laws, mourn the dead – were established in customary practices. These in turn were founded on an intricate web of understandings, traditions and beliefs that were particular to each people and to the land that supported them, and that had been tested over many generations.[2] From time to time, changes might be found necessary and desirable. But change would disrupt the customary ways and the supporting web of understandings, traditions and beliefs. It would always be risky.

The old stories therefore warned against the forces of change – against technological ambition, subversive ideas and experimentation with the untried, possibly untrue and potentially dangerous. Trying something new would get humanity kicked out of the Garden of Eden. Curiosity would open Pandora's box and release evils into the world. New technologies might bring important benefits, but there would be a price to be paid. Daedelus' ingenious wax and feather wings would allow him to escape the Labyrinth but kill his over-confident son when he flew too close to the sun. Even fire, that great gift to humanity, would destroy cities as well as warm the hearth.[3]

Hesitancy about innovation was accompanied by a general suspicion of wealth seeking, and for the same reasons. Unleashed acquisitiveness would be disruptive. Wealth might be accepted as an accompaniment of power and a signal of high position and plunder of an enemy's wealth might be celebrated, but until the modern era, wealth seeking as a purpose of life was condemned as sinful or ignoble or unworthy of a being endowed with the higher powers of creativity, contemplation or transcendence. So argued Socrates and Confucius, Buddha, the Biblical Testaments and the Qur'an. And so responded cultures of great diversity that in their many and various ways discouraged, restricted and suppressed gain seeking activities.

Material desirousness is now commonly assumed to be deeply entrenched in human nature, and perhaps the essence of it. But for more than 90 per cent of the human experience, devotion to acquisition was not feasible. During our countless millennia as nomadic hunting and gathering people, material wealth was a burden to be carried from place to place. When sedentary communities were established and material accumulation became possible, greed was quickly identified as a vice, an offence against the common interest. It was something to be blocked by custom and law. Most goods – especially those key to existence such as land and food – were distributed in predetermined ways. Social position was more or less fixed. Honour and reputation were won in other ways. Courage, oratory, wisdom, art, healing, holiness, beauty, endurance – all these were preferred to the skills of avarice. In the aboriginal communities of the north-west coast of North America, prestige was gained not be amassing valuable goods, but by giving them away (Jonaitis, 1991).

Underneath it all was concern for the maintenance of social order and ecological viability. The sustainability of old was profoundly conservative. It was sustainability in the service of customary life, stability and continuity. But that was then and this is now. While there is much to be learned from our many millennia of sustainability experience, the context today, in many ways and in most places, is very different. Things changed profoundly and probably irreversibly when progress was invented.

Groundwork for a new sustainability

Progress

In a wonderful but now mostly forgotten book published in 1920, the Cambridge historian J. B. Bury described how the idea of progress emerged. It was, he argued, one of the two great steps for humanity. The other was self-consciousness (Bury, 1955).[4] Before the modern era, views of the past and future varied considerably but nowhere included an assumption that human life had generally improved and could go on doing so. More common were notions of repeating cycles or gradual decline from an earlier time. In the beginning, humans and animals talked with one another, or the first couple occupied a garden of innocence, or semi-divine heroes fought in a Golden Age, or stalwart citizens founded the great city. After that things went downhill in alienation and sin, softening and decadence.

According to Bury, the idea of progress arose only a few hundred years ago. First the Renaissance had to reassert confidence in reason and interest in earthly life. Then the essentials of customary society had to be undermined by gradual acceptance of tradition's twin enemies: innovation and avarice. We can quibble about the details of the modern agenda and its various components. But the core certainly includes the modern scientific conception of nature as matter obedient to knowable laws and therefore able to be manipulated, and the modern economic conception of humans as desirous individuals driven to maximize their satisfactions. Together these two ideas meant that material improvement was possible and proper. They also provided the foundations for approval of profit seeking, encouragement of invention, commodification of land and labour, investment in industrial advance and proliferation of consumerism – the key components of modern practice that have defined and driven the world to the achievements and perils we now face.

Unlike the world of old sustainability, the new one is relentlessly dynamic. Change is the status quo and the characteristic changes recognize no barriers to application or ambition. The economy seeks growth in productive and consumptive activity. Science and technology seek expansion of manipulative capability. While neither is necessarily destructive of long-term human and ecological prospects, they certainly present challenges for sustainability that are fundamentally different from those faced by the elders and ancients who sought to maintain the well tested ways.

In 1920, when Bury wrote his account of the idea of progress, the previous century's confidence in consistently progressive advance had just been shaken by the Great War. The Victorians had assumed that rationality, knowledge, civilization, well-being and even virtue had increased and would continue to do so. Bury was less optimistic:

> *To the minds of most people the desirable outcome of human development would be a condition of society in which all the inhabitants of the planet would enjoy a perfectly happy existence. But it is impossible to be sure that civilisation is moving in the right direction to realise this aim. Certain features of our 'progress' may be urged as presumptions in its favour, but there are always offsets, and it has always been easy to make out a case that, from the point of view of increasing happiness, the tendencies of our progressive civilisation are far from desirable (Bury, 1955, preface).*

Over the following decades, the 20th century confirmed Bury's mixed review, bringing both remarkable advances and unspeakable horrors – electrification and Auschwitz, the end of smallpox and the introduction of Mutually Assured Destruction. While some of the ugliest destruction and degeneration could be blamed on new versions of old evils (totalitarian governments supplanting old autarchies, inequalities from technology and commerce replacing inequalities of inherited position), others were clearly products of modern ambitions and capabilities (Agent Orange, internet fraud, driftnet fisheries). Moreover, these 'offsets' of 20th century progress were of an unprecedented scale. The Depression, World War II and the Cold War that followed were global phenomena, enabled by economic dependencies, technological capacities and material ambitions at a planetary level.

Development and growth

The favourable side of progress – including marvellous advances in medicine and enormous increases in productive capacity – was clearly substantial and valuable. For most people in the industrialized world, the 20th century brought a shift from material privation to material comfort. It also brought the idea that the same could be provided for everyone, everywhere. The 'underdeveloped' countries could be helped to follow the path already taken by the rich, industrial ones, for the greater prosperity of all. US President Harry Truman's 1949 inauguration address is usually credited as the first confirmation of this development agenda (Sachs, 1999). It would be the new civilizing mission of the powerful. And it too would bring important gains, at least in some ways and to some people.

The negative side included a host of concerns, large and small, about the side-effect risks and damages, about evident failures to deliver on the promises of development, and about the plausibility of claims that growth could continue forever.

Risks and damages

Any hope and relief brought by the end of World War II were overshadowed by the demonstrated threat of nuclear warfare. The 'conquest of the atom' was clearly both a stunning scientific and technological achievement and a step towards global annihilation. As two hostile powers raced to expand their weapons capacity well beyond what was required to destroy human life on the planet, a war that would actually end all wars seemed almost inevitable – if not from a failure of diplomacy then from a failure in warning or control systems.

The nuclear age also brought the first of the global environmental degradation concerns. Atmospheric nuclear testing spread radioactive materials around the world. The strontium 90 found in cow's milk thousands of kilometres downwind of test sites was the precursor to a succession of other invisible health threats – carcinogens, teratogens, mutagens, immune and endocrine system disruptors (Carson, 1962; Commoner, 1972; Epstein, 1978; Colborn et al, 1996). These were accompanied by parallel and overlapping worries about the broader ecological effects of industrial activities and consumer products, including releases of toxic chemical wastes, acidifying precipitation, ozone depleting substances and greenhouse gases. The resulting widespread discomfort was deepened by worries about new technologies that promise substantial benefits but are inherently risky.

The severity of each of these problems was and continues to be debated. But in most cases an initial period of official denial and reassurance was followed by grudging recognition and response. Gradually the cumulative weight of evident damages and risks established grounds for more thorough anticipatory evaluations of new technologies and proposed applications. Whether these steps have been generally adequate has also been widely debated. Certainly, however, the responses have not been enough to dispel suspicions that ever more ambitious technological adventures – from synthetic chemicals and nuclear power to genetic engineering and nanotechnology – could bring ever more serious perils and that future equivalents to the Seveso, Bhopal and Chernobyl accidents could prove more disastrous. By the time food biotechnology options emerged, a more precautionary mood had been established; major European jurisdictions resisted adoption on grounds that the risks were too high.

Failures of development

The post-World War II campaign against underdevelopment began with optimism. After the success of the Marshall Plan for European reconstruction assistance, there were great hopes for broader development efforts applying western models of industrialization and infrastructure expansion to countries emerging from colonial status. The essentially simple idea, set out most notably in US President Harry Truman's 1949 inaugural address, was to speed the arrow of progress along the established western trajectory, bringing greater prosperity to all.[5] Unfortunately, development proved to be much more difficult in practice than in theory.

The following decades of development assistance had remarkable achievements, most notably through the 'green revolution' in agricultural production,
and the inoculations against infectious diseases. But there were also dramatic
disasters and an overall failure to bring greater prosperity to all. While global
material prosperity grew enormously between 1950 and 2000, it was increasingly concentrated in the hands of an advantaged minority of individuals
and nations. Those most in need were frequently the victims rather than the
beneficiaries of development (Sainath, 1996). Failed development initiatives
led to heavy debt burdens for recipient nations and by the mid-1980s, annual
debt payments from poor countries exceeded the value of new aid, loans and
investment. By the mid-1990s, the number of people trying to survive on less
than US$2 per day exceeded the number of people living on the planet in
1949 when Truman initiated the campaign against underdevelopment (Black,
2002).

Part of the problem was that Truman's announced agenda of 'development
based on the concepts of democratic fair dealing' had been quickly complicated
by other objectives related to the commercial and political self-interest of
'donor' nations. The Cold War contest between East and West left a Third
World of nations that were at least as much targets for influence as intended
beneficiaries of development. But development efforts also suffered from
insufficient respect for the complexities involved. Few gains were automatic.
Many of the big infrastructure projects failed technically and economically
while destroying the social and ecological systems that had been the existing
base of support for local livelihoods. Even broadly successful initiatives such
as the 'green revolution' agriculture projects tended to favour richer farmers
at the expense of poorer ones.

In 1968, international assistance allocations dropped for the first time and
the *New York Times* ran a series on the 'horror stories of development'. The
next year, when a World Bank commission on development problems, led by
former Canadian Prime Minister Lester Pearson, began its work, the foreign
aid climate was 'heavy with disillusion and distrust' (CID, 1969). Pearson and
his colleagues blamed unrealistic expectations and claimed that aid efforts
had helped foster unprecedented growth in many countries. But they also
recognized and lamented the still widening gap between rich and poor and the
decline in genuine, untied aid.

Over the following decades, a succession of commissions examined and
re-examined the failures to overcome poverty and recommended similar
packages of solutions. Repeatedly they advocated more consistent attention
to development requirements beyond technological advance and economic
growth – including needs to redistribute wealth, strengthen democracy, build
administrative capacity, foster political stability and enhance social cohesion,
all with greater sensitivity to local conditions and preferences.[6] Although
these observations had less influence than might be hoped,[7] they signalled a
gradually deepening appreciation of the complexity and interdependency of
factors that influence prospects for lasting improvements. In some corners of
trade liberalization advocacy, there is still a residual faith in spurring progress

simply by facilitating more economic activity. But in the professional and popular understanding of development experience that notion is increasingly a relic of the past.

The costs and limits to growth

The equation of economic growth and human progress still underlies core components of most national agendas. Simple addition of measured economic activities – the gross domestic product (GDP) – remains the standard indicator of national success. But faith in growth as progress has been besieged for decades. Ezra J. Mishan's 1967 book, *The Costs of Economic Growth*, set the stage, demonstrating how growth in real income could coincide with a reduction of human welfare. Mishan, a respected mainstream social welfare economist, noted that the conventional indicators were misleading: while material gains were typically measured and celebrated, many of the associated quality of life damages – social, ecological, cultural and aesthetic – were simply suffered. Where these costs were not ignored or denied, they were labelled as the unavoidable price of progress.

Mishan's work was soon complemented by that of other growth sceptics who argued, variously, that devotion to economic growth was fostering a culture of selfishness and anomie, that it was exhausting non-renewable resources and overwhelming renewable ones, that it was upsetting the necessary equilibrium of ecological and economic systems, that it was eliminating both cultural diversity and biodiversity in ways likely to be dangerous as well as impoverishing, and that it was leading to global scale challenges involving complexities, uncertainties and sensitivities beyond the demonstrated managerial capacity of human institutions (Boulding, 1966; Meadows et al, 1972; Hirsh, 1978).

Many of the critics' claims were challenged. Economic optimists argued that increased wealth provided the wherewithal to address undesirable effects, allowing richer nations to achieve better air and water quality than poor ones. Moreover, they said, any increasing scarcity of valued commodities would lead to higher prices and in turn inspire further discoveries, greater efficiencies and inventive substitutions. They pointed to technology's two centuries of success in frustrating Malthusian predictions. They celebrated human ingenuity (see, for example, Simon and Kahn, 1984). And in some applications they were well justified. Anticipated mineral shortages, for example, were avoided through use of new exploratory, mining and smelting techniques. Anticipated fossil fuel shortages too were pushed back, though unevenly and at some political as well as ecological cost.

But these responses were only persuasive in limited areas. While increased wealth did support important pollution abatement action, it tended also to introduce new hazards and higher volumes of use (cars, for example, became much more energy efficient and less polluting but also much more numerous). Corrective action was rarely automatic. Where effective controls proved difficult, as in ocean fisheries, resources were decimated. The biggest problems, however, proved to be systemic. Substitutions could often be achieved for particular resources such as tropical hardwoods, but not for the associated loss of ecosystem functions and services – species habitat, rainfall attenuation and flood control. Policing adjustments have countered particular criminal innovations, but where customary civility has broken down there have been no effective substitutes. Buildings damaged by hurricanes have been repaired or replaced, but we have no idea how to substitute for the current global climate system.

The growth debates persisted through the final decades of the 20th century. While devotion to economic expansion continued to dominate national agendas, the easy assumption that progress would necessarily ensue, without significant managerial effort and without substantial costs, ceased to be believable. An atmosphere of ambivalence prevailed, contributing to the century's broad legacy of uncertainty and unease. The benefits of new opportunities and more commodious lives were still attractive but expected to come with some cost. In the short term, growth was something still to be sought, but also guided and controlled. In the long term, the problems seemed likely to multiply. Despite the best efforts of the optimists, the prevailing public suspicion rested with the simple common sense view that there were limits, that infinite expansion of economic demands on a single, necessarily limited biosphere was simply not plausible.[8]

All this is just part of a much more complex story. The evolving concerns and controversies about risks and damages, development failures and limits to growth overlapped with each other and with a myriad of additional considerations all of which can be viewed from many different perspectives. Nevertheless, the basic themes are clear enough. Confidence in the agenda and inevitability of progress – already shaken in the first half of the 20th century – declined further in the second half. And it did so in ways that seemed increasingly to demand alternative approaches that would be more cautious and humble, more sensitive to multiple interacting factors and to specific circumstances, and more effectively devoted to equity and durability.

The idea of progress was not rejected. Perhaps, as Bury suggested back in 1920, progress has now joined self-consciousness as a permanent feature of our conceptual world. In any event, the disappointments of the 20th century did not shatter hope that we might be able to improve our behaviour and conditions. Certainly they spurred criticism of how progress was being defined and pursued. And certainly the criticisms included attacks on conventional growth with its ever expanding material demands and ecosystem stresses. But there was little serious interest in returning to the old sustainability of customary stability. Instead, the predominant focus was on finding more viable approaches to progress. The objective was to replace short sighted and merely economic growth with development options that promised more comprehensive and lasting gains.

This was the context in which sustainability re-emerged. Unlike the old sustainability, the new version had to be constructed not in a world of tradition and preservation of the tried and true, but in a world of change and devotion to improvement.

The second coming of sustainability

Sustainability as a term and rough idea appeared in the early 1970s, in response to the two previous decades' deepening worries about damages and risks, development failures and evident growth limits. When global environmental concerns were explored in the United Nations' 1972 Stockholm Conference on the Human Environment, questions arose immediately about how to reconcile environmental protection with advancement in well-being for the world's poor. In a book linked to the conference, Barbara Ward and René Dubos (1972) suggested 'sustainable development' as the way forward.

The idea was apparently premature. Where they went beyond agreeable environmental matters, the Stockholm diplomats did little more than paper over the tensions between the growth worries of the wealthy nations and the development aspirations of the poor. Professionals in agencies with conservation and development aid responsibilities continued to wrestle with their overlapping tasks, attempting linked approaches under various titles: 'environment and development', 'development without destruction', 'environmentally sound development' and 'eco-development'. None of these attracted much attention outside a limited circle of international agencies and associated non-governmental organizations, but they helped establish a foundation of thinking about the reconciliation of two unavoidable obligations.

Also in 1972, broader public attention to some of the underlying concerns was spurred by The Club of Rome's extraordinarily popular report on its computer projection of trends in resource use, pollution, food projection, population and industrial output (Meadows et al, 1972). The computer generated scenarios were primitive and vulnerable to misinterpretation as predictions of the future. But the report renewed attention to biospheric limits and spurred lively debates about whether and when economic growth and technological advance might contribute to solutions as well as to deepening problems.

Eight years later conservation interests came to the sustainability idea from a somewhat different direction. Gradually recognizing that wildlife could only be protected if habitats were maintained and that this was only possible if the local people had viable livelihoods, the International Union for the Conservation of Nature and Natural Resources, the World Wildlife Fund and the United Nations Environment Programme, issued a *World Conservation Strategy* with a subtitle, 'living resource conservation for sustainable development' (IUCN et al, 1980a). But this too was just a step in a gestation period.

The references to sustainability in the Ward and Dubos book, the conservation strategy document and several other works received limited public notice. It took some further years for the emerging concerns about growth limits, development failures and the risks and damages of technological adventures to merge and mature, and for a focus on problems to shift to a focus on what to do. By the mid-1980s, however, the time was ripe.

In late 1983, Norwegian Prime Minister Gro Harlem Brundtland was asked by the Secretary-General of the United Nations to chair an independent commission on how to deal with the tensions that had arisen in Stockholm. Her commission's mandate was to determine not just how to protect the environment but also how to eliminate poverty and promote general progress on one limited and already abused planet. It was not an easy assignment. Poverty and environmental degradation remained two of the great intractable global problems. Moreover, they appeared to demand opposing solutions. Overcoming poverty demanded expansion of economic activity and opportunity; protecting the environment entailed restraint. Any imaginable solution would have to be both highly creative and sharply at odds with business as usual. And it would have to win support not just from Brundtland but also from the Commission's 20 other members, representing as many different nations and consequently a great diversity of conditions and cultures, ideologies and interests. It would be a marvel if they could agree a description of the problems, much less an innovative prescription for the future.

At the same time, it was an entirely sensible assignment. For decades the United Nations and its associated agencies had struggled separately with development and environment. Both were life-and-death matters and increasingly they were interrelated. Continuing environmental degradation was leading not only to local and regional resource depletion and damage to essential ecological functions, but also to cumulative effects that aggravated poverty and threatened global well-being. Meanwhile, the failures or inadequacies of development initiatives in many places were leaving many people in destitution and insecurity while the gap between rich and poor widened. These dynamics, combined with a continuing rise in human numbers, pointed to an ugly future of increasingly desperate poor people with little choice but to eat into their remaining natural capital – in a world that apparently could not support everyone at even a moderate European standard with current levels of technological and distributional efficiency.

The Brundtland Commission's solution – announced in its now famous report, *Our Common Future* (WCED, 1987) – was sustainable development. It was at once necessary, brilliant, incomplete, filled with tensions and wildly popular.

Environment and development, the Commission argued, had to be addressed together because they are interdependent – both as problems and as solutions. Poverty cannot be overcome in a world of ecological decline and resource depletion. Environment cannot be rehabilitated in a world of deprivation and desperation. The aim of development must therefore be to build conditions and capabilities that will allow people to sustain themselves while also sustaining the environment that is the foundation for their lives and livelihoods. And the results must be lasting. It was hard to disagree. All 21 commissioners signed on to the concept, signaling and fostering widespread acceptance of the Commission's report and its argument.

The concept of sustainable development became the closest thing to an overnight hit that is imaginable for a product of international diplomacy. There were critics, certainly – arguing, for example, that the Brundtland agenda was contradictory, or too invasive or too soft on the rich. But the critics had little effect. Within months of the report's release, national governments and government jurisdictions at other levels began to embrace sustainable development. Sustainability became the featured objective of government pronouncements on development initiatives, domestic programme agendas and international aid targets. Major corporations and business associations also claimed adherence. Shelves of academic treatises, consulting reports and policy documents were prepared. Sustainability became a household term. By 1992, when the United Nations held its first world conference on environment and development, an unprecedented number of national government representatives were willing to travel to Rio de Janeiro to refresh their vows of commitment to the pursuit of sustainability. Today, sustainability is firmly embedded in the language of development – locally, globally and at every level between. It is in common use well beyond the fields of poverty reduction and environmental protection, and beyond the halls of formal government. It is a huge success.

And a continuing disappointment. The enormous popularity of the notion among the great and mighty has been accompanied by more verbal adherence than practical implementation. While thousands of specific initiatives have been undertaken at all levels from the neighbourhood to the planet, they have so far remained mostly counterpoints to the dominant practice. Certainly they have had far too little evident effect on the two key trends that agitated the Brundtland Commission – the continuing degradation of ecosystems and resources, and the expanding gap between rich and poor.

Agenda 21, the major product of the 1992 United Nations Conference on Environment and Development (UNCED) in Rio de Janeiro, was an ambitious compilation (40 chapters totaling 700 pages) of officially recognized needs for action (Robinson, 1993). The document set out detailed action programmes, with cost estimates for their implementation, to address a long list of sectoral concerns including poverty reduction, technology transfer, climate change and hazardous waste disposal. While not all items were well specified and not all observers were satisfied that the best strategies had been adopted, 'hopes were high and expectations were great' (WSSD, 2002).

A significant amount of international as well as local discussion and research about sustainability followed the Rio conference. Valuable work was done to understand better how ecosystems work and how their integrity may be sustained. Similarly admirable efforts went into designing and applying more promising ways of fostering efficiency and equity, of helping communities build on their own social and material resources to establish sustainable livelihoods, of addressing problems with intergenerational implications, of identifying appropriate indicators of human and ecological well-being for all sorts of communities and ecosystems, and of understanding how to design for and adapt to continuing uncertainties. The UN and associated bodies also held a series of 'Rio Cluster' international conferences to deal with issues ranging from trade and development, fish stocks, pollution and human rights, to climate change, biodiversity and desertification. At the same time, many more immediately practical positive steps were taken in neighbourhoods and communities, in local government councils and in progressive corporate board rooms. At all levels and in numerous fields, sustainability was becoming an increasingly visible part of planning and problem solving.

But by 2002, when the Rio+10 gathering – the World Summit on Sustainable Development in Johannesburg – was held, it was abundantly clear that few of the 1992 expectations had been met. Apparently because of widespread failures to achieve measurable improvements, few of the participating countries submitted progress reports. Trends away from sustainability, however, were evident enough. Conference organizers reported that in the ten years following the Rio gathering, 'poverty deepened in many areas and environmental degradation continued unabated' (WSSD, 2002). And the new steps taken at Johannesburg did little to dispel the disappointments. While the Rio commitments were reaffirmed, some additional targets were specified and new partnerships were announced, UN Secretary General Kofi Annan was putting the most positive face on it when he called the Johannesburg summit 'a beginning' (WSSD, 2002).

Sustainability today remains an idea with more potential than effect. It has been widely embraced not just in rough concept and language but also in a plethora of applications by a host of different players, including governments, businesses and civil society organizations. And no doubt it has contributed to important improvements in a wide range of areas. At the same time, sustainability commitments have had far too little practical effect on the major global concerns that they were meant to address. For example:

- About a fifth of the world's population (1.2 billion people) still live on less than US$1 a day, and almost half the world's population live on less than US$2 a day (UNEP, 2002).
- The 1997 Kyoto Protocol targets are not expected to be met, even though it is just a first small step in slowing the rise in atmospheric carbon dioxide concentrations which, at roughly 360 parts per million today, are already higher than they have been in half a million years and still climbing steadily (Torrie and Parfett, 2000; Watson, 2001; NASA, 2004).
- The richest fifth of the world's people consume 86 per cent of all goods and services, while the poorest fifth get 1.3 per cent (UNDP, 1998).
- World fisheries landings are declining; an increasing percentage of catches are from already depleted stocks, and fishing fleets are gradually fishing down marine food webs, targeting smaller fish as big fish populations are exhausted (Pauly et al, 2002).
- One-tenth of the world's grain harvest (about 180 million tonnes) is produced by unsustainable over-exploitation of ground water resources (FAO, 2002).
- Of the 4.5 billion people who do not live in rich countries, one-third lack access to clean water and nearly 60 per cent lack access to safe sewers (UNDP, 1998).
- In the 41 most 'heavily indebted poor countries', about 10,000 children under five years old die every day, most of them because of the easily preventable infectious diseases associated with poverty (UNICEF, 1999).

Some of the disappointment following Agenda 21 and other sustainability commitments is the product of unrealistic expectations for results that cannot possibly come quickly. Changing entrenched assumptions and practices is inevitably difficult, especially at the global level where the Rio commitments were made and where the big measurements are taken. More or less competing nation states and international bodies have an understandably limited capacity for decisive joint action even on more specific and conventional concerns. When the problems are very broad and the needed responses demand serious reorientation of objectives and methods, immediately effective international action is unlikely. Ten years is short space for a global turnaround.

At the national and regional levels, the possibilities for action are enhanced by the existence of governance bodies with effective authority and tools to facilitate and, if necessary, compel action. But for these bodies as well, sustainability challenges established interests and requires changes to existing institutions. Perhaps not surprisingly, many of the most noteworthy sustainability initiatives so far have been at the local and municipal levels where particular and well-recognized problems such as urban sprawl, smog and shortages of affordable housing can be the focus of collective attention. Here too, however, most innovations have faced resistance and sustainability planning has often been more impressive than sustainability implementation.

Whether more could have been accomplished over the past decade and a half is an open question. But it is an academic question except insofar as it might shed some light on the way ahead. Despite the disappointments, sustainability remains a lively notion. The language has permeated government, corporate and civil society activities and new initiatives continue to proliferate under the sustainability banner. Even when the claims are patently fraudulent, they reveal the power of the notion. Sustainability has been adopted, and has power, as a representation of widely shared expectations for arrangements that will deliver progress and continuity – richer and safer lives, fairer distribution and a protected environment. The expectations may be fuzzy, and some formulations may be self-contradictory, but they have emerged from a comprehensible history and after a decade and more of deliberation and experimentation, a good deal has been learned about what sustainability means and implies.

From this have come insights not only about the basic requirements for sustainability but also about the uncertainties and variations. Both, as we shall see, are crucial for the purposes of sustainability assessment, which needs some foundation of shared agreement but must also serve as a means of working out the specifics of sustainability needs and possibilities for particular places and circumstances.

Debating the concept

In the years immediately following release of the Brundtland Commission's report, many scholars and activists doubted that a useful definition of sustainable development or the pursuit of sustainability was possible – to them the concept seemed to be too fuzzy, too contradictory and/or too generally ambitious to be useful in practice. These doubts became deeper worries when it became clear that the idea might become influential as well as popular, and proponents of various positions launched into a great contest over which interpretation would prevail.

Box 3.1 Sustainable development multiple choice

Sustainable development is:

(a) a redundancy, since unsustainable activities cannot provide true development;
(b) an oxymoron (a self-contradiction) that amounts to believing that you can have your cake and eat it too;
(c) a case of developers getting the noun and environmentalists being left with the adjective;
(d) a dangerous delusion, promoted by those who are unwilling to recognize that we are already overstraining our planet's capacity to withstand our impositions;
(e) one of the landmark steps in human history, following opposable thumbs, the discovery of fire and the invention of progress;
(f) an exceptionally popular term, invoked favourably by all manner of otherwise incompatible individuals;
(g) a term that everyone can support, largely because no one knows what sustainability means and/or no one agrees on what development means;
(h) a term that offers an accommodation of opposing forces – suggesting that responsible stewardship of nature and continuing gains in human material well-being are compatible.

The sustainability debates proceeded in word and in deed. Acres of literature were produced. Some of it was largely theoretical and speculative. But much of the focus was on implications for practice. Beginning in the late 1980s, policy initiatives and projects of great diversity were undertaken, or re-labelled, and discussed as exercises in applied sustainability. The participants included defenders of entrenched interests as well as devotees of bold exploration and, not surprisingly, the associated debates about the meaning and implications of sustainability were to some extent a competition among competing interests attempting to co-opt the term and promote or defend their own established priorities and understandings. Sustainability was a loose enough idea to accommodate them all.

Especially in the early years of these sustainability debates, differences were more evident than commonalities. The huge numbers of books, articles, consulting reports and policy papers offered countless competing positions on the proper definition of the term and its implications for action. There were even many thoughtful works proposing taxonomies to help readers sort through the many competing options.

One early typology that has enjoyed continued popularity is summarized in Table 3.1 (Pearce and Turner, 1990; Moffat, 1995). It identifies four basic positions following a worldview continuum from technocentric to ecocentric. This depiction suggests that the key difference is between underlying ethical stances. However, the same taxonomy is often also labelled as positions along a weak to strong sustainability spectrum, with the core distinction being more managerial than ethical. The debate turns on whether or not we should have much confidence that economic capital and technical innovation will be able to provide substitutes for the resources and other services of relatively natural biophysical systems (Schrecker, 1995, cited in Hodge et al, 1995).

Table 3.1 *Pearce and Turner's sustainability spectrum*

	Technocentric (or weak sustainability)		Ecocentric (or strong sustainability)	
	Cornucopian	*Accommodating*	*Communalist*	*Deep ecology*
Green labels	Resource exploitation; growth oriented	Resource conservationist; managerial	Resource preservationist	Extreme preservationist position
Type of economy	Unfettered free market	Green economy; environment economic instruments	Steady state economy; environmental protection prioritized	Heavily regulated economy; minimized resource use
Management strategies	Economic policy objectives; maximize gross national product (GNP) growth; Trust the markets; full substitution between forms of capital	Modified economic growth; green accounting; reject substitutability; constant capital rule	Zero economic growth and population growth; systems perspective and ecosystem health important; small-scale, community-level focus	Reduced economy and population; environmental ethics central
Ethics	Anthropocentric; instrumental value in nature	Wider notion of stewardship for nature; intergenerational equity considered	Extension of ethical responsibilities to non-humans; strongly communitarian	Acceptance of bioethics; intrinsic value in nature; millennarial stand

A second, oft-cited taxonomy, presented in Table 3.2, takes a somewhat different approach, identifying clusters of literature that emphasize managerial, technical or philosophical/political solutions (Pezzoli 1997). It too recognizes underlying critiques and ideology as well as more obvious emphases on particular means of responding to the evident challenges, but does not imply any simple links between particular ethical positions and willingness to use certain methods and tools for change.

Table 3.2 *Pezzoli's ten categories of literature on sustainable development*

Cluster	Category
Applied perspective with managerial focus	1 Managerialism, policy and planning Legal-institutional terrain and state initiatives; civil society and NGOs; urban and regional planning and development; natural resources and rural development; indicators of sustainable development
	2 Social conditions Population; human behaviour and social learning; environmental health
	3 Environmental law Property and development laws; legal issues concerning environmental racism, equity and justice
Technical perspective: the hard sciences of sustainability	4 Environmental sciences
	5 Eco-design and the built environment
	6 Ecological economics Environmental and resource economics; eco-tourism; industrial ecology
Philosophical or 'structural-transformative' perspective	7 Eco-philosophy environmental values and ethics Epistemology, science, culture and language; philosophy, policy and development; environmental justice and racism; eco-feminism
	8 Environmental history and human geography/ecology
	9 Utopianism, anarchism and bioregionalism
	10 Political ecology Globalization and eco-politics; urban and regional development; rural studies; critical social movements and empowerments; theory building and agendas for research and action

Perhaps the most familiar taxonomies are those that adopt an architectural metaphor, suggesting that sustainability rests on a number of interconnected pillars (Mebratu, 1998). There have been lively debates about whether it is best to conceive of sustainability resting on two intersecting pillars (the ecological and the human) or three (social, ecological and economic) or five (ecological, economic, social, political/institutional and cultural) or more.

The differences reflect contrasting preoccupations. The two pillar version, built on the environment and development concerns of the Brundtland Commission (WCED, 1987), has been popular among nature preservation advocates and other environmentalists who wish to stress that ecological concerns are at least equivalent to human ones. The popular three pillar version (Table 3.3) distinguishes between economic and social needs, and is therefore pre-

Table 3.3 *The three pillar version*

Pillars	Proponents	Emphases
Economic	Conventional corporate and government interests; institutions for trade liberalization	• Sustainable economic expansion to provide wealth to deal with environmental and social issues. • Efficiencies and substitutions to address ecological damage and resource depletion concerns. • Global market discipline and selected government interventions to encourage efficiencies and innovations (WBCSD, 2000).
Ecological/ biophysical	Environmental NGOs, greens, ecology activists	• Growth as the enemy of sustainability. • Reduce demands on already overstressed biosphere. • Efficiencies not enough. • Must protect and rehabilitate natural systems, avoid invasive technologies, cut over-consumption by the rich, build basic economic security for the poor and stabilize or lower human population (Goodland, 1995; Rees, 1999).
Social	Advocates of social justice and development reform	• Recognize the rich as well as the poor as problems for sustainability. • Wealth/poverty not just economic: must enhance social and political as well as material equity. • Strengthen the assets, opportunities and powers that allow people and communities to pursue sustainable options more successfully in their own ways and in their own places (Sharma, 1994; Sainath, 1996; Sachs, 1999).

ferred by those who emphasize that material gains are not sufficient measures or preservers of human well-being. Similarly, the addition of cultural and political or institutional pillars is most common in international development applications, where authorities see a need to underline the importance of these factors in building durable foundations for improvement (CIDA, 1997a). As is indicated in Table 3.3, even within the various versions there are differences of option about the relative importance of the recognized pillars.

Focusing on these pillars is convenient because they are traditional fields of policy making, scholarly enquiry and specialized research. Also, most available data on sustainability-related conditions and trends fit smoothly in the usual pillar categories, making them particularly popular in initiatives centred on sustainability indicator development and reporting (for example, GRI, 2002). Unfortunately, this conventional convenience makes the pillars less well suited to encouraging substantial innovation. In the usual depictions, the pillars are recognized to be interconnected and interdependent. But in application, effective integration has been rare, at least in part because reliance on the traditional pillars makes it too easy to continue thinking only within the old administrative, academic and technical boxes.

Part of the problem may be the focus on categorization and emphasis. Because sustainability is a politically significant concept it is important to illuminate the differences among the various, potentially competing positions. And because use of the term has been plagued by fuzziness, it is useful to identify its constituent components. But any exercise that puts things in separate categories tends to obscure what is overlapping and shared. This is especially problematic for sustainability, which is essentially about linkages, interconnections and interdependencies.

As we have seen, sustainability emerged as a popular notion from an enquiry into the relationships between environment and development. The sustainability literature, too, features wide agreement that the genius of the concept lies in its recognition of the ties between objectives usually assumed to be at odds. This conflicts with the divisive tendency of separate pillars. In response, many authorities on sustainability have proposed ways of seeing how the various pillars of sustainability fit together.

The 'deep green' depiction of the fundamental relationship between human cultures and the biosphere relies on concentric circles (as shown in Figure 3.1). The implication is that if anything in the smaller circles undermines the larger, it is weakening its own basis for existence. Most simple are two circle versions with the realm of human activities inside and dependent on the larger realm of nature. The World Conservation Union (IUCN), for example, favours 'the egg of well-being' in which the yolk of people is immersed in the white of ecosystems (Guijt et al, 2001). More complex versions distinguish between human economy and society, putting the circle of economy inside the circle of society, which is in turn inside the circle of ecology. In one form or another, such an understanding seems to have characterized most of the human experience (Frankfort and Frankfort, 1949: Polanyi, 1959). It was a foundation of the old sustainability.

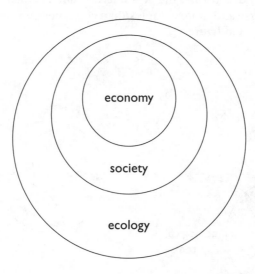

Figure 3.1 *Circles of sustainability*

Today, the old sustainability is mostly gone and the opposite ordering prevails
– economic imperatives rule, social arrangements are judged by how well they
serve the economy, and the biosphere is treated mostly as a source of resources
and services. The ancient understanding of the dependence of economy on
society and ecology still retains a certain truth. But now that humans play a
huge role in the character and functioning of many biophysical systems, depictions suggesting uni-directional lines of dependency are insufficient.

The usual alternatives to the concentric circles of sustainability are various
numbers of intersecting circles (Figure 3.2). The most common approach over-
laps three of the pillars discussed above – ecology, society and economy – in

a construct that is architecturally odd but conceptually helpful. The pillars/circles represent human activities in the identified sectors. Contributions to sustainability are asserted only in the area where all the pillars/circles intersect. In the usual depictions, that area is small relative to the whole, suggesting that little of what we now do is compatible with viability in the long run.

The pillars are still based on entrenched areas of mandate and specialization, typically resistant to integrative thinking and unlikely to be much moved by depiction of a small area of positive overlap. Nevertheless, the image of intersecting circles is valuable, if only because it encourages attention to interdependencies and the cheerful possibility of expanding the range of activities that offer multiple, mutually supportive gains.

All of the categorizations and depictions surveyed above are simplifications. The sustainability debates and the positions defended in them have been much richer, more diverse and more complex than could possibly be captured in any small set of tables and figures.

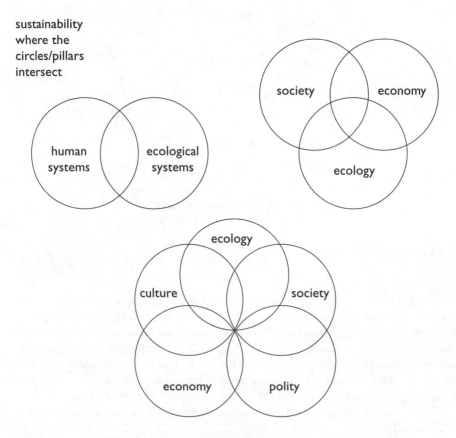

Figure 3.2 *Intersecting pillars of sustainability*

While there have been and remain fundamental differences between the ethical foundations and strategic preferences of sustainability advocates of one stripe and another, few of the positions taken are utterly at odds. Arguably, most of the disagreements have been about priorities and emphases, about the grounds for confidence that a proposed approach will be feasible or sufficient, and about what should be included in the list of key considerations when choices are being made on practical policy and project undertakings. Moreover, the years of experimentation as well as deliberation by the full diversity of sustainability adherents have gradually clarified both the objective of lasting betterment and the possible means to it.

The essentials

The concept of sustainability has certainly demonstrated some staying power. Nearly two decades since the Brundtland Commission completed its work, still increasing numbers of governments, corporations and civil society bodies claim to be moving in ways informed by sustainability commitments, and practical applications continue to proliferate. Durability alone does not prove that the concept is coherent and useful. But it suggests that there is good reason to consider what qualities have contributed to the lasting interest in sustainability and whether these qualities might also be its defining essentials.

For our purposes, the essential qualities of sustainability – the shared basics of the concept – must be those that lie at the core of the idea and that should inform its application anywhere. They must be rooted in its origins and evident, at least implicitly, through the range of competing interpretations. They must be minimally controversial. They must not just recognize problems but also offer some guidance for positive response. And, if sustainability is to be established as a fundamentally coherent concept (however much conflict and diversity there may be in particular applications) for the purposes of practical application in sustainability assessments at many scales from the local to the global, the essentials must together form a roughly complete whole.

Fortunately, it is not difficult to identify characteristics of sustainability that meet this test.

First, as we have seen, *the concept of sustainability is a challenge to conventional thinking and practice*. It was formulated as a broad response to persistent and fundamental concerns about the adequacy and long-term viability of the prevailing approaches to progress, development and well-being. Most immediately, it arose out of linked worries about environmental degradation and development failures, but it was also rooted in more comprehensive critiques of decision making that gave little attention to the costs and limits to growth, to the risks of increasingly ambitious manipulations of nature, or to the complex and particular realities of communities and ecologies targeted for development. The concept represents the need for positive alternatives to the present, unsustainable path.

Second, as a response to these concerns, *the concept of sustainability is in all its formulations concerned about long as well as short-term well-being*. It addresses persistent threats and it values potentially durable solutions.

Third, *sustainability covers the core issues of decision making (the pursuit and maintenance of necessities and satisfactions, health and security, diversity and equity, ecology and community, preservation and development, etc.)*. Arguably, sustainability is the proper central concern of decision making. It is not one item of a list of relevant considerations, but a broad conceptual framework and set of general values for integrating the full suite of relevant considerations. Some of the literature and practice has focused more narrowly and still usefully on, for example, environmental sustainability or community level sustainability. The full concept, however, is comprehensive of all factors, at all levels, that may affect the desirability and durability of future conditions.

Fourth, *sustainability demands recognition of links and interdependencies*. The key message of the Brundtland Commission, and of countless other serious deliberations about the prospects for human life on this planet, is that human and ecological well-being are effectively interdependent. However many layers of artifice we may construct, humans are ultimately and unavoidably dependent on biospheric conditions that are friendly to human life. And humans now play a huge role in manipulating biospheric conditions. Consequently, there is no serious strategy for preserving and enhancing ecosystem integrity that does not also involve ensuring human well-being. And vice versa. To some commentators on the Brundtland Commission's work, the crucial interdependencies involved an apparent contradiction. On the one hand, the Commission saw that it would eventually be suicidal to allow a further undermining of ecological life support systems, locally and globally. On the other, they saw that development was also required to eliminate destitution, ensure material security, and allow individuals and communities more choices and more power to exert greater control over the factors affecting their lives. Accordingly the Commission advocated development with sustainability: initiatives designed and pursued in ways that would protect resources and ecological integrity over the long term while greatly improving human well-being, especially among the poor. Not everyone has been persuaded that this is possible. Some have argued for more emphasis on redistribution to avoid additional exploitation of nature. But sustainability adherents of all persuasions have accepted that interdependencies are powerful and must be respected.

Fifth, *sustainability must be pursued in a world of complexity and surprise, in which precautionary approaches are necessary*. The debates about sustainability and its implications have coincided with growing recognition that human and ecological considerations are linked in open, dynamic, multi-scalar systems, which are complex beyond full description. In such a context, prediction of future conditions is at best uncertain, and surprise is likely. Efforts to anticipate and avoid problems, and to pursue positive opportunities remain desirable and potentially effective. But overconfidence is perilous and precaution (in the form of back up plans, avoidance of unnecessary risk, planning for reversibility, etc.) is wise.

Sixth, *the concept of sustainability recognizes both inviolable limits and endless opportunities for creative innovation.* A child of 20th century ambivalence, it respects perils and risks, but also diversity and possibility. The concept's ancestry includes appreciation of biophysical limits to growth, the many indicators of vulnerability to social as well as ecological collapse, and the precautionary inclination. But sustainability has also been embraced as a reaction against single-minded economism, cultural uniformity, analytical narrowness and administrative convenience. Its adherents have attempted to expand and link models, frameworks and methodologies from many disciplines.[9] And sustainability-centred inspiration has helped to spur an extraordinary range of local and larger initiatives – slow food and urban growth management strategies, microcredit and wind farms, traditional knowledge preservation and car-free days. Arguably, this diversity in thinking and practice is as crucial to the pursuit of sustainability as precaution, appreciation of interdependency and concern for the long term.

Seventh, *sustainability is open-ended.* It is a set of principles to apply and processes to follow, not a state to be achieved. Sustainability must be pursued in a dynamic and complex world where there will always be unexpected stresses, emerging opportunities and shifting preferences, and where there will always be uncertainty and surprise. In such a world, no single, lasting solution is possible. Not even the goals are fixed (Robinson et al, 1990; Ravetz, 2000; HKPD, 2000; HKSDU, 2002).

Eighth, *the means and the ends are necessarily intertwined.* Sustainability is not just a matter of putting in place a system of compatible relations among social, ecological and economic factors. It is also a matter of culture and governance. How we build relations with each other, what habits of thought and behaviour we establish and how we go about making decisions are central to sustainability.

Finally, and perhaps most importantly for a discussion of assessment applications, *the concept of sustainability is both universal and context dependent.* The points above refer to the essential qualities or characteristics shared by the many and various versions of the concept. In the interests of providing a basic set of criteria for sustainability assessment decision making, Chapter 5 will go even further by proposing a short but broadly applicable list of core requirements for progress towards sustainability. To this extent, sustainability has a universal aspect, relevant not just to consideration of global scale issues but also local and regional ones, wherever they may be and whatever the particulars of the case. At the same time, however, sustainability offers no common blueprint, no single paradigm. While the shared characteristics discussed here and the core requirements outlined in Chapter 5 have some substantive weight, they are all dependent on elaboration and specification in context. As noted above, the concept arose in part as a response to the failures of narrow impositions and context-insensitive development. It is not the banner of a new civilizing mission to be led by the mighty and the expert. The concept of sustainability is perhaps best conceived as a substantively important but minimal framework requiring specification in and for particular places.

In other words, sustainability cannot be defined as one set of characteristics and requirements. While there are some core basics, the implications and applications differ from one context to the next. In defining and applying the sustainability concept, the core basics are necessary but insufficient. Specification in context is also needed.

Box 3.2 The essentials of the concept of sustainability

The concept of sustainability is:

- a challenge to conventional thinking and practice;
- about long- as well as short-term well-being;
- comprehensive, covering all the core issues of decision making;
- a recognition of links and interdependencies, especially between humans and the biophysical foundations for life;
- embedded in a world of complexity and surprise, in which precautionary approaches are necessary;
- a recognition of both inviolable limits and endless opportunities for creative innovation;
- about an open-ended process, not a state;
- about intertwined means and ends – culture and governance as well as ecology, society and economy;
- both universal and context dependent.

Initial implications for assessment regimes

These essentials of sustainability have some obvious implications for the design and application of assessment policies, laws and processes. They suggest, for example, that assessments ought to encourage a turnaround from unsustainability and that the test of acceptability for new undertakings should be, as it was in the Voisey's Bay case, more demanding than mere mitigation. The essentials also demand that the scope of concern must extend into the long term and beyond merely biophysical considerations. Assessment should cover the full suite of factors, because they interact and the interrelated effects of all of them will determine whether our futures are more viable, desirable and durable.

Perhaps most important is the universal and context dependent aspect of the concept, which has a contrasting pair of implications. Sustainability assessments have the double role of vehicles for the general pursuit of sustainability and contributors to defining the specifics of sustainability in particular circumstances. Because the concept of sustainability has an identifiable core, we should be able to set out general sustainability criteria to be applied in assessment evaluations and decision making. But because specification in context is required, each assessment must help establish an understanding of the local particulars and what the pursuit of sustainability means and entails there.

A good deal more needs to be said about sustainability's implications for assessment processes: about the basic agenda and design for assessments; about how they can cover the full range of sustainability issues and still be manageable; about how they might specify sustainability considerations and integrate them together; about approaches to dealing with conflicts and uncertainties; about suitable links between strategic and project level work; and between assessments and other initiatives for sustainability. But before that can be done properly, we need to be clearer about sustainability as a basis for evaluation and decision making in assessments.

Assessments are exercises in evaluation and decision making. They involve countless choices – on whether an undertaking merits detailed review, whether an anticipated effect is likely to be significant, whether one option is preferable to another, whether a design change is acceptable, whether a monitoring programme is addressing the most important concerns, and so on. For such purposes, it makes a difference when the basic test is whether the undertaking is likely to make a positive contribution to the pursuit of sustainability. And it helps to understand that this involves a long-term view, integrated consideration of all relevant factors and appreciation of the particular circumstances. But these alone are unlikely to provide a satisfactory foundation for clarity, consistency and cumulative effectiveness in sustainability-centred assessments. For that we need a basic shared understanding of the key considerations that underlie the basic test so that we can build a working set of general sustainability criteria for evaluations and decision making.

It is possible to extract a broadly supported set of sustainability decision criteria directly from the literature about what sustainability means. Many authors and organizations have already offered definitions of sustainability and provided lists of guiding principles for decision makers. A selection of these, spanning over two decades, is included in the surveys of sustainability concepts and approaches in the appendices at the back of this book. These lists vary in detail and ambition. But most of them are intended as steps from definition to application. They are as much about how to pursue sustainability as about what the concept means. Moreover, some of the lists are for specified decision makers (business corporations, development agencies, international finance institutions, forest product certifiers, mine developers, ecovillage creators, urban and regional planners, etc.). They combine general sustainability considerations with a more or less profound understanding of particular practical requirements. Together they provide a reasonably strong practical as well as theoretical base for identifying the core criteria for sustainability-centred decisions.

The question can, however, be approached from a quite different direction. Along with the broad literature and the various lists of guiding principles, there have been many experiments in applied sustainability. Some of these have been initiated by people already familiar with and committed to the concept of sustainability. But many others have been more directly driven by the specifics of the situation. The next chapter examines five examples of circumstance-driven sustainability. While they are not necessarily more valuable indicators of the 'true' nature of sustainability requirements than the broader conceptions and principles lists in the literature, they do provide a window into sustainability on the ground and a transition from sustainability as an idea to sustainability in decision making.

Notes

1   For the purposes of this book, the two terms are synonymous. They have been used differently, but there is no evident consistency of difference. The debates about whether and how the usages have differed or should differ are unresolved. There is not even much agreement on which term is broader, or which carries more undesirable baggage. The term 'sustainability' is adopted here solely because it is shorter.

2   Among the Inuit of the Canadian high arctic, seal liver is a traditional delicacy. It is eaten raw. This is important because raw liver retains exceptional nutritional value, especially as a source of vitamins A and C (Inuit Tapiriit Kanatami, 2004). But vitamin science was not a part of traditional Inuit knowledge, which instead offered spiritual reasons for the customary practice. Jill Oakes (1987) has explained the spiritual aspect as follows:

> *A spirit of plenty is believed by some to live in the seal liver; therefore the liver must be eaten raw in order to release the spirit back to the earth where it is passed on to the sky and eventually returns to the sea. When the spirit is kept alive and allowed to circulate through the land, air and marine ecological systems, it provides a bountiful harvest to the Inuit hunters.*

In the traditional Inuit world, customary practice served spiritual, ecological and nutritional ends all at once.

3   In Hesiod's version of the 'how humans got fire' story, the Titan Prometheus steals fire from Zeus and gives it to the mortals. In response, Zeus not only punishes Prometheus horribly, but also ensures that humans suffer as well. Zeus says to Prometheus [Hesiod, Works and Days 55]:

> *Prometheus, you are glad that you have outwitted me and stolen fire ... but I will give men as the price for fire an evil thing in which they may all be glad of heart while they embrace their own destruction.*

4   Self-consciousness, at least in some views, distinguishes humanity and defines our origins. In the Judaeo-Christian tradition, it came near the beginning, with defiant consumption of fruit from the tree of knowledge. It is, like progress, an ambivalent accomplishment, associated with sin and loss as well as with liberation and enrichment.

5   In his inaugural address, Truman presented the argument as follows:

> *...we must embark on a bold new program for making the benefits of our scientific advances and industrial progress available for the improvement and growth of underdeveloped areas.*
>
> *More than half the people of the world are living in conditions approaching misery. Their food is inadequate. They are victims of disease. Their economic life is primitive and stagnant. Their poverty is a handicap and a threat both to them and to more prosperous areas.*
>
> *...Greater production is the key to prosperity and peace. And the key to greater production is a wider and more vigorous application of modern scientific and technical knowledge.*

6   A typical recent statement of the main lessons of the last 50 years of development experience was provided by the Organisation for Economic Co-operation and Development's (OECD's) Development Assistance Committee (1996):

> *...we have learned that successful development strategies must integrate a number of key elements: they require a sound and stable policy framework; an emphasis on social development; enhanced participation by the local population, and notably by women; good governance, in the widest sense; policies and practices that are environmentally sustainable; and better means of preventing and resolving conflict and fostering reconciliation.*

7   Improved awareness of context and complexity has, however, been offered as a key explanation for the gradual improvement in World Bank aid effectiveness over the past decade. See Johnston and Battaile (2001).

8   An indicator of the shift from Mishan's time to the recent past is the reception given to the Danish statistician Bjorn Lomborg. In his 2001 book, *The Skeptical Environmentalist*, Lomborg argued that growth induced global environmental problems were trivial or well managed. In 1967, Mishan's questioning of growth had been an extraordinary challenge to the received wisdom. By 2001, Lomborg's growth defending views were characterized as 'contrarian'.

9   Approaches to sustainability based on interdisciplinary application of multiple paradigms were advocated and applied even before the concept gained popular recognition. See Redclift (1987).

4

Practice

Sustainability in Illustrative Initiatives

Theory and practice

The sustainability essentials set out in Chapter 3 are drawn from what we usually call the theoretical literature. This literature is not all theoretical, of course. Writers on sustainability over the past decade and a half have drawn as much from experiment as from philosophy, and many of the theoreticians are practitioners as well. Nonetheless, the references in Chapter 3 are mostly to works of overview, synthesis and conceptual review by authors who have wrestled with the big issues of meaning and implication. Their works have great strengths. They reveal much about a very difficult concept that incorporates and affects an enormous breath of relevant considerations. They offer insights from evidently deep and careful thinking about matters of knowledge (and ignorance), about logical consistency and ethical justification, about the evolution of ideas and the broader context of history. In contrast to their counterparts in too many other fields, the works on sustainability theory are remarkably free of terminological pomposity. And clearly most of the authors have a practical bent. They have been as much concerned with application strategies as with conceptual alternatives and they have both contributed to and learned from implementation efforts.

Still, an examination of sustainability assessment as a practice as well as an idea should be built on a sense of what has been happening on the ground as well as what is in the literature. This chapter therefore explores applied sustainability. It relies mostly on stories – short accounts of particular cases from the hundreds of thousands of sustainability-centred initiatives undertaken over the past few years by neighbourhoods, communities, government bodies, private corporations, and combinations of one sort or another.

There was no science to the selection of the stories for telling here. The chosen cases are meant to be diverse in components, locations and participants. They have not all been undertaken explicitly under the label of 'sustainability'. They differ in initial driving concerns and hopes, and in scale, funding and ambitions. What they share is a broad agenda centred on long-term improvement and more or less simultaneous, if not integrated, attention to the interrelated factors that evidently characterize sustainability as an idea. In addition, since the exercise is meant to illuminate implications for sustainability assessment, the selection has favoured cases where some form of assessment has been involved, though more often implicitly in the course of events than explicitly as assessments.

Stories

Sustainable livelihoods in Madhya Pradesh[1]

Since 1995, traditionally marginalized residents of a dozen villages in the Bundelkhand region of Madhya Pradesh in India have been participants in and beneficiaries of a gradually expanding set of small-scale, sustainable, local employment enterprises. These now include tile making and building material production, energy generation, water management and other activities – all using local resources and building on the capabilities of local people. Previously disadvantaged women, particularly *adivasis* (tribal people) and *dalits* (members of the 'untouchables' caste), have been especially important participants.

The initiative began with a modest, handmade paper production unit introduced by Development Alternatives, an Indian non-governmental organization (NGO), with funding from Canada's International Development Research Centre. But recognition of local assets and priorities, and consultation with the local people, led to a continued process of reconsideration and adjustment as problems and opportunities emerged.

Even before the paper unit was set up, the Development Alternatives staff worked with residents to build a small check dam on a stream near the building site for their TARAgram technology centre. The dam was intended to increase water availability for the centre and to help recharge local wells, but it also regenerated stream side vegetation and supplied irrigation water for adjacent farm fields. Invasive plants cleared from the site were used to make charcoal, which was mixed with clay and cow dung to make a briquette fuel that slowly became popular as a fuel wood alternative. Invasive vegetation in the stream was also harvested to feed a biogas-driven electricity generator.

Eventually, the manufacture of roof tiles and other building materials became the centre's main productive enterprise, again using local materials that were otherwise problems. The microconcrete roof tiles are made in part from stone dust that had previously been dumped as an industrial waste from stone-crushing operations in the region. As an affordable local product, the tiles are increasingly popular in house construction and repair, and the expanded market has inspired production by other independent microenterprises in the area.

At the TARAgram centre, the tile-making unit is run by local women who were initially unskilled and underemployed. Training and involvement in decision making have characterized all aspects of the initiative. As well, the employment component has been complemented by a larger set of efforts to enhance livelihood security and choice, and to address practical issues as they emerged. For example, when the employment of women in the production operations led to reduced school attendance by their oldest daughters (who dropped out to take care of their younger siblings), the project adapted by establishing an on-site daycare centre for the young children of working mothers. The project also uses its van as a school bus, has initiated saving circles for microcredit, and has gone into partnerships with local artisans, retailers and contractors to expand participation and benefits.

As a case of development assistance for sustainability, this initiative in Bundelkhand is remarkable for its use of modest outside intervention in the form of expertise and resources to strengthen and make use of local capacities and material assets, for its emphasis on working with local people, especially the most marginalized, and for its ability to achieve mutually reinforcing benefits through undertakings with multiple objectives. A report on the case concludes:

> *Much of the TARAgram project success in enhancing sustainable local livelihood opportunities rests on its integrated character – linking local employment with adult training and child education, ecological restoration, reliance on local materials and markets, opportunities for women, and partnerships with local entrepreneurs. The results so far are impressive and should continue to build on each other. They include reduced seasonal migration to cities for casual employment, improved local availability of basic need items such as alternative cooking fuels and building materials, more purchasing power for local people, a local economy that is more self-reliant, and an environment that is less degraded (Vaidyanathan, 2002).*

As a case of sustainability assessment, it is an example of an initiative with multiple general objectives and a broad understanding of their interconnections but also deep appreciation of the importance of the specifics of the local context. It is also an example of integrated, iterative and adaptive planning. Sustainability assessment in this case was continuous, with particular objectives adjusted, and new opportunities and options evaluated, as the project evolved. The approach to development and decision making also recognized that a participative process had value in itself as a means of building capacities, as well as a substantive value in identifying problems and possibilities and setting priorities.

Both the development and assessment accomplishments in this case are vulnerable to influences from beyond the villages involved. Villages everywhere now are subject to outside commercial, political and cultural influences that may affect even projects like the ones in the Bundelkhand region focused on building self-reliance (for example, through tile making that uses indigenous resources and meeting local needs). Such projects and assessments, however exemplary, may need to be complemented by and linked with efforts at the larger strategic level aimed at ensuring that the outside influences support local aspirations.

Traditional knowledge in Lutsel K'e[2]

Lutsel K'e is a remote community of indigenous Denesoline people at the east end of Great Slave Lake in Canada's Northwest Territories. Traditional hunting, fishing and trapping are still important economic and cultural activities in Lutsel K'e and these both require and reinforce traditional knowledge, experience and values. For the Lutsel K'e people, traditional knowledge is also important as a basis for their efforts to protect their lands by exerting informed influence in land use decision making with government and industry officials. Finally, insofar as traditional knowledge can be maintained and continuously rejuvenated, it is a vehicle for cultural preservation, for linking young and old, history and present, people and land.

Experience all over the world has demonstrated that maintenance of traditional knowledge and local influence in decision making is rarely easy. As the benefits and costs of modernity spread even to the most isolated places, languages are disappearing more quickly than species, and millennia of handed-down understandings are dying with the elders of countless indigenous communities. Lutsel K'e is no exception. But it has responded to the challenge of cultural sustainability with particular dedication and creativity through its Ni hat'ni initiative.

Over the past decade several major new diamond mining operations and associated infrastructure projects have been initiated in the region north of Lutsel K'e, bringing new economic opportunities but also the danger of adverse cumulative effects, social and cultural as well as biophysical. The community, organized as the Lutsel K'e Dene First Nation, has recognized aboriginal rights and opportunities for participation in environmental assessments and other deliberations on a variety of land use permitting and approvals processes related to such projects. The community elders have found, however, that even in nominally equitable co-management bodies, their roles and the use of their knowledge have been limited by translation difficulties, a deep-seated tendency to favour conventionally gathered scientific data, and poor understanding of traditional knowledge as a combination of information and worldview.

To ensure more effective gathering, retention and communication of their traditional knowledge, and to enable more powerful application of this knowledge in environmental assessment, regulation and management practice, the Lutsel K'e elders and other community leaders developed the Ni hat'ni programme for monitoring ecological and socio-economic changes in the community's traditional territories. It has two main components. First, the observations and analyses of traditional land users are now recorded on the land as well as in the community, transferred to computer based reporting systems using geographic information systems (GIS) and other software, and continually updated. Second, procedural steps have been taken to maintain community control over the data and their application.

The concept uses indicators that reflect the community's priorities, established values and ways of knowing but that are also recordable with modern monitoring technology. Elders provide, analyse and interpret the ecological information in light of their long-term collective memory of conditions in the area. They look particularly for evidence of apparently unnatural change. Socio-economic information is also collected, analysed and reported. All the findings are used by the community to assess changes and to guide initiatives to mitigate negative trends and encourage positive ones.

An important objective and design feature of the Ni hat'ni community monitoring initiative is the involvement of young people as researchers and computer database managers. This reflects the community's commitment not just to integrate the best of the old and the new but also to maintain the inter-generational transmission of traditional knowledge and understanding. In this way the project is as much an exercise in cultural sustainability as an effort to identify and address potential threats to ecological and socio-economic objectives.

The close association of, and joint attention given to, ecological, social, economic and cultural concerns is another notable feature of the Ni hat'ni approach, though not a unique one. Livelihoods, traditions and activities on the land have long been inseparable for aboriginal people, and at least in the Canadian north, aboriginal communities participating in planning and project deliberations continue to treat these concerns together.[3]

As a sustainability initiative, the Ni hat'ni project has enhanced the credibility and acceptance of traditional knowledge and traditional knowledge holders. Early findings have already been used effectively in negotiations on the mitigation of adverse mining industry effects and are playing a part in discussions with federal government officials on the establishment of a major national park in the area. Eventually, the approach is expected to be adopted by other communities and to provide a much enhanced foundation for ongoing cumulative effects monitoring in an area where conventional scientific research is typically limited by cost and climate to brief summer field seasons.

The project's parallel contributions to the preservation and intergenerational transmission of culture will not be determined for some time. However, the strategy of using youth and elders, men and women, traditional harvesters and GIS database technicians in a community-based monitoring venture seems well suited to the purpose. The Ni hat'ni project combines the traditional and modern in objectives, participants, methods and tools – all of them with some tensions but also all of them potentially reinforcing in positive ways. In the terminology of Chapter 3, the project combines pursuit of both old and new sustainability.

As a case of sustainability assessment, the Ni hat'ni project has the odd status of an undertaking that is meant to contribute to assessments (of cumulative effects as well as new projects) but that is itself the product of what amounts to a continuing assessment process. That process was community initiated and remains broadly participative. It originated in multiple interrelated concerns and objectives that were widely shared and long discussed in the community. And it began with a series of initial research projects that involved traditional land users, community leaders and younger people with suitable technical skills who together explored monitoring methods and priorities, possible key indicators and means of recording and storing the information.

Broad engagement has clearly been key, not just to the project's development but also to its success in the community so far. At the same time, the project has been designed to strengthen the community's hand in activities, deliberations and decision making with other parties, especially territorial and federal government agencies, mining companies and other development interests. The project's initial design and continuing assessment in application have involved consideration of how the monitoring work would fit with broader regulatory and planning efforts, other project assessments and cumulative effects studies. In effect the project level assessment of the monitoring initiative had to be linked to the strategic level of decision making affecting the larger region. In this, as in other aspects, the approach taken by the Lutsel K'e community combined a practical and cultural inclination to integration of considerations (traditional and modern, local and regional, young and older, social and ecological) while designing a monitoring project that would be well enough focused to produce clear and specific findings, and simple enough to be manageable in a small community with modest resources and plenty of other issues to address.

Growth management in Greater Victoria[4]

The Capital Region of British Columbia – the city of Victoria and 15 adjacent municipalities and electoral districts at the southern end of Vancouver Island on Canada's west coast – occupies one of the most beautiful and benign locations on the planet. It is prosperous, has advanced urban amenities and abundant cultural opportunities, and yet retains a measure of rural and recreational character that is uncommon in large cities. The quality of life is high.

But it is also vulnerable. Because of the area's attractiveness, and the usual economic and other pressures for expansion, the population has been increasing steadily. While this has contributed to the communities in many valued ways, it has also increased demand for new housing, brought more vehicles, and placed heavier burdens on existing infrastructure, services and public goods. All of these threaten the established quality of life. Moreover, while the area is far from fully urbanized, it is bordered on three sides by water and on the other by mountains. And much of what remains undeveloped is recognized for its ecological, agricultural and resource value, leaving little room for uncontested urban growth.

In 1996, the Capital Regional District (the regional authority of the area municipalities) responded by starting a growth management strategy development process. Because urban growth management is a concern in many urban areas, there is a considerable literature in the field and an increasing body of experience. Moreover, a growth management framework had recently been established in provincial legislation.[5] But in the Capital Regional District, much of the initiative and direction came from municipal leaders, the district's planning staff and perhaps most importantly the extraordinary number and variety of residents' and citizens' groups committed to preserving the area's quality of life.

The immediate objective was to produce a strategy document that would be, in effect, a regional plan of considerable influence. The more specific Official

Community Plans of the participating municipalities would have to comply with it, as would implementation agreements with provincial agencies (for example, concerning major transportation projects). The bigger and longer term objective was regional sustainability or at least sufficient progress in that direction to protect the most valued aspects of existing quality of life while pursuing new opportunities and accommodating new residents.

Regional planning staff, directed by a committee of the Capital Regional District Board, led the process. But because regional districts in British Columbia are essentially creatures of the participating municipalities (whose representatives constitute the district boards), the giving of direction involved a good deal of intermunicipal deliberation. Important roles were also played by a public advisory committee and an advisory body with representatives from other governments and agencies (federal, provincial, First Nations, etc.). And throughout the process, public views were sought on concerns and objectives, strategic options, technical evaluations and drafts of the strategy.

In all the process took seven years, from 1996 to 2003, just to reach agreement on a growth management strategy. The key steps included:

- initial background research on needs, concerns and options;
- examination of the nature and implications of continuing with current trends and plans;
- a public survey and priority identification exercise by elected officials;
- preparation of an initial objectives and framework document;
- technical and public evaluation of four basic growth strategy options;
- selection of a favoured (hybrid) option by elected officials;
- preparation of a draft Regional Growth Strategy;
- a public hearing on the draft strategy;
- negotiations among the municipalities and use of conflict resolution mechanisms, including mediation, to resolve differences;
- final approval and formal adoption of the strategy as a regional bylaw (CRD, 2003).

On the basics, agreement was achieved easily enough. The broad agenda of the provincial growth management law was accepted and the municipalities had no great difficulty approving a set of key objectives for their region: urban containment and rural protection; green/blue space protection; more complete communities; balanced regional transportation; stronger regional economy; and improved housing affordability. It was clear that the key issues would be the placement and firmness of the containment boundary, the locations chosen for densification within the boundary, and the associated implications for transportation infrastructure, housing, industry and natural and agricultural area. Once they had projected the future along the prevailing trend lines, and had heard the public reaction to that scenario, the municipalities were also agreed on the regional unacceptability of business-as-usual.

Four more promising options were developed and examined: a base strategy (current municipal plans plus a regional urban containment boundary; a 'metropolitan core and major centres' option (densification concentrated in the Victoria downtown and a few other existing hubs); 'transit-linked towns' (densification along a rapid transit corridor); and a 'hierarchy of walkable centres' (densification around a multitude of village centres throughout the region). After detailed technical analysis of option implications, advantages and disadvantages, the municipal politicians chose a hybrid version of the 'metropolitan core and centres' option with components from the 'transit-linked towns' approach.

Reaching final agreement on the specifics of the strategy was more difficult. Commitment to serious change was not shared evenly among the municipalities and the deeply embedded tradition of municipal autonomy was not easily overcome. Achieving consensus required some sacrifice of growth management effectiveness.

The length of the process was also frustrating for some. But it may have been unavoidable, given the anticipated power of the strategy, the divergent interests of the municipalities and the need for consensus on the strategy. For many participants, politicians as well as members of the public, the process was an exploration of unfamiliar ground. Some time for learning was required and the educational process is far from over. Actual implementation through adjustments to the official community plans, provincial–regional agreements, economic development initiatives, transportation and housing ventures, and strategy monitoring will continue for many more years. No doubt there will be conflicts, delays, frustrations and learning in these matters too.

As an urban growth management initiative, the Capital Regional District's efforts have not been entirely comprehensive of the concerns usually associated with sustainability. Equity and uncertainty, for example, have been given little prominence, and effects beyond the region have been mostly neglected. Nevertheless, the key regional objectives list reflects a broad, long-term agenda and the deliberations reflected an understanding that these elements were interconnected. The main strategy development work, especially the elaboration and evaluation of alternative scenarios (the four options), presumed that any useful response to the objectives had to be conceived as a package. Beyond this joint pursuit of multiple good planning benefits, the strategy development process fostered learning about growth management possibilities and served as an incubator of broader communication and cooperation. In so doing it helped develop the understandings and habits required for successful pursuit of sustainability.

As an assessment process, the strategy development exercise had the advantage of a conscious place in a larger multi-level planning structure. It was initiated in the framework of provincial law, and relied not only on that law's objectives and tools (the strategy concept, the implementation agreements, etc.) but also on its provisions for provincial mediation and other conflict resolution. In turn, however, the strategy would provide the framework for more specific municipal level plans, as well as particular agreements on infrastructure funding and other implementation matters. Both aspects helped to clarify the role and enhance the manageability of growth strategy development at the regional level.

No less significantly, the strategy process applied multiple intersecting approaches to its task. The work began with a broad set of sustainability objectives and gradually specified these into regional objectives, future preferences and strategy components. These specific objectives remained core considerations in the technical evaluations, public deliberations and political negotiations. But this objective-led focus was combined with elaboration and comparison of alternatives, extensive open debate and consensus-seeking conflict resolution – effectively combining several attractive approaches to decision making on complex matters.

A biosphere reserve for the Rhön[6]

In some places the threat to sustainability is not growth but decline. The case of the Rhön Biosphere Reserve in central Germany is illustrative. A 185,000 hectare area of low mountains at the conjunction of three Länders – Hesse, Bavaria and Thuringia – the Rhön reserve lands are mostly rolling hills with open meadow pastures, hedges, bogs, woodlands, orchards and a few small settlements. In ancient times it was a beech forest, but centuries of clearing and grazing have produced a relatively open landscape supporting exceptional biodiversity and a tourist industry based on the region's pastoral aesthetic. Maintenance of this biodiversity and industry, however, depends on maintenance of the traditional agricultural practices.

In the early 1990s, at the time of German reunification, it became clear that the traditional agriculture of the Rhön would never be able to compete with modern farming practices. Farm incomes were decreasing and fields were being abandoned. Further agricultural decline would mean depopulation and probably, under European Union agricultural policy, active re-afforestation. While return of the primaeval forest might be desirable from some perspectives, it threatened the established natural and agricultural biodiversity of the cultural landscape and the livelihoods of local residents. There was, consequently, broad interest in an initiative to preserve the existing socio-ecological system.

As a first step, the federal and länder authorities sought recognition of the area as a specially protected area under the United Nations Educational, Scientific and Cultural Organization's (UNESCO's) biosphere reserve designation. The biosphere reserve concept was first applied in the 1970s to exceptional land or coastal ecosystems where scientific research on human–environment relations might be valuable. More recently, and especially since the 1992 Rio Conference on Environment and Development, they have been a focus for exemplary initiatives to establish and maintain sustainable human–environment relations. Safeguarding ecological values, including biodiversity, is always involved. Environmental education, research and monitoring are also typical. But increasing emphasis is placed on efforts to combine protection and development in ways that strengthen the lasting integrity of the socio-economy and ecosystem. Often a zoning approach is used, with a well-protected core natural area surrounded by a buffer zone of greater human activity and a development zone where less compatible land uses are concentrated. And management is usually through cooperative action by government authorities at various levels, volunteer organizations, conservation groups, landowners, businesses and other local interests.

In the Rhön, the core natural area remains very small – about 2 per cent of the region, mostly peat bog and forest. Of the reserve, 40 per cent is grassland buffer and the rest is the development zone. This allocation reflects the character of the Rhön as a cultural landscape and the key challenge of strengthening the economic activities that can keep the landscape open and diverse.

To do this, the authorities in the three länders, along with other government agencies and local participants, began by designing a general framework for sustainable development in the area and by initiating a planning and implementation process that combines economic expansion and landscape protection. So far the economic side has involved three overlapping phases. First came efforts to identify the region's main assets and to undertake pilot projects that would promote those assets with greatest potential for strengthening traditional land uses. The second phase centred on building broader partnerships and the third is essentially a more comprehensive marketing campaign emphasizing labelling of the Biosphere Reserve's products and services.

Landscape protection has addressed natural and agricultural biodiversity, both of which were identified as threatened, but also part of the solution for the Rhön. Preservation of natural biodiversity, for ecological and tourism purposes, is pursued mostly through the broad zoning and more detailed decision making at the local plan level. However, environmental education, guidance of tourist traffic away from stressed areas, and work with farmers to retain hedgerows and other key habitats and corridors have also been important. Preservation of genetic diversity in agriculture centres on recognizing, re-establishing and marketing use of local animal breeds and cultivars, especially the Rhön black faced sheep and several heritage apple varieties.

The Rhön sheep, well adapted to the region and known for excellent wool and meat, were too slow growing for modern agribusiness purposes. Their numbers declined sharply (in Bavaria from 30,000 ewes in 1950 to 300 in 1970). Conservation organizations started a preservation flock in 1984 and, after 1991, biosphere reserve authorities and associated groups began to build partnerships with restaurants, wool marketers and other businesses to re-establish demand for Rhön sheep products. This sheep project is now considered a remarkable economic and ecological success, integrating interests in gastronomy, agriculture, tourism and landscape preservation.

The Rhön apple initiative focused similarly on traditional local varieties. In 1996, experts identified 170 varieties of apples, plus 38 kinds of pear and 12 plums, most of them with little potential for modern mass marketing but valuable for regional cuisine and genetic diversity, as well as for maintenance of traditional village aesthetics. Here too a partnership approach was adopted combining several purposes, players and projects. Orchardists and biosphere reserve authorities, scientists and restauranteurs, a tourism agency, a garden centre, a brewery and a fruit juice bottler, among others, worked to expand the market for heritage fruit. They also promoted understanding of generic resources, fostered local employment and encouraged organic farming methods to improve marketability and protect wildlife habitat.

A 'biosphere reserve business partners' initiative was introduced in 1998 in part as a step towards quality labelling for Rhön products and services. The partners must serve biosphere reserve objectives and meet specified local criteria (for example, minimum number of local products in a grocery store or on a restaurant menu) as well as appropriate European Union standards (for organic food production or environmental management and auditing, etc.). From a marketing perspective, the essential idea has been to combine ecologically responsible innovation and valued tradition in a way that wins recognition for particular quality. But the same combination is also expected to build a dynamic form of socio-ecological sustainability.

Other projects undertaken within the biosphere reserve framework and intended to serve its intersecting objectives include:

- entrepreneurial training for rural women;
- research on reintroduction of regional train services to reduce truck traffic;
- cooking contests featuring local products;
- encouragement of traditional building styles and materials linked to green housing criteria, including energy and water conservation;
- mountain biking route development with consenting stakeholders;
- a model community competition;
- a woodland and wood processing cooperative of carpenters, sawmills, local authorities and the biosphere reserve association in Hesse using sustainably harvested beech wood;
- facility development and promotion of farm and village tourism;
- landscape guide training.

Many of these projects have been partnership efforts. While the biosphere reserve administrative authorities in the three länders have often played co-ordinating roles, they have recognized the importance of engaging all of the regional stakeholders. As a result, municipalities have often taken the lead in new initiatives, as have citizen groups, private businesses and landowners. This increasingly broad base is likely to become even more important as outside support from state and European Union funding programmes declines.

As a sustainability initiative, the Rhön case demonstrates powerfully how environment and development can be deeply interdependent even at the obvious and immediate local level. The participants in Rhön biosphere reserve sustainability efforts have faced significant challenges including competition with conventional industrial agriculture and maintenance of effective coopera-tion among three separate administrative bodies in the participating länders. But they have had relatively little difficulty establishing the importance of mutually supportive development and preservation.

As a case of sustainability assessment, the Rhön experience seems not to have followed a clear and simple path of conception, evaluation, decision and implementation. The key framework document, prepared after adoption of the flexible biosphere reserve model, is a comprehensive but general management plan with no legal status. Much of the implementation has been through individual projects tied only loosely to the plan. Mostly, the Rhön participants have used an adaptive approach, starting with pilot projects, experimenting with alternatives, undertaking and then linking a variety of small initiatives. They have emphasized monitoring and learning from their successes and failures. Nevertheless, the overall package of Rhön activities so far is remarkably coherent.

This coherence seems to be the product of several factors, including the consensus based approach to the framework plan, the focus on partnerships, the early availability of outside project funding, the evident need to integrate protection and development, and the respect accorded to the authorities involved. The result, however achieved, has been effective agreement on the problems to be addressed, the core objectives to be pursued and the essential character of the actions to be taken. And this strategic foundation has been sufficient to guide the various participants in producing a set of initiatives that suit the local circumstances, complement each other well and cover most of the usual sustainability considerations.

The global mining industry and the Tahltan mining strategy

In 1998, when nine of the world's largest mining companies initiated a review of their industry, their interest in sustainability was not altruistic. They were concerned about prospects for their own well-being in the face of growing pressures and expectations from host countries and communities, civil society organizations, investors, insurers and employees. Several well-publicized tailing dam failures and the spread of local resistance to new mining projects had darkened the industry's reputation in capital markets as well as in the public mind. Credibility was eroding and costs were rising.

Some in the industry had noted the chemical sector's response to similar circumstances a decade earlier. After a series of serious contaminant discharges and waste disasters (Seveso, Love Canal, Bhopal, etc.) the industry in many countries signed on to a 'Responsible Care' programme promising environmental performance beyond regulatory requirements. While the results were imperfect, even the industry's critics recognized improvements and the industry's overall reputation rose.

For the mining companies, the situation was somewhat different. The prevailing concerns were about the industry's social and development performance as well as its environmental responsibility. Moreover, the intervening years had brought increased public scepticism, higher expectations for transparency and for delivery of benefits, much faster global communication, and much more able organization of action campaigns when problems emerged. Recognizing that their response would therefore have to be broader than Responsible Care, miners looked to sustainability.

Assisted by the World Business Council for Sustainable Development, the industry leaders initiated the Mining, Minerals and Sustainable Development (MMSD) project. It was a global undertaking, complemented by four more or less separate regional groups, a host of research undertakings and multi-stakeholder deliberations. Overall independent management was provided by the London-based International Institute for Environment and Development. Not all relevant parties agreed to participate, and not all participants agreed with the final conclusions. It was not a consensus process – for the stakeholders involved or even for the industry participants. The project's final report (MMSD, 2002) instead summarizes the project findings and outlines ways by which mining companies, related government authorities and other actors could move towards sustainability.

Overall, the report anticipates a dramatic transition from a secretive industry often associated with land use conflict, benefits for the rich and a legacy of ghost towns, poverty and pollution to an exemplary sector devoted to transparency, equity, social and ecological responsibility, and durably positive effects (MMSD, 2002).

To accomplish this, the report offers a set of suggested actions and mechanisms for application globally, nationally and locally. These include:

- sustainability-centred policies and management systems for mining companies and related government, labour and non-government organizations;
- capacity-building initiatives for industry players to enhance cooperative action, with appropriate guiding principles and codes of conduct (for example, for emergency response preparation);
- community engagement plans, community involvement in integrated impact assessments, dispute resolution mechanisms, and links between project plans and community sustainable development plans;
- integrated planning for closures, including efforts to sustain benefits in community health, education and housing;
- national-level cooperative and government action to ensure access to information, effective public participation, clarification of land regimes and fair resolution of indigenous land claims, just treatment of displaced people, proper environmental and financial auditing, and prevention of corruption;
- special arrangements for small-scale and artisinal miners;
- inclusion of organized labour in sustainability agreements and other initiatives;
- strategic plans for maximizing, sustaining and ensuring fair distribution of long-term benefits;
- supportive global efforts in standard setting, trade reform, skills and technology transfer, cost internalization, financial surety, conflict resolution, product stewardship, corporate reporting, and overall redistribution of benefits (MMSD, 2002).

Individually and as a package, these are clearly admirable suggestions. As a response to the practical sustainability challenges facing a whole industrial sector, it is impressively coherent and comprehensive. But it is just a set of proposals and there are libraries of such documents that have failed to inspire much effective action. While the mining sector's leaders see good reasons for action, there are plenty of barriers to implementation. Many of the individual proposals are likely to seem less agreeable when disruptive and costly actions are specifically required. Moreover, action on the package as a whole depends on broad participation, which in turn depends on understanding and motivations that are now uncommon.[7]

At the same time, there is a reasonably conventional mining business case for many sustainability-centred initiatives, even without collective support. And mining companies are not the only parties with an interest in practical implementation. One example of MMSD implementation, directly involving sustainability assessment, was driven not by the industry but by an aboriginal authority dealing with mining ventures in their traditional lands (MMSD-NA, 2002; Hodge, 2004; Tahltan First Nation/IISD, 2004).

The Tahltan First Nation's traditional territories cover nearly 100,000 square kilometres in northwestern British Columbia's rich, diverse and largely unroaded Stikine watershed. The Tahltan people mined copper, obsidian and jade for trade purposes long before Europeans arrived and the area has attracted outside miners since the 1860s. Only one hard rock operation – the underground Eskay Creek gold/silver mine – is now active, but several other mines have operated sporadically and exploration work continues. Many ventures have been marginal, with mines opening and suspending production in response to global market shifts and local cost factors. Limited access to transportation and power grids adds to the economic difficulties. Nevertheless, the mineral potential of the area is great and mining seems likely to remain a source of opportunity and challenge for the Tahltan well into the future.

In 2003, Tahltan First Nation leaders convened a special symposium with representatives of active mine exploration and development interests and relevant government agencies to develop a strategy for establishing mining as a contributor to sustainability. The initiative was part of a long history of efforts by the Tahltan to secure more significant and lasting benefits from mining on their lands. Some of the Tahltan have many years of experience with the mining industry, in direct employment and in the provision of related services. These include the Tahltan Band chief, Jerry Asp, who has an international reputation for his efforts to enhance indigenous people's engagement in and gains from mining activities. But relations have included conflict as well as cooperation and the effects have been mixed.

The Tahltan had to block an access road to the Golden Bear mining property before they succeeded in having the road re-routed away from prime moose habitat and won project subcontracting roles. An agreement with the Eskay Creek mine has brought welcome employment and training opportunities but the income has been associated with substance abuse and related social problems. Mining roads and other infrastructure have provided conveniences but also easier backcountry access and more pressure on wildlife. As well there are continuing concerns about acid mine drainage and other mine environmental effects threatening fisheries and other key foundations for Tahltan life (EMCBC,1999; Tahltan FN/IISD, 2004).

The sustainability focus of the mining symposium reflected its broad agenda. The Tahltan wanted multi-interest acceptance of a strategy covering all aspects of mining activity management/co-management that might affect them. In particular, the strategy would aim to distribute benefits, costs and risks fairly among the various parties, and ensure proper attention to ecological, health and socio-cultural effects. As a framework for considering the issues and options involved, the Tahltan adopted a sustainability assessment methodology centred on 'seven questions to sustainability'.

The seven questions approach had been initially formulated for assessment of a controversial mine re-opening on the Taku River, just north of the Tahltan territory. But it had been elaborated and publicized by the MMSD North America working group for application to mining activities anywhere. The seven questions were designed to guide sustainability assessments of mining activities through their full cycle – from exploration through development (design, construction and operation), temporary and permanent closure and post-closure:

1   Are engagement processes in place and working effectively?
2   Will people's well-being be maintained or improved?
3   Is the integrity of the environment assured over the long term?
4   Is the economic viability of the project or operation assured, and will the economy of the community and beyond be better off as a result?
5   Are traditional and non-market activities in the community and surrounding area accounted for in a way that is acceptable to the local people?
6   Are rules, incentives, programmes and capacities in place to address project or operational consequences?
7   Does a full synthesis show that the net result will be positive or negative in the long term and will there be periodic reassessments? (MMSD-NA, 2002)

In the Tahltan case, each question was posed for exploration, operation and closure activities to assess past and present performance and to clarify desired future conditions. The findings, presented in matrix form, were then translated into identified needs for improvement and incorporated into a new Tahltan mining strategy. The strategy, accordingly, addresses the entire mining cycle and the full suite of issues covered by the seven questions. It deals with capacity-building, communications and education, youth opportunities, ecosystem well-being, co-management arrangements, and development of Tahltan corporate capacities for delivery of exploration, restoration, monitoring and other services. It puts particular weight on health, social and cultural considerations that had received little attention in the past. But it also includes integrative measures, for example, combined socio-cultural and environmental monitoring and an anticipated generic framework for negotiating agreements governing mining activities on Tahltan traditional territory. In addition to matters for Tahltan action, it provides short lists of actions to be taken by government agencies and industry.

As linked sustainability initiatives, the MMSD project and the development of the Tahltan mining strategy were odd partners. The mining sector's concern about sustainability had been driven in part by a record of conflict with host communities and the Tahltan were hosts whose relations with the industry had not always been smooth. Certainly, the Tahltan entered their mining strategy process with a perspective sharply different from that of the mining industry participants in the MMSD process and in the Tahltan symposium. At the same time, the very broad sustainability concept apparently provided a viable common basis for discussion. The symposium and the strategy process may have adopted a framework from the MMSD exercise, but they also continued a long history of Tahltan efforts to be more influential participants in and beneficiaries of mining, while protecting their lands and communities from its negative effects. Both global context and local history affected the work.

With application of the seven questions framework, the analysis and the resulting strategy were more explicitly comprehensive and detailed than those of previous Tahltan initiatives. The framework helped the Tahltan to integrate attention to their long-standing concerns about social effects and cultural preservation as well as environmental stewardship, jobs and other economic opportunities. A focus on overall long-term gains extending beyond project closure was also encouraged by the seven questions. But the specifics of the Tahltan strategy were clearly informed by local priorities and experience and these were already pushing the Tahltan to adopt a more comprehensive, integrated and long-term approach.

As cases of sustainability assessment, the MMSD and Tahltan efforts connected the global and the local without leaving the strategic realm. In contrast to the frequent depiction of strategic level assessments guiding project level deliberations, the MMSD-Tahltan cases illustrate the no less common potential for broader strategic work informing more specific strategy development. The two cases are also remarkable for the minor role of conventional government bodies. While both involved multiple stakeholders, industry led the MMSD initiative and the Tahltan application of the seven questions was by a First Nation that has some recognized status as a government, but is not the main authority for land use policy, mining regulation or assessment in the region.

The two assessments were linked by the seven questions methodology, by multi-stakeholder discussion, and by a shared underlying belief that mining could contribute to sustainability despite its often regrettable history. But they differed dramatically in process complexity. The MMSD assessment was big not merely because of its global scope but also because it was meant to be a vehicle for educating the industry. In contrast, the Tahltan sustainability assessment was simple, quick and direct. Past and existing problems were identified; needs for action were listed and follow-up steps recommended. A multi-stakeholder symposium was held but, in the immediate exercise, there was no public review of scenarios or any detailed evaluation of competing policy options. No doubt part of the difference lies in the limited resources available for the Tahltan process, and in their use of an existing framework that encouraged attention to an already well-considered list of sustainability and mining issues. But it is probably also important that for the small Tahltan communities, with their long history of relations with the mining industry, this particular strategy exercise was just one wave in a river of deliberation about current problems, future possibilities and alternative approaches to change. For the Tahltan, as for many people facing persistent livelihood issues, sustainability assessment is an on-going process.

Lessons from the stories

These five stories could be supplemented by countless others. The background files collected for this book include notes on livelihood building by communities of the Brazilian landless movement, sustainability assessment of Ghana's poverty reduction strategy, the combined social and ecological initiatives of Husky Injection Moulding Systems Ltd, the ecological rehabilitation work of the Gaviotas intentional community in Columbia, eco-community design in Fredensgade, Denmark, and Alphen ann der Rijn in The Netherlands, the healthy community and sustainable livelihoods initiatives in rural Woolwich Township, Canada, urban brownfield redevelopment planning for Southeast False Creek in Vancouver, sustainable transportation innovations in Hasselt, Belgium, and several certification cases involving sustainable forestry and fair trade coffee. It would have been easy to find documentation on many more.

Probably, a larger selection of stories would have illuminated additional diversities as well as more general lessons. But it seems likely they would also further confirm the following general observations about sustainability in practice.

- All the sustainability-in-practice stories told here combine changes not just in what goals are set and what concerns are addressed, but also in how decisions are made and by whom. By definition, practical sustainability initiatives involve challenges to conventional conditions, trends, thinking and practice. In the villages of Bundelkhand and the Stikine valley, in Victoria, Lutsel K'e and the Rhön, people have sought better futures than the ones that otherwise loom. The participating leaders and citizens have responded to what they themselves have identified as threats to sustainability and this has led them to think and act a little differently. They have tried to exercise more influence over their futures. They have engaged more and different people in their deliberations and have taken a wider range of concerns into consideration. They have typically defied convention not only by combining protection and advancement but also by taking a more inclusive and participative approach to decision making.
- At the same time, the challenges to business-as-usual in these cases (as in the theoretical literature) have not involved a comprehensive rejection of current understandings, structures, motives and practices. Although the cases reflect continuing disagreements about the potential roles of market mechanisms, technological innovation, central authority, law, custom,

religion and many other more or less conventional tools, the common approach is to use all of them to some degree and in some forms in the pursuit of sustainability. Similarly, the participants act on a familiar mix of inclinations to innovate and conserve. Only their understanding of how these fit together and where they should lead is uncommon.

- As challenges to convention, the sustainability initiatives described here are broadly comprehensive and integrated. This is hardly surprising – the cases were selected in part because they combined attention to protection and advancement, and aimed for overall, durable improvements. But in the cases reviewed, it is not just a matter of seeing connections between economic and ecological well-being. Each of the stories covers a broad range of concerns – health, security, equity, economic opportunity, ecological protection and/or restoration, maintenance of culture and cherished traditions, links between old and young, sense of community and, of course, continuity – and addresses the interconnections among them.

- Despite the great differences in the cases, they share a remarkably similar basic agenda. Each of the sustainability initiatives has involved a more or less evident set of shared, broad objectives, though they may not be fixed or formally stated. Predictably, these objectives vary in substance as well as emphasis and priority. But in each case – among the mostly wealthy in Victoria and the very poor in Bundelkhand, facing economic decline in the Rhön and expanding resource extraction around Lutsel K'e – the objectives reflect the common concerns enumerated above.

- This basic similarity of objectives seems to have little to do with the influence of the sustainability literature. In each case the effective sustainability concerns emerged from the particular circumstances, not from adoption or imposition of a sustainability-oriented ideology. At least in the beginnings there was no great reliance on the concept of sustainability. Related frameworks were involved. Development Alternatives working in Bundelkhand had an approach based on years of experience fostering community level development. The Rhön had the biosphere reserve concept. Lutsel K'e and the Tahltan could draw both from an integrated aboriginal tradition and from a more recent history of tested approaches to protection of land and title. The Tahltan also chose to apply the MMSD's seven questions approach to sustainability assessment, and Greater Victoria used the sustainability-informed framework of the provincial growth management strategy law. But these were used chiefly as tools for consolidating and clarifying an agenda already present.

- Most cases involved messy iterative processes rather than conveniently structured logical steps following a standard framework, with a well-delineated beginning and end. There were significant differences in approach. Development Alternatives and their project participants in the Bundelkhand villages used an especially informal and incremental approach, relying on gradual learning about local assets and priorities as well as about what would and would not work there. Growth management strategy development in Greater Victoria, by contrast, followed the well-travelled path of rational planning, guided by legislated prescription. But even here, the seven years of deliberations included a good deal of backtracking, reconsideration and adjustment. And none of the stories has a clear beginning or end. Arguably, all of the initiatives discussed rose out of a long history and all of them are on-going today.

- Also in every case, some characteristics of the process were valuable, even crucial, for reasons peculiar to the circumstances. In the greater Victoria region growth management case, for example, the long history of jealously guarded municipal autonomy was a key factor. Development and approval of a potentially effective growth management strategy would have been highly unlikely without the delicately balanced framework of consensus-based decision making supported by subtle provincial encouragements and a series of increasingly firm conflict resolution mechanisms. It would also have been much less likely in the absence of wide agreement among the citizenry that their quality of life was high and vulnerable. In the Rhön case, similarly, the particular circumstances were crucial. The evident interdependence of the local landscape ecology and the traditional economy made it unusually easy to recognize needs to integrate preservation and development. And this made a relatively cooperative, partnership based approach much less difficult than it might have been otherwise.

- Despite the great differences in approach, all the cases have involved some form of systematic and principled sustainability assessment. In each of the sustainability initiatives, the process included:
  - a more or less evident, broadly shared set of interrelated objectives, though they may not have been formally stated, and may have been gradually clarified and adjusted over time;
  - some consideration of alternative futures;
  - evaluation (again not necessarily formal) of competing options for positive action;
  - open discussion and participative engagement of local residents;
  - flexible application, with iterative re-examination and adjustment, and a succession of decisions rather than a single approval focus;
  - pursuit of multiple benefits, in line with the shared objectives;
  - an open-ended result with continuing attention to implementation as experimentation for learning and adjustment.

- In all cases, sustainability assessment was integrated into discussion, experimentation and decision making. Sustainability was the core consideration, the package containing the key objectives. Assessment work was typically continuous and difficult to distinguish from the succession of discussions and decisions involved. Even when particular evaluations were undertaken as identifiable, distinct initiatives – as in the Victoria and Tahltan cases – they were clearly in the mainstream of deliberations, not tributary inquiries contributing to some other agenda. Sustainability assessment and case decision making were effectively merged.

- Each case involved tensions and trade-offs. While the broad objectives may have been compatible, means of reaching them often conflicted. Sometimes the tensions and trade-offs involved the expected friction between economic and ecological or social imperatives. In Greater Victoria, for example, municipalities seeking an expanded tax base pushed to expand urbanization into areas of ecological importance. But many of the most significant conflicts were not between economic and social or ecological aspirations. More often they were between immediate and longer-term gains, between some beneficiaries and others, or between bolder action and more complete consensus. In the Bundelkhand villages providing new opportunities for marginalized women raised domestic problems. In the Rhön local product certification options threatened to help some area producers and disadvantage others. In Lutsel K'e, the whole initiative struggled over conflict between traditional and conventional scientific knowledge systems. Even the urban boundary discussions in Greater Victoria were to a large degree tensions within the economic sphere, between the immediate municipal gains from expansion and the long-term regional costs of sprawl.

- Finally, all of the stories here have involved other stories, larger and smaller. In all cases, what could be accomplished locally was influenced by activities at a larger scale – in the global economy, through national policy, because of larger pressures, possibilities and constraints. The Tahltan, for example, have been able to pursue a bigger agenda in discussions with the mining companies in their region in part because of changes sweeping the global mining sector. Traditional farmers in the Rhön have been facing decline due to economic globalization and associated changes in agricultural technology. At the same time, the potential success of sustainability initiatives by the Tahltan and in the Rhön Biosphere Reserve, will depend on what happens with a multitude of smaller projects – arrangements with particular mining operations, results of particular local product promotions. No initiative is autonomous. While none of the cases discussed here hoped to have much effect on the larger world, or to assume dictatorial authority over the smaller scale implementations, all of them recognized the importance of influences from above and below.

Considering that these are stories of sustainability initiatives that emerged from particular circumstances, not efforts to apply a theory, it is remarkable how closely the character of these initiatives in sustainability parallels the essentials of the sustainability concept. As presented in Box 3.2, the concept as variously presented in the literature can be distilled into eight characteristics:

1 a challenge to conventional thinking and practice;
2 about long- as well as short-term well-being;
3 comprehensive, covering all the core issues of decision making;
4 a recognition of links and interdependencies, especially between humans and the biophysical foundations for life;
5 a recognition of both inviolable limits and endless opportunities for creative innovation;
6 an open-ended process, not a state;

7   a means and end; culture and governance as well as ecology, society and economy;

8   both universal and context dependent.

All of them are evident in the sustainability-as-practice cases. Moreover, the cases confirm the fundamental logic of the sustainability idea – that protection and rehabilitation of the environment and improvements in human well-being can (and should) be mutually supporting.

The stories told here also shed light on the processes for considering and preparing sustainability-oriented undertakings. As noted above, each of the cases incorporated some rough version of sustainability assessment. The forms of sustainability assessment have varied greatly to serve in very different circumstances. Nevertheless, some shared basics have been evident.

Thus both the process and the concept appear to have an essential core as well as a need for particular elaborations to fit various circumstances. In the cases described in this chapter, exemplary initiatives were undertaken with little guidance on sustainability assessment. Arguably they did well enough without it. But that is no justification for leaving others to start from scratch as well.

For sustainability assessment, clarification of the essential core of the sustainability concept would provide the basic criteria for evaluations and decisions. Clarification of the essential core of the process would supply basic guidance for future applications. Neither core criteria nor basic process guidance can possibly be sufficient. Both will have to be built upon in diverse ways for various circumstances. But if experience in conceptual and practical deliberations so far has revealed a common base, it would seem reasonable to examine this base and see what useful implications might be identified for the next generation of sustainability application pioneers. That will be the agenda of the following chapters.

Notes

1   This account is based largely on information from Geeta Vaidyanathan, an architect who was one of Development Alternatives' on-site participants. See especially Vaidyanathan (2002).

2   This account is based largely on LKDFN and Ellis (2004), and Ellis (2005).

3   This was evident in the first major assessment process in the Canadian north – the hearings on the proposed Mackenzie Valley natural gas pipeline (see Berger, 1977) – and in virtually all such processes since, including the Voisey's Bay case discussed in Chapter 1. See also Roue and Nakashima (2002).

4   This account is based largely on Boyle et al (2003 and 2004), CRD (2003), plus other documents available on the website of the Regional Growth Strategy Division of the Capital Regional District's Regional Planning Services Department – www.crd.bc.ca/regplan/rgs/index.htm

5   The 1995 *Growth Strategies Statutes Amendment Act,* was subsequently incorporated into the province's *Municipal Act* (British Columbia 1996). The core contents are summarized in Appendix 2.
6   This account is based largely on Popp (1997), Pokorny (1999a, 1999b, 2001a, 2001b) and Biosphärenreservat Rhön (2004).
7   The authors of the MMSD report recognized the importance of collective effects and the danger of non-participation:

> *Corporate performance in the minerals sector, measured against any indicator, is variable. Some good companies are improving, but the bad are inexcusable, and the past record is even worse. Action by companies, individually and collectively, is clearly required. In an open trading and competitive world, a 'rush to the bottom' caused by 'free riders' is a real danger. In many areas, small companies are crucial to the standards of large ones. If, for example, projects near closure are simply sold by multinationals to private, less visible entities, other routes are opened to avoid obligations. Collective action must include companies of all sizes in order to produce positive results (MMSD, 2002).*

5

Criteria

Sustainability Requirements as the Basis for Decision Making

The need for decision criteria

All this discussion of sustainability, in the theoretical literature and in practical applications, has presumed acceptance of a debatable assumption. It is that sustainability assessment needs to be guided by a set of core insights about the purposes to be served and the consequent criteria to be applied in evaluations and decision making.

The need for some agreement on basic purposes and criteria may seem obvious. Assessments are exercises in evaluation and decision making. They involve countless choices – on whether an undertaking merits detailed review, whether an anticipated effect is likely to be significant, whether one option is preferable to another, whether a design change is acceptable, and whether a monitoring programme is addressing the most important concerns. And in all these evaluations and decisions, criteria of some sort underlie and guide the choices. The criteria may be implicit; indeed they often are. In jurisdictions all over the world, a good deal of actual decision making, even on important policies and projects, appears just to bumble along, guided by no clear vision or agenda, adjusting semi-consciously to the winds of the moment. But no decision making is neutral about purposes and not even the most bumbling choices are simply random.

In formal deliberative processes – in mandated sustainability assessments, for example – questions about what purposes will be served are answered in part by what is written into the defining framework. The driving law or policy will focus on a narrowly environmental or more broadly comprehensive set of concerns. It will seek mitigation of significant adverse effects or encourage net gains. It will be sensitive to uncertainties or confident that science can deliver decisive evidence. It will require broad public engagement or rely on technical expertise. It will impose firm rules or allow flexible adjustment to the specifics of individual undertakings, participants and locations. And so on. These characteristics affect who gets heard and what gets considered and how some concerns come to be favoured over others in the resulting deliberations.

Decision criteria are also imposed or influenced by prevailing ideologies, decision making traditions, government agendas and other factors in the broad context. Case specific factors play important roles as well. A long established strategy for transportation network expansion may dictate key choices in the assessment of a proposed new highway. A biotech corporation's competitive priorities may affect its evaluation of risks from a proposed field test. The preferences of certain cabinet ministers may be anticipated in a ranking of pollution abatement regulatory options. Some of these guiding criteria may be set out in public documents. Some may be a matter of guesswork, even for the assessors involved.

Taken together, these framework components, broad contextual influences and case specific factors establish the effective decision criteria. They determine what objectives are favoured, which options are considered and preferred, what effects are judged desirable, acceptable or intolerable. The criteria may be unstated and unclear; they may be hopelessly muddled and contradictory. But there will always be decision criteria of some sort. For sustainability assessment purposes, the question is not whether there should be decision criteria, but which ones should be used, how they should be selected, whether and when they should be set out explicitly.

Carefully chosen, openly debated criteria

Advocates of sustainability commonly assume that a shift to more sustainability-focused decision making is needed and that one prerequisite is specification and adoption of suitably enlightened guiding principles. Not content merely to urge such action, they have drafted, and in some cases tested, many lists of core decision criteria. These criteria lists, which may be presented as fundamental objectives, key challenges, essential strategy components, foundation principles or design imperatives (see Appendix 1), are rarely meant to be the final word. Moreover, virtually everyone recognizes that local differences matter and that case specific additions and elaborations are needed. But, with few exceptions, sustainability advocates are convinced that setting out a basic working set of explicit general criteria is both possible and valuable.

In the literature about assessment processes, the similarly dominant position is that we should think carefully and openly about our bases for decision making, and that rationales and criteria for decisions should be visible and available for debate. This approach, it is argued, facilitates broader and more effective participation and fosters better informed, more coherent and more consistent decision making. It also serves the interests of accountability, process credibility and learning from mistakes (Sadler, 1996; Senécal et al, 1999; Dovers, 2001; Wood, 2003).

The combination of these convictions in sustainability assessment brings no surprises. All but one of the approaches to sustainability assessment surveyed in Appendix 2 provide or require explicit decision criteria of some sort.

Even the exception – the Equator Principles of major financial institutions investing in large scale development infrastructure projects – includes a 'topics of concern' list that implies a reasonably clear set of tests. This insistence on clear sustainability-centred decision criteria rests in part on the arguments favouring participation, coherence, accountability and learning. But it is also driven by awareness that sustainability is a challenge to business as usual and by suspicion that if assessment proponents, practitioners and authorities are left to their own unsupervised preferences, they will slide back into the old unsustainable ways. Clearly specified decision criteria, publicly discussed, widely published, and complemented by legally enforceable requirements for open justification of decisions, seem to be the best, perhaps the only potentially effective means of ensuring reasonable adherence to a sustainability agenda.

These are persuasive arguments. But as with most things, the story is not so simple and there are some additional considerations to ponder.

Difficulties and caveats

There is an attractive, simple elegance to the idea of first setting objectives and then trying to attain them. It enjoys a tidy 'first socks, then shoes' logic. But the world in which this logic must be applied is not simple or linear. On the contrary, it is messy – complex, evolving and full of contradiction and conflict – and this messiness is far too great to allow fully rational and comprehensive planning (Lindblom, 1959).

Many of the profoundly regrettable actions of the modern era have been characterized by the hubris of authorities attempting to impose a single, simple vision of enlightenment, civilization and/or progress, defying if not destroying local difference and local choice. A long list of these authorities and their works have been undone by tenacious resistance, neglected considerations and unanticipated consequences. Colonial empires, the 1000 year Reich, the Politburo, aboriginal assimilation, Rostow's five stages of economic development, DDT, maximum yield from the North Atlantic cod fishery, and the legendary aid experts whose unsuitable tractors are still rusting in the fields of Africa – all were once representatives of a scientific certainty or universal truth. This is not a path we might wish to follow.

The extreme version of the corrective is to reject all universal claims in favour of situated discourse. For practical decision making in a world facing sustainability problems at multiple intersecting scales, reliance on locally situated discourse alone is not workable.[1] But the underlying concern remains. No one is in a position to dictate a set of global rules for sustainability decision making. The grounds for such confidence are too soft, the differences of context too great, and the history of impositions too ugly.

Part of the problem is the inevitable inadequacy of our knowledge. We cannot possibly anticipate all the intersecting factors that may affect whether one possible future is more desirable or attainable than another. Even our grasp of current conditions is more or less tenuous (Gunderson et al, 1995). Our working understandings, unavoidably based on partial and imperfect information, are therefore, at least to some degree, socially constructed rather than objective (Berger and Luckmann, 1967). This reality undermines confident claims about what is true and good, and erodes justifications for imposing general rules, including broadly applicable decision criteria.

A closely related large difficulty is the diversity of contexts. The physical and social circumstances in which new initiatives are proposed and undertaken are always significant factors in their successes and failures, and these circumstances vary greatly. Even within particular communities the differences may be large. Global differences – in culture and ecology, assets and deficiencies, history and prospects, stresses and resiliencies, preferences and possibilities – are immense. Decision criteria for assessments must respect this. Indeed, any general list of decision criteria must be adjusted and elaborated in and for the circumstances of application.

Finally, there is the problem of conflict. The simple objectives-to-solutions model assumes a world of convenient agreement. Unfortunately, the multiple positive objectives that underpin the usual lists of sustainability-based decision criteria can seldom be met all at once. Sustainability may depend on success on all fronts and such success may be possible as well as necessary in the long run. But in the short run, achieving one worthy priority will often conflict with achieving another. Immediate poverty reduction may put more pressure on already stressed resources; preserving cultural diversity may make achieving gender equality more difficult; setting higher standards for sustainable forestry or agriculture may reduce the number of participants drawn into a process of improvement. For resolution of such conflicts, lists of positive objectives do not provide enough help. As we will see in Chapter 6, it is possible to go beyond the broad objectives and set out general guidance for decisions about conflicts, compromises and trade-offs. But here too the particular circumstances of application are crucial and there are few clearly defensible universal rules.

None of this means that we should abandon hope for general guidance in sustainability assessment. We can recognize complexity and uncertainty, accept the importance of context and the likelihood of conflict, and still agree that we should always think carefully and openly about our bases for decision making. We can keep our decision criteria visible and available for debate. Clear and openly debated criteria and explicit rationales for evaluations and decisions at least serve the interests of greater accountability and easier learning from mistakes. Hopefully, in most cases they will also foster better initial decisions.

Still, the caveats are important. There is good reason to be tentative in assertions about what is necessary for sustainability, to suggest rather than impose general rules, to emphasize sensitivity to particular circumstances, and to treat it all as work in progress.

Beyond the Voisey's Bay test

The great innovation of the Voisey's Bay mine environmental assessment was to introduce decision criteria centred on sustainability. The project proponent was asked to show how the undertaking would make 'a positive overall contribution towards the attainment of ecological and community sustainability, both at the local and regional levels' and was required to defend its case in public hearings. As we have seen, most environmental assessment processes have aimed much lower, focusing on avoiding or mitigating significant adverse effects. And even this modest objective has often been superceded. Environmental assessment findings have usually served as information for more comprehensive deliberations leading to overall decisions that have often accepted very negative environmental effects as a price to be paid for anticipated economic and/or political benefits. Whether these benefits were considered carefully and found overwhelming, or simply preferred for some anticipated immediate advantage, has not often been easy to determine since the core decision making has rarely been open to public scrutiny or guided by explicit criteria. The overall results, however, suggest that careful attention to sustainability objectives has been uncommon.

A clearly important first step towards better decision making would be consistent imposition of the higher test from Voisey's Bay – requiring the proponents of each new or renewed project, programme, plan or policy to make a persuasive public case that the undertaking deserves approval because it would contribute to prospects for desirable and durable futures, local and global. That step alone would probably have a substantial positive effect on decisions and decision making. It would require integrated attention to the full suite of core considerations (rather than one set of concerns that might be superceded by others), facilitate public scrutiny, and apply decision criteria focused on lasting gains. Proponents and decision makers would be encouraged to make a conscious, public effort to specify and use sustainability-centred criteria and to justify options they choose and the trade-offs they accept in light of these criteria.

But while this would be a positive step, it has some serious limitations as an isolated initiative. Perhaps the most important problem is the vagueness of the 'contribution to sustainability' test. For practical application in evaluations and decisions, more specific sustainability-centred criteria are needed. As we saw in Chapter 3, the years of debate and experimentation have helped to clarify sustainability basics enough that there may now be sufficient agreement on the shared foundations for sustainability to permit a general framing of broadly appropriate criteria for sustainability assessment work. Similarly, the initiatives surveyed in Chapter 4 suggest that common themes underlie practical efforts to establish more desirable and durable futures in a wide diversity of places and circumstances.

The problem of specifying sustainability-centred criteria must be addressed in two complementary ways. For some overall consistency of direction we need clearer presentation of the broadly applicable basic criteria for sustainability assessment evaluations and decisions. That is the topic of this chapter. But for particular applications there is also a need for more detailed specification of the criteria so that they recognize the particularities of context. Such specification can only be accomplished in the context. Often it will need to be an initial component of the assessment process itself, with the early consideration of needs and alternatives for a new undertaking accompanied by work to specify the criteria by which these apparent needs and evident alternatives will be evaluated. That will be a matter for discussion in Chapter 7, which considers the fundamentals of how assessment processes should be designed to ensure they serve sustainability purposes effectively.

The overall and case specific unsustainability of prevailing current practices will not be corrected merely by imposing and specifying a higher test in decision making processes. A turnaround to sustainability will also require a host of other initiatives to strengthen appropriate incentives, to gain better information and stronger analytical tools, to foster greater humility, and to link assessment work with initiatives in complementary areas such as green accounting, sustainability indicator development, corporate social responsibility, ecological tax reform, new approaches to conflict resolution and interdisciplinary education. But an unavoidably key role will be played by the accumulation of individual decisions on new (or renewed) projects, programmes, plans and policies. It is sensible to begin with some clarification of the 'contribution to sustainability' test for these decisions.

The objective here is modest. It is to propose, on the basis of experience and proposals thus far, a rough set of basic, common considerations for assessment decision making. As noted above, these core considerations would have to be elaborated in various ways for particular applications and contexts, and supplemented with guidance for making compromises and trade-offs. The set of core criteria will serve mostly to indicate the key issues that require attention, the common realities to be respected and the broadly shared objectives to be pursued. The intent is not imposition of one grand agenda. Realistically, there is no serious prospect of one set of core criteria winning widespread adoption. Nor is any one set of criteria likely to be found satisfactory for long. As sustainability assessment practice expands and experience increases, any initial set of criteria will be found wanting. Revisions of approaches, categories and formulations will be needed again and again.

That said, there is good reason for care and rigour, even in setting out tentative rule-of-thumb criteria. The criteria should consolidate and make use of what we have learned so far. They should also help increase the odds of mutually supportive benefits from the many decisions on individual sustainability assessment cases from the local level to the global. However significant individual cases may be, the main hope for progress towards sustainability lies in the combined, cumulative effects of better decisions. While similarly guided decisions will not necessarily reinforce each other, some rough consistency is likely to be useful.

We are not starting from scratch. There is, as we have seen, a huge literature on sustainability. Although much of it is theoretical, focused on definition, devoted to identification of useful indicators and imperfectly suited for the kind of integrated application demanded in sustainability assessment, there is an enormous wealth of thought and insight. And despite the diversity of viewpoints and emphasis, there is much basic agreement. In addition, many sustainability-centred approaches to evaluating options and making decisions have been proposed and tested. Here too there is great diversity but also the makings of fundamental agreement. It should not be too difficult to identify a working set of core principles for sustainability assessment.

Beyond the pillars

Much of the sustainability literature and many practical applications construct an understanding of sustainability on a number of intersecting pillars (as shown in Figure 3.2). The pillars – usually three (social, economic and ecological), though some authorities advocate two (ecological and socio-economic) and others add more (cultural and/or political) – are conventional modern policy and disciplinary categories used to represent the main broad areas of concern for sustainability initiatives. They have been valued as a simple way of presenting the range of sustainability considerations, as useful groupings of relevant players in sustainability negotiations (for example, FSC, 2004b), and as convenient categories for the structuring of sustainability indicators that use existing data sets about conditions and trends (for example, GRI, 2002).

Because the pillar areas seem comprehensive and are a familiar way of dividing up responsibilities and expertise, they are also attractive as organizing categories for sustainability assessment criteria. Indeed, they have been so used. However, the pillars have proved more useful for categorizing and separating than for linking and integrating. Practitioners have often found it necessary to add supplementary criteria to deal with cross-pillar issues or an additional layer of analysis to address the interconnections (for example, Lawrence 1997 and others outlined in Appendix 2). Where this extra work has not been done, decision makers relying on pillar-based evaluations have often found themselves struggling to understand the overall implications of separate ecological, social and economic assessment reports that are integrated only by the staples holding the documents together.

The pillar categories reproduce the deeply entrenched divisions of policy mandates and research expertise that have long frustrated more integrated thinking. And they encourage a focus on conflicts, especially between the economic and ecological pillars, which are often assumed to be the foundations of warring houses. As a result, pillars-based approaches to sustainability planning and evaluation tend to concentrate attention on competing objectives, rather than on opportunities for positive accommodations of interrelated human and ecological interests. While conflicts among sustainability objectives are serious matters that merit careful consideration, it is no less crucial to uncover openings for mutually supportive initiatives, for positive feedback and for multiple benefits.

Whatever tensions may lie between various particular areas of concern, the crucial reality is that they are all effectively interdependent. The interwoven threats to human and ecological well-being demand similarly interwoven and mutually reinforcing responses. Any useful set of sustainability criteria therefore has two roles. The criteria individually must identify areas where damage must always be avoided and lasting improvements always sought. The criteria together must encourage and facilitate attention to positive linkages. There are, of course, formidable questions to be faced in each individual category – about what counts as a benefit, and about whether we are often able to predict effects, positive or negative, with adequate reliability for the purpose. But the most difficult and most crucial issues are about cross-category concerns in a world of connections and interdependencies. The divisive, pillars-based approach is not well suited to deal with these.

For sustainability assessment, which needs a basic set of broadly applicable criteria for a host of choices and evaluations, there is a better alternative to criteria organized under the pillars. This approach rejects the established categories of mandate and expertise and instead focuses directly on the key changes needed in human arrangements and activities if we are to move towards long-term viability and well-being.

Requirements for progress towards sustainability

The essential requirements for progress towards sustainability can be and have been set out in countless different ways. Any such list is debatable and there will always be openings for learning and revision. Nevertheless, after years of deliberation and experimentation, it is not difficult to discern a limited number of common themes and broadly accepted general positions.

The eight points that follow constitute a minimal set of core requirements, all of which would have to be elaborated on and specified for particular places and applications. The list is based on a synthesis of arguments drawn from the sustainability literature and practical experience very broadly categorized as sustainability-centred. It integrates considerations from ecological systems theory, corporate greening initiatives, growth management planning, civil society advocacy, ecological economics, community development and a host of other fields, as well as shared insights from a diversity of implementation efforts. As a set of core criteria for sustainability assessments, these points are proposed tentatively and largely for illustrative purposes. The eight could easily be subdivided or reorganized into a dozen or a score. But they should be at least indicative of the approach proposed and the main factors to be addressed.

Socio-ecological system integrity

Build human–ecological relations that establish and maintain the long-term integrity of socio-biophysical systems and protect the irreplaceable life support functions upon which human as well as ecological well-being depends.

Human well-being is utterly dependent on the integrity of biophysical systems, at every scale from the local to the global. We rely on the key life support functions of these systems, and on the resources and conditions that these systems maintain. At the same time, we are active participants in the world's biophysical systems and will remain so under any plausible scenario that does not dramatically deplete the human population (Vitousek et al, 1997). One consequence is that we must establish and maintain socio-ecological systems that can provide a viable context for human life (expression, advancement, happiness) over the long term.

The 'systems' terminology here reflects the growing understanding, emerging from many fields, that we live in a world of enormous complexity, not just of conditions and components but also and more significantly of relationships (Bertalanffy, 1968; Nicolis and Prigogine, 1977, 1989; McHarg, 1998; Checkland, 1981; Flood and Carson, 1988; Funtowicz and Ravetz, 1993; Clark et al, 1995; Gunderson and Holling, 2002). Many of these relationships are established in lasting forms and functions that we can identify, for example, as particular forests, watersheds or urban economies. But they are also interconnected at many scales from the microscopic to the cosmological with links that involve both positive and negative feedback. And, subject to all these influences, systems change, sometimes in dramatic, surprising and non-linear ways. For sustainability, the objective is not to prevent system change but to organize and manage our activities so that the changes we influence still preserve the system conditions and services upon which we rely. That means preserving the 'integrity' of systems – their ability to adjust and reorganize in ways that maintain their key functions.

Social and biophysical systems are not the same. Conscious human choice makes the character and possibilities of social systems quite different from those with simply biophysical relations. But the basic concept of systems integrity applies to both and the two together (Waltner-Toews and Lang, 2000; Gallopín et al, 2001; Waltner-Toews, 2004). It recognizes that the conditions and relationships involved at any scale, and between and among scales, are highly complex and dynamic, that we will never understand fully how they work or how they will respond to human interventions of various kinds, and that we cannot preserve current conditions and relationships in some fixed state (Gunderson et al, 1995; Kay et al, 1999). We can, however, work to maintain the dynamic integrity of these systems – by protecting system resilience, by reducing stresses that threaten to force catastrophic shifts, and by fostering systems' capacity to adjust, reorganize and renew in ways that retain key life support functions. We can, for example, work to preserve diversity and redundancy as part of systems' wherewithal for self-organization (Kay and Schneider, 1994).

This is not just a question of taking ecosystem integrity into account in human decision making. Human activities are major components in most global systems. At least since the initial aboriginal use of fire to influence ecosystem change, our actions have been important factors in nature. Today, our intentional and unintentional influences clearly stress and alter biophysical systems, and degrade or deplete crucial resources at the global as well as regional and local scales. The massive Millennium Ecosystem Assessment project has recently reported worldwide declines in 'nearly two-thirds of the services provided by nature to humankind' (MEA, 2005). Moreover, many of the most serious human sources of threats to global and local system integrity are expanding. Energy and material consumption levels, waste generation including greenhouse gases, human population numbers and consequent demands for material sufficiency and luxury are now growing and are expected to continue to grow for some time, even under the most optimistic scenarios for environmentally responsible correction.

These phenomena are rooted in human social systems with political, cultural and economic aspects that are just as complex, dynamic and interconnected as those of ecological systems. It makes sense to consider the integrity of human social systems – their ability to deal with stresses and their capacity to adjust or reorganize in ways that retain key life support functions. Moreover, because social and biophysical systems are now interconnected in complex, dynamic ways, they effectively constitute one big system at the planetary level and multiple intersecting socio-ecological systems at national, regional and local levels (Costanza et al, 2001; Berkes et al, 2003). The challenge of maintaining system integrity applies to these wholes as well as to the social and biophysical parts.

The current situation is not entirely gloomy. Not all human activities are undermining the integrity and potential long-term viability of the whole. Not all resources are over-harvested and while all ecosystems are yet subject to stresses, not all are in immediate danger of losing their essential integrity.[2] Openings for substitution and rehabilitation will permit extension of some current practices (though there is much debate about what substitutions may be reasonably expected and systemically viable, and considerable discussion about the potential adequacy of rehabilitations). And there may well be positive opportunities (as well as additional perils) that we do not yet see.

Overall, however, the big indicators suggest that we are now on the brink and that we are obliged for self-preservation as well as by prudence to pay much more attention to preserving biophysical and ecosystem integrity (UNEP, 2002; WWF, 2004; MEA, 2005; Reid et al, 2005). The rules for this are not well understood. We know much less about biophysical systems and our influences on them than we need to know for confident prediction, intervention and manipulation. Part of the necessary response will involve reducing specific negative impacts and solving bigger individual problems (for example, discharges of persistent toxins, mining of groundwater, and destructive over-harvesting of wild fish stocks). But as the inquiries into climate change have so clearly revealed, it is the complex interlinking of a host of ecologically insensitive human activities that is the underlying problem. And addressing these inevitably takes us into matters of priority, power, fairness, capability, cooperation, conflict and incentive that characterize the realm of human systems.

In the current circumstances, then, the integrity requirement entails more than just reducing human-induced stresses on ecological systems, though this is important. Maintaining the integrity of these systems and associated life support functions also entails examining the complex systemic implications of our own activities. We need to reduce the indirect and overall, as well as direct and specific, threats to system integrity and life support viability. To do this we need to adjust and reconstruct our own human systems to establish more modest, sensitive and flexible relations with the biophysical systems upon which we depend. The key for all this is acceptance that maintaining the planet's life support functions involves attention to the integrity of the human–ecological whole.[3]

Livelihood sufficiency and opportunity

Ensure that everyone and every community has enough for a decent life and opportunities to seek improvements in ways that do not compromise future generations' possibilities for sufficiency and opportunity.

At the time of the Brundtland Commission, the sustainability concept centred on the interdependence of ecological preservation and human development objectives. The core position merged two arguments. The first was that reducing and reversing ecological degradation is necessary for immediate human well-being and for human survival over the long term. The second was that enhancing human well-being, especially for people who lack the key prerequisites for a decent life, is a practical necessity for ecological preservation. Sustainability therefore requires a positive combination of environment and development initiatives.

Today we might phrase this a little differently. As we have seen in the integrity discussion, the human and ecological sides are not really separate. We need to go beyond ecological protection to establish viable socio-ecological systems. And we need to recognize that human well-being involves environmental conditions as well as material goods and services. Nonetheless, it remains clear that socio-ecological systems cannot be built and maintained when many people lack access to basic resources and essential services, have few if any satisfactory employment opportunities, are especially vulnerable to disease, and face physical, environmental or economic insecurity.

The difficulty is that the usual paths to material improvement of human well-being have been damaging to the biophysical environment. Although increased wealth and technological capacity have brought environmental gains as well as losses – air and water quality, for example, have improved with income growth in some places (Grossman and Krueger, 1995) – the overall effects have included important negatives such as accelerated decline of biodiversity, altered atmospheric chemistry, and over-exploited fisheries and groundwater sources. Some calculations suggest that human material demands are now exceeding the planet's ecological carrying capacity by as much as 30 per cent (Rees, 2001; WWF, 2002).[4] And there are deeper worries ahead, since these current demands do not include adequate attention to the basic needs of everyone – half of the human population, roughly 2.8 billion people, are living on US$2 per day or less (UNDP, 2001)[5] – or take into account the anticipated rise in human population – from about 6.3 billion today to about 8.9 billion in 2050 according to the UN's mid-range scenario (UNPD, 2003).

None of this makes it impossible to meet more needs and reduce stresses on the biosphere at the same time. Both remain necessary and many practical openings have been identified. The few outlined in Chapter 4 are mere indicators of countless possibilities. But given the evident challenges, it will be important to be as clear as possible about what needs must be met, overall as well as in particular circumstances.

There is a very long history of enquiry into human 'needs' and associated or overlapping desires, aspirations, confusions and pathologies (Lao-Tse, 1979; Aristotle, 1998; Bentham, 1834; Maslow, 1970; Illich, 1978; Durning, 1992; Nussbaum and Sen, 1993). It is well established as a fascinating but slippery subject. Needs evidently vary. They depend on the context of culture and ecology. Although people can be confused about their own needs, there is no easy distinction between real needs and false ones (Leiss, 1976). Nor is there a clear line between essential needs and supplementary ones or between poverty and well-being (Sharma, 1994). Imposing one culture's view of essential or higher needs on people of another culture is at best risky. But ignoring destitution, oppression and desperation is unsustainable as well as morally unacceptable.

Needs must therefore be addressed.[6] This must be done recognizing the multiplicity of conceptual perils and appreciating the diversity of circumstances. But it is not too difficult to find agreement on some raw basics. The Canadian International Development Agency is surely not going too far when it observes, citing international declarations and covenants on human rights:

> *Performing the basic functions of life (the intake of adequate nutrition, maintenance of health, protection, reproduction, growth) and taking part in the socio-economic and cultural life of the community (learning, understanding, communicating, producing, exchanging) are considered to be people's most basic needs (CIDA, 1997b).*

The short statement of the 'sufficiency' and 'opportunity' requirement as set out above may not capture all the fundamental prerequisites of a decent life. But it does recognize that human requirements involve mind and body, individuals and collectives, timeless basics and dynamic possibilities. It also stands as a minimum claim. Wherever they may be, people do inevitably need what qualifies as enough for a decent life in that context. And that clearly extends beyond mere material survival. The basic wherewithal for a human life also includes the necessities for positive exertion of powers and capabilities, for doing and being as well as having and existing (Macpherson, 1973; Nussbaum and Sen, 1993; Narayan et al, 2000a, 2000b).[7] What qualifies as an improvement of opportunity depends on context and choice and will vary no less than what qualifies as material sufficiency. But as active, striving beings, humans need both.

The sustainability qualifier is that the pursuit of livelihood sufficiency and opportunity is a long-term as well as immediate imperative. Future generations will also need sufficiency and opportunity. This constrains what can be accepted as means of meeting immediate needs. It also affects the nature of appropriate decision making. Because choice is crucial, so is involvement of those whose present needs are allegedly being addressed or potentially being affected. But the interests of those not yet born are also relevant.

Future needs and their implications are even more difficult to define and represent than present ones. For example, uncertainties about the likely nature of coming technological developments, and their negative as well as beneficial effects, make it difficult to know what depletable current resources will be most important in the future. We can, however, confidently assume that maintenance of key biophysical systems and ecological functions will be critical, and that while some technological innovations will find substitutes for current resources, other discoveries will identify valuable new uses for these resources.

Applied to future as well as present generations, the sufficiency and opportunity requirement incorporates a key tension. It recognizes the need to provide expanded economic and other goods to many people today but provides no safe justification for continued degradation of resource stocks and undermining of biophysical systems. Thus it both constrains and guides what is acceptable.

As with the integrity requirement, needs for sufficiency and opportunity must be specified for particular circumstances. It is important nonetheless to keep the global situation and associated sustainability requirements in mind. This is perhaps especially true in applications to wealthy countries and communities.

Specification of well-being objectives has already been undertaken in a host of initiatives, loosely related to sustainability assessment, that have set out basic well-being indicators, criteria and/or guiding principles (see Appendix 2). Some of this work has been done in poor countries or communities, or by development aid agencies and others with a focus on places typified by insufficiency and limited opportunity. But the bulk has been in relatively wealthy jurisdictions. While these places too have legitimate reasons for concern about sufficiency and opportunity, the implications are different.

In places where the basic material and social conditions for a decent life are inadequate or immediately insecure, provision of greater sufficiency and opportunity should be a means of reducing desperation, facilitating a longer term perspective and thereby enhancing prospects for sustainability. The situation is very different in places where the level of material consumption and associated biophysical system burdens is already disproportionately high, and where insecurity is centred on the protection of property rather than the absence of it. In such circumstances, serious contributions to sustainability require a shift in emphasis from yet more material gain to minimally material improvements, perhaps especially in the social, cultural and ecological environments. In other words, the sufficiency and opportunity requirement in wealthy contexts demands a decoupling of well-being from material growth (Robinson and Tinker, 1998).

A shift of this sort may be an obvious prerequisite for sustainability and broadly consistent with some existing trends (for example, greater support for environmental initiatives in times of economic confidence). But even in the most wealthy jurisdictions, the long-standing emphasis on yet more material expansion is still deeply rooted in the social, economic and political institutions. This is a telling example of a situation where the specification of a sustainability requirement must do more than adjust to the particular context. The interpretation of needs for livelihood sufficiency and opportunity must respect the global and long-term imperatives, which centre on enhancing long-term prospects but ensuring enough for all.

Intragenerational equity

Ensure that sufficiency and effective choices for all are pursued in ways that reduce dangerous gaps in sufficiency and opportunity (and health, security, social recognition, political influence, etc.) between the rich and the poor.

World agriculture today produces enough food to ensure adequate nutrition for everyone, but over 800 million people do not get enough to eat (FAO, 2003), and every year malnutrition is an underlying factor in the deaths of about half of the 10.7 million children who die before their fifth birthday (WHO, 2000). The situation for other basic physical requirements – for example, safe drinking water (WHO, 2004) – is probably not much different. At least for now there is or could be enough supply. The key failures lie not in inadequate resources and technology but in inequalities rooted in economics and politics. The victims are economically and politically poor. They suffer material deprivation, economic insecurity and tightly constrained opportunity. And, typically, they have limited influence in collective decision making at all levels from the family on up. This treatment is not just highly unequal, it is also profoundly inequitable. It is unfair to disadvantaged people today and, because it is likely to foster abuses and conflicts that undermine prospects for the future, it is unfair to the generations to come.

Current trends on matters of inequality are mixed. The gap between rich and poor is not widening everywhere. But the overall situation is bleak. According to the United Nations Development Programme, the income gap between the richest tenth of the world's people and poorest tenth rose from 19:1 in 1970 to 27:1 in 1997 (UNDP, 2001) and the richest fifth of the world's people are now consuming 86 per cent of all goods and services, while the poorest fifth make do with 1.3 per cent (UNDP, 1998). Quite aside from the moral repugnance of this situation, it entails vulnerability to environmental abuses and breeds tensions likely to be destructive to both rich and poor, sooner or later.

In the dominant institutions of economic authority today, the main strategies for improving conditions for the poorest of the poor are centred on economic growth achieved largely through expansion of material production, consumption and trade (for example, OECD, 1997a). Some scenario builders expect that general growth will eventually lead to an evening of distribution, among and within nations (OECD, 1997b).[8] But recent trends towards deeper inequality even in some of the wealthiest countries (for example, the US, the UK and New Zealand) suggest this is an unreliable expectation, at least in the absence of dedicated efforts to ensure more even distribution. Moreover, reliance on general growth ignores or denies biophysical limitations.

As noted above, ecological footprint calculations indicate that human economic activities are already exceeding the planetary carrying capacity (WWF, 2002) and extending average North American material standards to everyone would demand the resources of two to three additional Earth-equivalent planets (Wackernagel and Rees, 1996; Rees 2001). These analyses assume current technologies, which are open to substantial improvement (see the discussion of efficiency, below). But they also assume current population, which is expected to grow, and current consumer expectations, which are growing even faster. With only one already stressed planet available, continued devotion to overall growth in production and consumption – with overall expansion of material and energy throughput (Daly, 1996) – does not offer much hope for material improvements where they are needed most. The more likely results will further undermine ecological assets and increase the insecurity of people already most vulnerable. It seems, then, that poverty and inequality must be addressed directly through measures that deliver material improvements where there is deprivation, and material demands must be cut elsewhere.

Even modest redistribution of presently available resources would have considerable corrective potential. The United Nations Development Programme (UNDP) reports, for example, that annual American spending on cosmetics is US$8 billion and the estimated annual total needed to provide basic education for everyone in the world is only US$6 billion. Similarly, while the annual total needed to provide clean water and safe sewers for the world's population is US$9 billion, annual European spending on ice cream is US$11 billion (UNDP, 1998).

But simple redistribution is unlikely to be effective by itself and is rarely achieved or maintained without accompanying efforts to build sustainable livelihoods that include practically available livelihood choices and the power to choose. Moreover, significant willing redistribution from the rich and usually powerful to the less advantaged has been uncommon, except where the recognized alternative (for example, the threat of revolution) seemed worse. Whether the ecological and social threats arising from unsustainable inequities can be widely recognized as a clearly worse option is open to debate (UNDP, 1994; Athanasiou, 1996; Homer-Dixon, 1999; Elliot, 2002).

A more positive argument about openings for greater material equality focuses on alternatives to consumer satisfactions. It holds that acquisitive spending by the affluent often fails to contribute much to actual well-being, and that a less materially and energy intensive approach to personal satisfactions would permit both more equitable distribution and greater overall well-being (Linder, 1970; Daly and Cobb, 1989; Sachs, 1999). Certainly there is evidence that a good deal of current material consumption is largely for status rather than for more directly functional purposes (Easterlin, 1974; Hirsch, 1976; James, 1993; Brekke and Howarth, 2002). It is also evident that other, less ecologically threatening means of achieving belonging and respect are available. Here again the potential for significant change in the desirable direction is not well established, but worth pursuing.

Greater material equality is, however, only part of the story. It is needed to eliminate deprivation and material insecurity, to reduce envy, and to make better use of limited resources and ecological capacities. But greater material equality is unlikely to be achieved or to be lasting unless it is accompanied by greater political equality, in the broad sense of power to participate effectively in decision making in a context of real choices. There is plenty of evidence, particularly from studies of gender inequality, that powerlessness, vulnerability and deprivation are intertwined (Benería and Bisnath, 1996; Sainath, 1996; UNFPA, 2002). Moreover, powerlessness is widely associated with individual and collective pathologies, including violence, that undermine crucial aspects of community integrity, socio-economic well-being and global security (May, 1972; Galtung, 1975; Sachs, 2001). These in turn contribute to ecological damage that worsens poverty and insecurity (Renner, 1996; Dalby, 2002; Martinez-Alier, 2002). It is a viciously unsustainable circle.

The positive alternative that is required for sustainability might best be called livelihood equality, extending political and material equality to include the overlapping concerns of health, valued employment, respected knowledge and community security. These factors have been common themes in practical sustainability initiatives (see Chapter 4). They are also well recognized in the literature that distinguishes development from mere growth, and advocates processes in which the least advantaged are empowered as active participants in their own development (Singh and Titi, 1995; Wignaraja, 1996; Hoon et al, 1997; Narayan et al, 2000b).

Intergenerational equity

Favour present options and actions that are most likely to preserve or enhance the opportunities and capabilities of future generations to live sustainably.

Equity for sustainability is a matter that stretches well into the future. Indeed intergenerational equity is fundamental to the concept of sustainability and inevitably one of the most significant considerations in sustainability assessments (George, 1999). The basic idea is remarkably uncontroversial. Applied concern for the well-being of future generations has characterized most cultures (perhaps because the ones that ignored it did not survive), and has been encouraged for many reasons.[9] Today it is most commonly associated with an extension of basic fairness concepts – treat as you would be treated, the benefiter should pay, etc (Jacobs, 1991; Thompson, 2003).

The difficulties arise in determining just what is fair for future generations, human and otherwise. Direct representatives of future interests are not available to exert influence or clarify their preferences. Present decision makers may share a broad moral commitment to the future but have divergent views on what actions today might threaten or enhance future prospects. And the main disagreements cannot be resolved with much confidence because they rely on more or less speculative predictions about the future effects of present actions.

The most common, and perhaps the most important, intergenerational equity debates centre on what the economists call substitution: can gains in human capital (wealth, knowledge, technological advance) substitute for associated ecological losses incurred by the 'development' initiatives that contributed the new human capital (Pezzey, 1989; Ayres et al, 1997; Franceschi and Kahn, 2003)? In practical cases this often takes the form of a choice between preserving and exploiting. Do we retain and protect current ecological systems and resources for the continued benefit of future generations? Or do we use (and in some ways degrade) these systems and resources now in the expectation that the returns will build economic, technical and/or intellectual capacity for replacing exhausted resources or improving the environment in the future?

Although mountains of theoretical analyses have been devoted to substitution questions, few easy general answers have emerged. Substitutions have certainly been made. The historical record contains many examples of wealth- and technology-assisted resource replacements (plastics and metals replacing wood, synthetic fertilizers replacing dung) and broader socio-ecological system shifts (local farming supplanting hunting and gathering, global agribusiness supplanting local farming). And the results include much valued and lasting improvements in human well-being. The catch is that they have not had consistently positive or fairly distributed effects. Whole civilizations (Sumer, the Maya, etc.) have collapsed because they wrecked their ecological foundations through what amounted to substitution failure (Wright, 2004). And very often the attractive results have been accompanied by unanticipated damages (as in the recent cases of DDT, tall emission stacks, large dams and chlorofluorocarbons (CFCs)).

As the solutions have become more ambitious (from crop hybridization to genetic modification, hydro dams to nuclear power, regional reciprocity to global trade liberalization, and perhaps from slide rules to nanobots), they have stirred rising worries about risks and vulnerabilities (Borgmann, 1984; Beck, 1999; Joy, 2000). And because extractive economic activities are now pressing or exceeding the potential capacity of ecological systems globally, it seems clear that more substitutions of the conventional sort are not sustainable.

None of this establishes that substitution initiatives are inherently undesirable, but they are not automatically beneficial either. Their viability and desirability depend on the particulars of complex circumstances, and are likely to be undermined if important determinants of long-term effects are ignored. Part of the problem is that the usual market- and economy-centred decision making does not give adequate attention to ecological factors, common goods, system behaviour or future implications (Daly and Cobb, 1989; Norgaard, 1995). The task of sustainability assessment, guided by commitment to intergenerational equity, is to do a better job of this, recognizing that the future effects of substitutions proposed today will not be predictable with much certainty.

At least for sustainability assessment purposes, recognizing intergenerational equity as a requirement for sustainability does not favour any general position for or against substitution of human for natural capital. It demands only that assessment participants in each case give careful attention to potential future effects, considering the particulars of the case, that they respect the inevitable uncertainties, and that they ask what choice future generations might prefer, if they were represented at the table.

We cannot know what future generations would prefer. As a best guess, however, we can surmise that they would subscribe to the basics of sustainability. Their interests would, for example, be served by application of a fundamental commitment to retaining or enhancing socio-ecological integrity. The integrity requirement respects the dynamic evolution of choices as well as possibilities and it favours avoidance of risk to resilience and self-organizing capacity. This supports the precautionary bias to be discussed below and should help to guide judgements on intergenerational equity as well as more immediate desirability. But there are still difficulties of prediction and of judgement about the relative merits of competing uncertainties.

The requirement for intergenerational equity is, perhaps more clearly than the other sustainability prerequisites, a matter of applied moral choice where the interests of the unrepresented must be served. While better understanding – of particular project effects and general factors influencing long-term socio-ecological integrity, for example – will help, there can be no adequate technical means of identifying the proper choices and no substitute for open deliberation.

Resource maintenance and efficiency

Provide a larger base for ensuring sustainable livelihoods for all while reducing threats to the long-term integrity of socio-ecological systems by reducing extractive damage, avoiding waste and cutting overall material and energy use per unit of benefit.

The Brundtland Commission placed heavy emphasis on technological and economic changes that would deliver major improvements in material and energy efficiencies. According to the Commission's calculations, a five to tenfold increase in material production would be needed to raise conditions in developing countries to current industrial country standards and to meet the needs of an expanding human population (WCED, 1987). To deliver this increase while reducing already unsustainable stresses on ecosystems and resources, production (and subsequent consumption) would have to become much more careful in the extraction of resources, much less profligate in the use of materials and energy, and much more successful in the control of discharges and residuals.

This focus on efficiency has been particularly popular among industrial advocates of sustainability (DeSimone et al, 1997; Anderson, 1998; WBCSD, 2002). A large portion of the literature and initiatives addressing private sector responsibilities concentrates on doing more with less – optimizing production by decreasing material and energy inputs, cutting waste outputs through product and process redesign, and shifting emphasis from products to services. Such improvements would permit continued economic expansion, with associated employment and wealth generation, while reducing demands on resource stocks and pressures on ecosystems (OECD, 1997c; Hawken et al, 1999; McDonough and Braungart, 2002; Hinterberger et al, 2004).

While there is considerable debate about what is needed, what is possible with current technologies and what is plausible with imagination and creativity, leading works in the area suggest that material and energy efficiencies could be increased by a factor of four or even ten, without much strain on existing technological and administrative capacities (Weiszacker et al, 1997; Gardner and Sampat, 1998; Schmidt-Bleek, 2000). Calls for factor 10 improvement (a 90 per cent overall reduction in materials/energy per unit of product or service) accept that progress towards sustainability demands a halving of present resource use and a substantial further reduction by the rich to make room for needed improvement of material conditions among the poor (Schmidt-Bleek, 2000) and for regeneration of now over-stressed natural capital (Daly, 2002). Important policy changes (for example, shifting subsidies from hydrocarbon extraction projects to energy demand reduction programmes) would be required to change incentive structures and draw attention to opportunities for efficiency gains. Advocates nevertheless hold that no great change in the dominant capitalist form would be needed (Hawken et al, 1999).

Efficiency strategies face a number of difficulties. While theoretically there is plenty of room for efficiency gains, capturing them often involves enormous political as well as technical complexities. For example, a factor 10 efficiency gain in transportation seems quite plausible given that only about 1 per cent of the energy in fuel consumed by average automobiles actually moves the passengers. But because these vehicles are deeply entrenched in global corporate practice, consumer expectations and infrastructure design, rapid transition to other options, even to substantially more efficient private automobiles, is unlikely to be achieved by efficiency initiatives alone.

A second serious challenge is the 'rebound effect' that occurs when the savings from efficiency gains are spent on more production and consumption (Jevons, 1865; Patterson, 2000; Hertwich, 2005). If savings in one area merely facilitate more material or energy consumption elsewhere, there is no net gain. If the savings go into more consumption by the already affluent, which is mostly what is happening now, prospects for sustainability are likely to decline. Here again, efficiency by itself cannot be enough. It must be combined with efforts to direct gains to those in material need and to shift the demands of the affluent to less materially and energy intensive satisfactions (more massages, fewer Mercedes).

A related problem arises with proposals for ecological tax reform. The idea of shifting taxes from employment and income to pollution and resource use is attractive as a means of encouraging efficiency investments. But it is problematic if it means the end of progressive income tax regimes, which draw more heavily from the wealthy and advantaged. Progressive income taxes have been one of the few effective mechanisms for reducing the gap between rich and poor. A similarly powerful replacement would have to be introduced. Or a much smaller but more steeply progressive residual income tax would have to be retained. Otherwise, the efficiency gains from ecological tax reform would be negated by sustainability losses resulting from deeper inequity.

Efficiencies also offer no release from the ultimate limits of biospheric capacity or the laws of thermodynamics. Because so many of our current productive and consumptive activities are highly inefficient, we may well be able to achieve 90 per cent overall reductions in materials/energy throughput for each unit of many products and services. But 100 per cent reductions are not possible. Nor is continued expansion of the overall quantity of material and energy extraction, production, consumption and waste. Even if we combine efficiencies with other impact reducing measures (less damaging extractive practices and substantial cuts in the generation and use of toxic substances, etc.), we come up against the limited residual resilience of biospheric systems upon which we depend. A 1986 calculation found that humans were already appropriating about 40 per cent of net terrestrial primary production (Vitousek et al, 1986). More recent 'ecological footprint' studies suggest that human demands now exceed the planet's biological capacity by about 20 per cent (WWF, 2004). These estimates are imperfect and debatable. But they are useful reminders of the presence and likely proximity of unforgiving overall limits.

Finally, commitments to efficiency must be tempered with respect for uncertainty and integrity. Efficiency initiatives typically include efforts to maximize yield and minimize redundancies. But in ill-understood complex systems, where the limits to resiliency are not clearly identified and where surprise is common, maximizing yield entails a risky form of brinkmanship. As bitter experience with several ocean fisheries has demonstrated, it is dangerously easy to cross the invisible threshold between maximum sustainable yield and system collapse. It is wiser by far to maintain a substantial cushion. Similar considerations favour retention of redundancies. In complex systems, redundancy is a form of back-up capacity, available to maintain functions in response to new perturbations. Such redundancy is worth preserving despite loss of some immediate efficiencies.

Recognizing these difficulties, it remains that substantial efficiency improvements are possible and necessary as part of the sustainability agenda. But initiatives to reduce material and energy throughput will be beneficial only if designed and implemented within a more comprehensive package of approaches that seek overall gains and consider the distribution of benefits.

Socio-ecological civility and democratic governance

Build the capacity, motivation and habitual inclination of individuals, communities and other collective decision making bodies to apply sustainability principles through more open and better informed deliberations, greater attention to fostering reciprocal awareness and collective responsibility, and more integrated use of administrative, market, customary, collective and personal decision making practices.

Better governance is a prerequisite and probably also a product of steps towards sustainability. As the discussion so far has confirmed, there are few easy answers in the pursuit of sustainability. Even the initial items in the requirements list – dealing with the dynamic complexities of interlinked socio-ecological systems, ensuring sufficiency and opportunity, moving towards intra- and intergenerational equity, and designing efficiency strategies that can win lasting overall gains – demand much more than our present decision-making structures and processes have been able to deliver. At every scale from the individual to the planet we apparently need to be more thoughtful, open and flexible, and to examine our capacities and objectives in a more integrated way, with more humility, more far-sightedness, and more commitment to continuous learning and adjustment.

Fortunately we have more tools available than we usually recognize. Most discussions about the pursuit of sustainability centre on what might be done by government authorities and adjusted markets. In the long history of human socio-economic and ecological relations, however, we have more often relied on customary practice and deliberate choice. The four together – government, markets, custom and choice – provide the makings of governance arrangements for sustainability.

For each of the four there is now a more or less extensive body of theory and discourse, housed in its own disciplinary tradition (political science, economics, anthropology and sociology, philosophy and psychology). In practice, however, at least beyond the face-to-face scale, decision making on matters of collective interest has almost always relied on an interweaving of all four. Especially for sustainability, we need to mobilize all the positive forces available, in well-considered combinations.

Governments and markets are clearly powerful and unavoidably necessary. At the same time, their limitations have become increasingly evident. Governments are and will remain crucial as our best, widely mandated and potentially legitimate means of defending and advancing the common interest. But faith in the capacity of governments (of any ideological persuasion) to be ably comprehensive central planners and managers was destroyed in the 20th century. And their adequacy in many less ambitious assignments is widely doubted. Markets too are indispensable – responsive to important demands and attractively automatic in their adjustments. Probably no complex society could do without them. But markets have proved to be neglectful of goods that are unpriced, long term, collective or sought by those who lack the means to pay. As a result, advocacy of fully unleashed markets survives only in theoretical isolation.

Today, most regimes are depicted as hybrids with markets given more or less wide scope and governments expected to facilitate, regulate and compensate as necessary. Over the last few decades, however, confidence in government market arrangements has been undermined by a variety of unsettling developments. Corporations, international trade organizations, advertising media and other market players have extended a global reach into all commodifiable realms, with a scale of operations and a range of side-effects increasingly beyond the repair and gap filling capabilities of established governments. The great successes in generating more wealth and technological innovation have been accompanied by horrible maldistribution, large regions of development failure, persistent and in some ways worsening global insecurity, and cynical expectation of untrustworthy assurances and broken commitments. While there are many probable causes, an important part of the story is that new problems and expectations are being generated too quickly, and with too little respect for national boundaries, administrative mandates or the demands of credible technical analysis. The problems to be faced and the expectations to be met have become too numerous, too complex and too vast for the established mechanisms to manage adequately (Dryzek, 1987; Paehlke and Torgerson, 1990; Ludwig, 2001; Paehlke, 2003).

No doubt there has been exaggeration of the bad news.[10] Certainly, some claims about the general impotence of governments have been wildly overstated (McQuaig, 1998). Nonetheless, it seems clear that even relatively capable governments and market institutions have done an imperfect job of dealing with problems within national jurisdictions, and are doing a much more dangerously bad job globally. Not surprisingly, this has led to reasonable suspicions that the combination, by itself, will never be up to managing a transition to sustainability.

Fortunately, there are additional resources. Governments and markets have always relied on the customary civility and more or less informed choices of citizens. The knowledge and trustworthiness required in trade and community relations, for example, have depended not so much on economic self-interest and obedience to the law as on education, culturally ingrained morality and collectively established norms of behaviour. Accordingly, many responses to the evident limitations of governments and markets recognize and strengthen citizen-based contributions.

Three are particularly important: insistence on decision making transparency and public involvement; the proliferation of non-government and non-market groups demanding or asserting significant roles in collective action; and greater attention to the glue of commitment and engagement that holds community together. These developments – often labeled as movements in democracy, civil society and social capital – mobilize new versions of the old public tools of collective concern, traditionally expressed as custom and choice (Dryzek, 1992; O'Riordan, 1996; Runyan, 1999; Swift, 1999; Putnam, 2000; Weber, 2003).

The effects are evident in a diversity of applications. At the leading edges of development work, the old focus on government capacity-building has been shifting towards building good governance. Efforts to strengthen democracy have extended beyond voting to transparency and participative openness. Devotion to modernization and material improvement has been combined with efforts to recognize and retain traditional knowledge, and build on existing social as well as physical assets. The language (though less often the practice) of development assistance has moved from development for the people to development with and by the people (CIDA, 1996; UNDP, 1997).[11]

Similarly, in the hugely expanded world of public interest groups, activists who once focused mostly on raising public awareness as a means of pressuring governments to act, have become recognized participants in multi-stakeholder governance at every level from the local to the global (ICLEI, 1996; Zarsky, 1999; Cardoso, 2004). Moreover, they have expanded their strategies to engage corporations and citizens directly. Campaigns now include consumer mobilization (against the purchase of blood diamonds, genetically modified foods, lawn pesticides, tropical hardwoods and old growth lumber, etc.), product certification (of sustainably harvested forest products, etc.), community social marketing (of energy efficiency options and alternatives to lawn pesticides, etc.), and alternative trade and exchange mechanisms (fair trade initiatives and alternative 'green money' mechanisms), all based on informed, personal moral choice (Bendell, 2000; McKenzie-Mohr, 1999; EFTA, 2002; Kotler et al, 2002).

In most jurisdictions, responses to government and/or market failures and resistance to undesired impositions have spurred reassertions of community and local culture. Some of these have involved ugly returns to narrow intolerance and ancient grievance. But many reflect a more admirable dedication to maintain a collective identity, to preserve establish networks of attachment, and support, and to express commitment to a social and ecological home (Ekins, 1992; Shiva, 1994; Douthwaite, 1996). Linked to this are large bodies of related work on ethics, education, spirituality, traditional knowledge, renewed citizenship and associated subjects that represent another large field of sustainability discussion and application that is, effectively, about governance (for example, Leopold, 1970; Friere, 1970; Tobias and Cowan, 1994; Berkes, 1999).

For sustainable governance, the central element is re-emphasis on the underlying importance of customary civility. Linked with other tools, including a reliable and reasonably equitable legal system and accessible public education, voluntary and habitual civility is the foundation for trust, fair treatment and mutual support (Nozick, 1992; Orr, 1994; de Soto, 2000). It is indispensable to any community and society that aspires to a decent quality of life and security of well-being, material and otherwise.

Normally, the concept of civility is a social one. But given that the social and the ecological are deeply interdependent, the needed civility must be extended, at least for sustainability purposes, to embrace both.

This is certainly achievable; indeed it has been widely demonstrated. Socio-ecological civility was, arguably, the essential message of traditional hunter-gatherer cultures and belief systems (Brody, 2000). Today, in a time of great, rapid and often necessary change, the old customs are depleted and insufficient. In most places, socio-ecological civility is something to be reconstructed as well as reasserted.[12] And that is as much a political as a cultural exercise in social learning (Milbrath, 1989; Relph, 1992; Alexander, 2002). In many, perhaps most cases, commitment to community and ecology is reasserted to protect valued assets, to force desired action and to reclaim denied authority. It is seen in efforts to rehabilitate the abandoned urban block, to take fisheries management back from the central authorities, to defend customary access to the forest, to favour slow food over fast food, and to save the familiar rural landscape from urban sprawl. Indeed there are libraries of cheerful reports on the persistence and rebirth of civility in the most unlikely venues.

Commitment to community and ecology is not enough, however. The many stories of persistent local civility are accompanied by as many counter examples of atrocity and horror also arising from devotion to tradition, history and collective identity, including ecological aspects. The Nazi appeal to blood and soil is only one example (Schama, 1996). To rise above exclusive solidarity, socio-ecological civility must be tied to global responsibility and to respect for shared rights. It must be supported in law, enabled by fair opportunity, and complemented by education. It must enrich and be enriched by the capacity for informed choice and the democratic opportunity to use it.

In other words, what is crucial is the evolving combination of habitual civility and informed choice with responsive authority and well-guided markets. A wide diversity of particular arrangements will serve. What is most needed, appropriate and workable will always depend heavily on the context. But virtually everywhere, effective governance for sustainability will depend on well integrated mobilization of all four components, with special efforts to ensure mutually supportive beneficial effects. Some openings for positive feedback are obvious. For example, government regulations and tax initiatives can be designed to force producers to include social and ecological costs in commodity prices, thereby helping consumers to exercise informed personal choice. Similarly, openings for participative governance experience can be designed to enhance community and ecological understanding, which should in turn feed habitually responsible behaviour.[13] And in many areas, the greatest gains are likely to be achieved by combining pressures and motivations – as we now can see in moves towards greater attention to corporate social and eco-logical responsibility driven by the simultaneous efforts of regulators, insurers, employees, concerned customers, downwind and downstream, neighbours and activist investors. Such initiatives may require innovative mechanisms and thinking outside the usual institutional boxes, but the concept itself is not difficult.

Precaution and adaptation

Respect uncertainty, avoid even poorly understood risks of serious or irreversible damage to the foundations for sustainability, plan to learn, design for surprise and manage for adaptation.

The principles above are generic, meant for universal application in the assessment of many kinds of undertakings, affecting many different communities and ecosystems. They are drawn from and reflect broad agreement in a wide base of literature and some practice. At the same time, they are imprecise and proposed tentatively. This is in part because there are many different ways to integrate and categorize the underlying considerations and points of agreement. But the fuzziness and hesitation also reflect the continuing weakness of our understanding about how it all works.

In sustainability deliberations, the key uncertainties arise from complexity. Even just the raw volume of things to consider is well beyond our current in-formation gathering capacity. Biodiversity experts, for example, estimate that we have so far identified only 1 per cent of viruses and bacteria and less than 14 per cent of all species (Giri et al, 2001). And identification is the easy part.

The difficulties multiply as we try to understand how these species behave, how they participate in larger biophysical processes, how the processes combine as dynamic and complex open systems at multiple intersecting scales, and how they all may be affected by further human interventions of the sort to be examined in sustainability assessments. It is easy to see why confident prediction is not often possible. And that is without taking into account the apparent non-linearity of complex system behaviour and the frequently surprising influence of tiny perturbations, or the peculiar problems that accompany us doing research on systems in which we are active participants (Holling, 1986; Midgley, 2003).

At least three sorts of uncertainty result: ignorance (we do not even know what to expect), vagueness (we have founded suspicions, a rough grasp, perhaps even a quite reliable working understanding, but at least some of the picture is fuzzy and we may be overlooking something important) and evaluation difficulties (we may be able to describe conditions, relations and changes but do not have any firm basis for determining their importance relative to other concerns) (Gunderson et al, 1995; Stirling, 2000, 2001; Harrernoës et al, 2001; Young, 2001). In this world of uncertainty, everything is a risk (Camus, 1956). But the risks are unavoidable and must be faced. The challenge is in knowing how to live in such a world, how to respect the risks, how to choose among the competing options for action.

While better science can help, even the most excellent science – well funded, carefully designed, appreciative of complexity and rigorously examined – will rarely be sufficient. Strategic and project level assessments, which turn on prediction of effects and comparison of competing options, are typified by uncertainties and more or less risky choices. In making these choices the key questions will not be what is correct or optimal or safe, but what is fair and what is the best option given the uncertainties and the perils (Stirling, 2000; O'Brien, 2000, 2003).

Two implications are evident. The first is that public engagement is crucial. On uncertain matters expert analysis can illuminate options, but cannot deliver correct answers. The choices to be made necessarily involve the application of values and the exercise of power. If the choosing is to serve broader sustainability objectives – if it is to build equality and enhanced democracy and civility – then the deliberating and decision making should be, to the extent possible, public exercises. They should reveal the difficulties of the choice making and reflect the preferences of those who must live with the results.

The second, even more obvious implication is that precautionary approaches are preferable. Because we are uncertain, we should be careful. Because the world is complex beyond confident prediction, we should expect surprise, prepare for error and act to avoid possible peril. This applies very broadly in the conception, selection and design of new projects and strategic undertakings of the sort properly subject to sustainability assessment.

The narrow version of the precautionary principle set out in the 1992 Rio Declaration requires that 'Where there are threats of serious or irreversible damage, lack of full scientific certainty shall not be used as a reason for postponing cost-effective measures to prevent environmental degradation' (UN, 1992, principle 15). More broadly, precaution involves willingness to act on incomplete but suggestive indications of significant risk to social and ecological systems that are crucial for sustainability (Bonilla et al, 2001). But this too is only part of the story.

We will be surprised by unanticipated effects. Because of the complexities and uncertainties that underlie the precautionary approach, we may often have only suggestive evidence about many emerging problems, and even less information about resulting effects that will ripple through complex socio-ecological systems. Moreover, there will be serious problems that we do anticipate but cannot find (or agree upon) ways to prevent. Global climate change is unlikely to be alone in this category. Prudence therefore involves avoiding options that might imperil important things – health, crucial ecosystem functions, valued community qualities – and favouring options that anticipate surprise and are designed for adaptation (Walters and Holling, 1990; Singh and Titi, 1994).

In sustainability assessment, the precautionary approach looks for multiple diverse solutions rather than one big one. It prefers safe-fail technologies (that can fail without causing serious damage) over fail-safe technologies (that require multiple safety systems because any failure could be catastrophic). It favours undertakings that are designed for flexibility and reversibility, that include mechanisms for effective monitoring, and that are accompanied by backup alternatives (Gunderson et al, 1995; Kay et al, 1999; Stirling, 2000).

Perhaps most importantly, the precautionary approach relies on and fosters learning. It recognizes that while uncertainty is inevitable, we can deal with it more successfully through continuous observation and adjustment. Because most key decisions will be matters of public choice rather than expert determination, applied precaution relies on a well informed citizenry. Accordingly, the most desirable undertakings are those that are most amenable to public understanding, monitoring and adjustment. And the most desirable processes are those that promote citizen engagement and learning about how to live in a world of complexity and uncertainty (Friedmann, 1973; Lee, 1993; Gunderson et al, 1995; Bolin et al, 2000; Lister and Kay, 2000; Diduck, 2004).

Immediate and long-term integration

Attempt to meet all requirements for sustainability together as a set of interdependent parts, seeking mutually supportive benefits.

The eight requirements for sustainability outlined above are both necessary and interconnected. Progress towards a durable and desirable future depends on gains in each area. But it is not just that every one of the requirements is crucial. They are linked – they overlap and are interdependent. What happens in one area affects what happens in the others. Gains in livelihood sufficiency and opportunity will collapse if the integrity of supporting socio-ecological systems is compromised and key ecological functions are not maintained. Gains in formal equality will remain vulnerable if democratic governance and customary civility are underdeveloped. Therefore the requirements for sustainability are not mere targets for the long run; they are a package of obligatory considerations for all decisions along the way. And in all of these decisions, consideration of the interconnections will be as important as attention to the individual requirements.

It is tempting to assume that all steps towards meeting the individual requirements will be mutually reinforcing. Certainly the interdependence of the parts suggests that positive feedback will be common. More devoted protection and restoration of socio-ecological system integrity will provide a stronger foundation for lasting opportunities and reliable sufficiency. Greater equity will support more citizen engagement, which will foster broader appreciation of complexities and uncertainties, which will encourage more cautious interventions, which will avoid costly and inefficient failures. And so on. In general, that is the nature of the requirements. But in particular cases, it won't be so simple. There will be conflicts and some trade-offs will be unavoidable. Moreover, in a world of complex and dynamic open systems with influences flowing back and forth between scales from the microscopic to the global and beyond, there will be counter-intuitive and perverse higher order consequences as well as positive feedback loops and mutually supporting gains. Integrated attention to all the requirements must include efforts to understand their interrelations and to prepare for surprises.

Integration does not mean balancing. Many ill-considered discussions of sustainability applications refer to a balancing of conservation and development, or of human and ecological imperatives. But balancing is usually a strategy of incremental sacrifice. In common practice, authorities claim to have balanced ecological and economic objectives when they approve an ecologically damaging undertaking but impose conditions that mitigate some of the adverse effects and sacrifice or delay some of the immediate extractive gains. Certainly a form of balancing is involved. However, the result is net ecological loss. As a continuing strategy this is not viable. Nor could sustainability be achieved through a balancing of the requirements set out here. For example, there would seem to be little long-term promise in a balancing strategy that accepted more incremental widenings of the gap between rich and poor on the grounds that it was softened by some equality-related restrictions in trade liberalization deals meant to serve wealth generation and efficiency goals. If both efficiency and equality are necessary for sustainability, then positive gains in both areas must be achieved.

The challenge for sustainability assessment is to find workable processes for pursuing all of the requirements at once, recognizing the interconnections and seeking positive overall gains even when trade-offs are unavoidable. The key probably lies in keeping all of the requirements in sight and always seeking the approach, option and design that will bring multiple benefits and net gains. But integration also means improving our means of seeing how the requirements are interconnected in particular circumstances, and finding ways of dealing with the unavoidable trade-offs that avoid the 'balancing' trap of continued incremental losses.

Characteristics, strengths and limitations of the requirements as decision criteria

The eight requirements set out in Box 5.1 and discussed above cover the key changes needed for progress towards sustainability. They should serve as the objectives underpinning every serious strategy for enhancing future well-being and they should inform the planning and review of every undertaking with potentially significant sustainability implications.

That is not to say this is the only valid set of basic sustainability criteria. There are countless other lists of sustainability components, principles and objectives (a few of which are summarized in Appendix 1). And there are many other ways of categorizing, describing and assigning emphases to the considerations recognized in the discussion here. Many alternative versions retain the same core values and ideas and would serve at least adequately as a foundation for decision making. In any event, application of a diversity of approaches is desirable as a way of testing the possibilities. Moreover, as sustainability assessment practice expands and experience increases, any initial set of objectives and criteria will be found wanting. Revisions of approaches, taxonomies and formulations will be needed again and again.

Nonetheless, it does matter which approach is adopted. The eight requirements here may not appear to be profoundly different from what has been presented in some of the more conventional pillar-based approaches. They address the usual set of key ecological, social, economic and other considerations. But the categorization and phrasing depart from the pillar conventions to stress interconnections and interdependencies among the pillar areas. Moreover, the thinking draws from sustainability-related discourses – for example, those related to complex systems, citizen engagement and precaution – that are not always incorporated successfully in the pillar-based sustainability literature and practice. While the approach set out here may still be incomplete, the eight listed requirements represent a careful attempt to incorporate all the main elements and interconnections of what is needed. More narrowly conceived sets of basic concerns are unlikely to provide a satisfactory foundation for sustainability assessment.

The main advantages of the eight requirements list are that it is short, comprehensive, demanding and difficult to collapse into conventional categories. The basics are simple enough to permit manageable implementation. And because the list covers all the key considerations for strategic and project level undertakings, it provides a foundation for consolidating the usual diversity of current evaluation and approval processes. At the same time, the demand for integrated attention to all eight requirements imposes a broader agenda than most proponents and public authorities now accept. The result should encourage simultaneous pursuit of multiple gains towards sustainability from undertakings that now typically have narrowly conceived objectives and too often have negative overall implications for long-term well-being on this planet.

Box 5.1 Sustainability requirements as decision criteria

Socio-ecological system integrity
The requirement:
Build human–ecological relations to establish and maintain the long-term integrity of socio-biophysical systems and protect the irreplaceable life support functions upon which human as well as ecological well-being depends.

Illustrative implications:

- need to understand better the complex systemic implications of our own activities;
- need to reduce indirect and overall, as well as direct and specific human threats to system integrity and life support viability.

Livelihood sufficiency and opportunity
The requirement:
Ensure that everyone and every community has enough for a decent life and that everyone has opportunities to seek improvements in ways that do not compromise future generations' possibilities for sufficiency and opportunity.

Illustrative implications:

- need to ensure provision of key prerequisites for a decent life (which, typically, are not now enjoyed by those who have little or no access to basic resources and essential services, who have few if any satisfactory employment opportunities, who are especially vulnerable to disease, or who face physical or economic insecurity);
- need to appreciate the diversity, and ensure the involvement of, those whose needs are being addressed.

Intragenerational equity
The requirement:
Ensure that sufficiency and effective choices for all are pursued in ways that reduce dangerous gaps in sufficiency and opportunity (and health, security, social recognition, political influence, etc.) between the rich and the poor.

Illustrative implications:

- need to build sustainable livelihoods for all, including practically available livelihood choices and the power to choose;
- need to emphasize less materially and energy intensive approaches to personal satisfactions among the advantaged, to permit material and energy sufficiency for all.

Intergenerational equity
The requirement:
Favour present options and actions that are most likely to preserve or enhance the opportunities and capabilities of future generations to live sustainably.

Illustrative implications:

- need to return current resource exploitation and other pressures on ecological systems and their functions to levels that are safely within the perpetual capacity of those systems to provide resources and services likely to be needed by future generations;
- need to build the integrity of socio-ecological systems, maintaining the diversity, accountability, broad engagement and other qualities required for long-term adaptive adjustment.

Resource maintenance and efficiency
The requirement:
Provide a larger base for ensuring sustainable livelihoods for all while reducing threats to the long-term integrity of socio-ecological systems by reducing extractive damage, avoiding waste and cutting overall material and energy use per unit of benefit.

Illustrative implications:

- need to do more with less (optimize production through decreasing material and energy inputs and cutting waste outputs through product and process redesign throughout product lifecycles) to permit continued economic expansion where it is needed, with associated employment and wealth generation, while reducing demands on resource stocks and pressures on ecosystems;
- need to consider purposes and end uses (efficiency gains are of no great value if the savings go to more advantages and more consumption by the already affluent).

Socio-ecological civility and democratic governance
The requirement:
Build the capacity, motivation and habitual inclination of individuals, communities and other collective decision making bodies to apply sustainability requirements through more open and better informed deliberations, greater attention to fostering reciprocal awareness and collective responsibility, and more integrated use of administrative, market, customary and personal decision making practices.

Illustrative implications:

- need governance structures capable of integrated responses to complex, intertwined and dynamic conditions;

- need to mobilize more participants, mechanisms and motivations, including producers, consumers, investors, lenders, insurers, employees, auditors, reporters;
- need to strengthen individual and collective understanding of ecology and community, foster customary civility and ecological responsibility, and build civil capacity for effective involvement in collective decision making.

Precaution and adaptation
The requirement:
Respect uncertainty, avoid even poorly understood risks of serious or irreversible damage to the foundations for sustainability, plan to learn, design for surprise and manage for adaptation.

Illustrative implications:

- need to act on incomplete but suggestive information where social and ecological systems that are crucial for sustainability are at risk;
- need to design for surprise and adaptation, favouring diversity, flexibility and reversibility;
- need to prefer safe-fail over fail-safe technologies;
- need to seek broadly comprehensible options rather than those that are dependent on specialized expertise;
- need to ensure the availability and practicality of backup alternatives;
- need to establish mechanisms for effective monitoring and response.

Immediate and long-term integration
The requirement:
Apply all principles of sustainability at once, seeking mutually supportive benefits and multiple gains.

Considerations:

- integration is not the same as balancing;
- because greater efficiency, equity, ecological integrity and civility are all necessary for sustainability, then positive gains in all areas must be achieved;
- what happens in any one area affects what happens in all of the others;
- it is reasonable to expect, but not safe to assume, that positive steps in different areas will be mutually reinforcing.

Illustrative implications:

- need positive steps in all areas, at least in general and at least in the long term;
- need to resist convenient, immediate compromises unless they clearly promise an eventual gain.

The eight requirements list nevertheless remains problematic and insufficient by itself. There are three particularly important limitations.

First, in the real world, compromises and trade-offs are rarely avoidable. The requirement for integration and simultaneous reconciliation may be reasonable in theory, but demanding positive results in all categories for every undertaking is likely to be overly ambitious when so much of what we now do, and regularly propose, satisfies none of the requirements. We must therefore anticipate the need for sacrifices and concessions. And that means providing basic guidance on what may or may not be tolerable, and how such judgements are to be made in particular circumstances.

Second, the requirements are only generally stated. For many of them there is limited consensus or practical experience in dealing with the real implications in actual situations. And there is an inevitable looseness about broad values such as integrity, civility, opportunity and equity. General requirements, accompanied by some careful exploration and explanation, may be all that is needed for redesigning overall planning, assessment and decision making processes. But for specific case use, no list of generic requirements is sufficient. Serious actual applications depend on appreciation of the particular activities under consideration and the particular ecologies, communities and socio-ecological systems to be affected. These elements of context play a key role in determining the substance of the issues to be considered, and the processes by which concrete objectives are developed, significance assessed, and trade-offs articulated. Assessment and decision making processes must therefore be designed to respect the specifics of context as well as to apply the basic list of general requirements. This is just part of living in a complex world. We must allocate our assessment resources sensibly, avoid risks to valued systems that we do not understand well, and learn and adjust as we go.

Finally, the package demands more sophistication than we normally demonstrate. Considerable knowledge, research and judgement are needed to elaborate and apply the requirements as practical decision criteria in particular situations. While the requirements can be used as a checklist of topics that must be considered in a planning process or a decision, they are not a simple list of items to be checked off as yes or no. In each case we will need to gain at least a rough understanding of the starting point – the socio-ecological context and the nature of present inefficiencies and inequities, risks and opportunities, assets and expectations. We will need to consider the purposes, alternatives and potential effects of the undertakings in question. And to do this we will need to draw from diverse sources of knowledge, and judge what expertise is appropriate and what weight to put on different kinds of evidence. Inevitably our time and resources for research will be constrained and our institutional capacities limited. We will therefore always need to set priorities and act on incomplete analysis as well as imperfect information. We will need to design our deliberative processes to respect these limitations and sometimes we will need to pass up opportunities simply because we do not have the capacity to evaluate their promises and dangers.

None of these difficulties is fatal. But each will have to be addressed carefully – in the preparation of guidance for decisions about compromises and trade-offs, and in the design of planning and assessment processes that respect particular contexts, demand only what real resources and institutions can deliver, and ensure fairness to the participants. These are matters to be considered in the following chapters.

Notes

1   Arguably it is not theoretically sound either. See, for example, David Beetham's (1999) discussion of this issue in the context of questions about universal application of democratic principles.

2   Arguably all ecosystems on the planet are now stressed to some extent by global climate changes and ozone layer depletion. More generally, the Millennium Ecosystem Assessment project (MEA, 2005) reviewed the global status of 24 key ecosystem services and found 15 in decline, and only 4 increasing.

3   Many environmentalists are inclined to go beyond imperatives rooted in human self-interest. They advocate eco-centred ethics, under which preservation of ecological diversity and integrity is pursued for its own sake, or at least not just for human purposes, immediate or long term. Just where and to what extent the implications concerning the maintenance and strengthening of ecological integrity would differ from those of enlightened human self-interest in the current situation is not entirely clear. But it would presumably affect discussions about any contemplated trade-offs between ecological objectives and more directly human objectives.

4   Such calculations are highly problematic due to data limitations, debates about appropriate measures and questions about potential substitutability of technology for natural capital. But even some who accept considerable substitution find reason to worry about current over-consumption (for example, Arrow et al, 2003).

5   Income is a highly unreliable indicator of poverty, sufficiency or well-being. Some people with very low incomes but access to resources and mutual aid may have materially as well as socially secure and fulfilling lives. Others with higher incomes but few opportunities and support may suffer serious deprivation.

6   'Needs' is probably not the best term to use here. In addition to the many confusions surrounding different (often unstated) definitions, it tends to emphasize deliverable goods for people as consumers rather than active opportunities for people as exerters of powers and capacities. Amartya Sen (1985) has suggested 'capabilities' and 'functionings' as potentially useful terms. Similarly, advocates of sustainable livelihoods approaches to development focus on positive 'assets and entitlements' (for example, Leach et al, 1998; Wanmali, 1998). These alternatives have important advantages. Since 'needs' is so widely used, imposing a different term now may bring more confusion than clarification. But it is important to insist that needs include both sufficiency and opportunity components.

7   This is, for example, the thinking behind the UNDP's Human Development Index (Panday and Mishra, 1998).

8   The 'Kuznets curve' expectation of gradually improving equality as a cheerful longer-term result of initial capital concentration, is still debated. However, a good deal of experience, dating back at least to the early 1970s, suggests the initially increased inequalities might well persist and act as barriers to growth as well as contributors to discord.

9   The usual religious and 'selfish gene' arguments only begin the list. Among the other motives are those of the ancient Greeks, for example, who saw that a viable future was needed to preserve the memory of present heroics (Arendt, 1958). Robert Jay Lifton (1969), after interviews with the survivors of Hiroshima, concluded that humans need confidence in a continuing future on Earth even to maintain belief in an afterlife.

10 The following comment is from Australian national science writer Julian Cribb (2003), in an assessment of community perspectives on risk:

> *For a number of years, I was a newspaper editor, and I knew, as most editors know, that if you print a lot of good news, people stop buying your paper. Conversely, you publish the correct mix of doom, gloom and disaster, and your circulation swells. I have done the experiment.*
>
> *The publication of 'bad news' is not a journalistic vice. It's a clear, unequivocal instruction from the market. It's what consumers, on average, demand. As a science journalist I found myself a 'good news journalist in a bad news industry', unable to publish stories of real merit because the overwhelming news demand was for stories of threats, crises, brawls and accidents.*

11 This is not to say that development thinking and practices have abandoned the traditional attention to government and market tools. On the contrary, many key development assistance agencies have concentrated much of their attention on new ways of working with recipient governments (for example, through multi-agency leverage in sector-wide approaches) and of promoting private sector involvement (for example, through public–private partnerships). But even here expectations have changed and initiatives that lack transparency and neglect civil society players are likely to face condemnation and resistance (OECD, 1996; CIDA, 2002, 2003; SIDA 2003a, 2003b).

12 This is evident, for example, in how Higgs (1997), relying in part on Cairns (1995), defines good ecological restoration as 'ecosocial restoration' that builds and relies on a renewed sense of place.

13 Such approaches have long been well supported by the literature on participatory democracy (for example, Pateman, 1970), gender equity (for example, Karl, 1995), transactive planning (for example, Friedmann, 1973), natural resource management (for example, Singh and Ham, 1995; Pimbert, 2000; Weber, 2003), and civic engagement in development (for example, UNDP 1993, 2002).

6

Trade-offs

Facing Conflict and Compromise

Pursuing sustainability in a messy world

The sustainability requirements set out in Chapter 5 are drawn and distilled from nearly two decades of discourse and experimentation. The list is also conceived specifically for application as criteria for decision making – especially concerning the kinds of undertakings that are now subject to environmental assessment obligations. Unlike the many explorations of sustainability that aim to further intellectual discussion or influence political priorities, the list of eight requirements is meant for direct practical use in the world of controversy and dispute.

Ideally, every undertaking that emerges from an assessment process would help meet every one of the requirements for sustainability. Every new project, programme, policy and plan would assist in the building of socio-ecosystem integrity, provide good jobs and other opportunities for a decent life, reduce inequities, cut overall energy and material use, strengthen democratic practice, foster habitual respect for people and nature, avoid risks and prepare for adaptation. These are the qualities we need for sustainability. None of them is expendable and neglect of any one will imperil progress on the others. If we are to reverse current trends towards deeper unsustainability, we need to deliver on all fronts consistently and persistently. Ensuring that every assessed undertaking offers gains in each category would be a good way of moving ahead.

It is also utterly unrealistic.

Consider, for example, one of the most positive undertakings of our time – the Kenyan tree planting initiatives of 2004 Nobel Peace Prize laureate Wangari Maathai. Village women mobilized by Maathai's Green Belt Movement have planted 30 million trees, re-established indigenous crops and kitchen gardens, reforested degraded lands, empowered women, created new economic opportunities, built local food security, and become a national force for democracy (Lappé and Lappé, 2004). This is an impressive set of multiple benefits, achieved through an upward spiral of mutually reinforcing gains.

In one way or another, it includes contributions to each of the sustainability requirements listed above. But the experience was not all sweetness and light. The Movement's work threatened established powers and practices. Maathai and many of her colleagues were beaten and jailed. Sacrifices were made so that the gains could be won. Certainly there were trade-offs here. Indeed, that bloodless term of barter and exchange seems too weak for the case.

Conflict and compromise are likely even in much less contested circumstances where all parties are broadly committed to the pursuit of sustainability. It may not be possible to convert from climate threatening coal thermal power plants to renewable sources without adding new ecological burdens. Or to ensure precautionary duplication and back-up options without some loss of energy and material efficiency. Or to provide basic sufficiency for everyone today without some reduction in the resources available to future generations. Such dilemmas may not arise in every assessment. But they will be common enough that few proponents and assessors will be able to deliver undertakings with positive contributions to all of the requirements for sustainability.

While applications of sustainability decision criteria must be rigorous and demanding, they must also be able to deal with real circumstances, real tensions and real limitations on the possibilities for rapid improvement. It will not be enough simply to set out general decision criteria for sustainability assessments. Since the very core of sustainability lies in the necessity of addressing a multiplicity of goals at the same time, there must be directions for dealing with potentially conflicting objectives and priorities. As a starting position, it is reasonable to be generally hostile to trade-offs and compromises. Nevertheless, preparations for sustainability assessment must anticipate unavoidable trade-offs and provide guidance for dealing with them.

Unavoidable trade-offs

Dealing with trade-offs has always been a major factor in assessments and related decision making on important new undertakings. Given limited resources, we are always deciding which objectives to emphasize and, at least implicitly, which ones to neglect. We are always choosing between making a speedy decision or considering more options, building a more detailed understanding or consulting more comprehensively. These decisions typically involve a host of potentially relevant considerations, many of them involving value-preferences or requiring speculation about an uncertain future. Not surprisingly, they are often made arbitrarily and without much careful reflection or explicit justification.

We now have environmental assessment law in most jurisdictions because without it decision makers had tended to give scant attention to environmental concerns. In the old pre-assessment days, environmental considerations were, in effect, traded-off as the price to be paid for lower initial costs and less disruption of conventional practice. When the resulting ecological, social and longer-term economic damages became politically intolerable, assessment requirements were imposed. But there was no change in the fundamental perception that environmental objectives conflicted with the financial, technical and political concerns that had normally prevailed. While the assessment requirements now forced decision makers to consider the environmental implications of proposed undertakings, and encouraged them to avoid serious environmental harm (Gardner, 1989; Wood, 2003), designers of environmental assessment regimes assumed continuing conflict between environmental objectives and the old priorities. Conventional environmental assessment processes are built with that conflict firmly in mind (Sadler, 1996).

In the Canadian federal process, for example, 'significant adverse environmental effects' are to be identified and mitigated where possible, but the law anticipates that such effects may be 'justified in the circumstances' (Canada, 2003b). While these 'circumstances' are not defined in the law or in any explicit policy, the provision clearly rests on the simple presumption that environmental protection is likely to restrict economic advance and that in some circumstances, even where significant adverse environmental effects are predicted, the environmental objectives may be sacrificed.

This is what happened, for example, in the case of the proposed Cheviot coal mining project near Jasper National Park in Alberta. The joint Canada/ Alberta environmental assessment review panel determined that the project would have some significant adverse environmental effects that could not be adequately mitigated. However, they also found that the project 'is economically viable and in the public interest ... and will generate significant positive economic and social benefits with the region generally and to the Town of Hinton in particular'. The panel recommended approval, stating that:

> ...sufficient information was provided for it to be able to determine that the majority of the environmental effects, including socio-economic effects, are either positive or where adverse, are not significant. Where the environmental effects were considered to be adverse and significant, they were generally considered to be justified in the context of the project as a whole (AEUB/CEAA, 1997).

Such trade-offs presume a world of environment–economy opposition and where this model prevails the core goal for environmental assessment is to facilitate a balancing of these competing ends. Where decision makers are still inclined to ignore environmental considerations, ensuring a reasonably fair balancing is an obvious step forward. But there is no future in it. As we saw in Chapter 5, balancing is not the path to sustainability. At best, balancing slows our decline. For progress to sustainability, we need to recognize the interdependence of economy and environment, and find ways of making mutually reinforcing gains on all fronts. That is the integration requirement.

It does not follow that all environment–economy conflicts can be avoided. Certainly some can. There is plenty of evidence that environmentally enlightened practice is often economically beneficial even for corporate actors with narrow and short-term objectives (Porter and van der Linde, 1995; Kerr, 1999). Broader policy initiatives in the public interest are even more likely to be strengthened by emphasis on the interconnections rather than the conflicts between environmental and economic objectives (Esty and Porter, 2001). Moreover, as we saw in Chapter 5, the fundamental requirements for sustainability do not fall conveniently into the established economic and environmental (or social or political) categories. The individual requirements – for socio-ecological integrity, overall throughput efficiency, intra- and inter-generational equity, etc. – cross the usual boundaries. Nevertheless, serious tensions remain. While the more sophisticated understanding of environment–economy relations and sustainability requirements suggests that the old environment–economy balancing model can be replaced, conflicts are still likely and difficult trade-off decisions will still be needed.

Finally, trade-offs may be unavoidable even concerning implications for a single sustainability requirement. Consider, for example, options for high level radioactive waste disposal. Because these wastes will remain dangerously radioactive for hundreds of thousands of years, very secure and very long-term disposal is crucial. The wastes now in temporary storage facilities pose an unacceptable longer-term threat to socio-ecological integrity. But all of the proposals for more permanent disposal are controversial. None of them might make a positive overall contribution to socio-ecological integrity except in the sense of being less negative than the others. And each option involves integrity trade-offs – reduction of hazards at the current temporary sites but introduction of new worries at the permanent sites and along the transportation routes between them.

These are familiar problems. Indeed we have a host of analytical and decision tools designed for, or at least often used in, the comparison of competing options where trade-offs are involved. Cost–benefit analysis, matrix-based appraisal methodologies, multi-criteria assessment, multiple accounts analysis, ecosystem-based planning, integrated assessment, backcasting, scenario comparison, life-cycle analysis, total economic value calculations, risk assessment, alternatives assessment, systems analysis, multi-stakeholder negotiation – all of these and more have been used in the identification, elaboration and comparison of trade-offs. Perhaps each one of them has already been applied, more or less usefully, in cases involving sustainability objectives. And each probably has something to offer in future sustainability assessments. But most of the applications so far have been ad hoc and partial. Few have been guided by an assessment framework that combined specified sustainability criteria with clear guidance on the application of these criteria in trade-off decisions.

Trade-offs of substance and process

Trade-offs allow some adverse effects in the interests of securing important gains. The adverse effects take us further from meeting the substantial demands of one or more of the requirements for sustainability. Permitting additional stress on a fragile ecosystem would qualify. So would accepting more inequitable distribution of livelihood opportunities in a community where the gap between the advantaged and the disadvantaged is already great. But these substantial effects are not the only considerations.

There are also matters of process. Progress towards sustainability requires broad expansion of understanding, involves public choices and relies on building mutually supportive, positive links among many activities. A sacrifice of public opportunities to learn and to choose, or a restriction of attention to possibilities outside the narrow boundaries of an individual undertaking, will compromise prospects for sustainability. It too may be accepted only if there are good grounds for thinking that the loss is necessary to achieve a more significant step forward.

Substantive and process compromises are often intertwined. Rapid and authoritarian decision making, for example, is typically rationalized as a route to quicker approvals and more immediate substantive benefits. And it is frequently condemned for longer-term substantive failures, which are normally attributed, at least in part, to process weaknesses, including inadequate public consultation and superficial exploration of relevant needs, conditions, opportunities and options. Substantive and process compromises should therefore be considered as a package. For the purposes of initial elaboration, however, it may be helpful to look at them separately.

Substantive trade-offs (trade-offs among the options)

Trade-offs are made in comparative evaluations and in the selection among competing options. In any serious assessment, this happens often. There are different possible purposes, different general approaches to serving the selected purpose, different locations and designs, different packages of mitigation and enhancement components, and different implementation plans. At each stage there are choices to be made, usually among several possibilities with each possibility offering a different package of advantages and disadvantages – a different set of trade-offs. Even in primitive assessment regimes where the only question on the table is whether to accept or reject a proposed undertaking, there are still two options. Accepting and rejecting promise different sets of gains and losses, and the choice rests on some evaluation of their relative merits.

In sustainability assessments, the basic framework for identifying and evaluating the options is a set of criteria based on the requirements for sustainability, specified and elaborated to respect the particular context. Anticipated positive effects enhance socio-ecological system integrity, livelihood sufficiency and opportunity, intra- and intergenerational equity, resource maintenance and efficiency, socio-ecological civility and democratic governance, and/or precaution and adaptability, preferably in mutually supporting ways. Anticipated negative effects retreat from one or more or these requirements, or block desired progress. The significance of the effects, positive and negative, is judged in light of their intensity, severity, scale, extent, duration, frequency, permanence, importance relative to the conditions and priority concerns of the context, and/or likelihood of broader spin-offs. The significance of any trade-offs involving these effects rests similarly on their implications for sustainability requirements, in context.

Substantive trade-offs are involved whenever there are positives and negatives that must be weighed against each other. If a municipality proposes to extend a road through a wooded area to permit construction of a new housing subdivision there, the temporarily positive effects on building trade employment and the longer positive effects on housing availability are traded off against the negative ecological effects of woodland loss and disruption of aquifer recharge, and the adverse community, efficiency and civility effects of urban sprawl. As an alternative, the municipality might consider support for an undertaking that would rehabilitate a contaminated urban core site to provide the same number of new housing units as was promised by the subdivision proponents. The trade-offs here would put positive implications for urban core regeneration, transit viability and urban growth management against concerns about initially higher municipal costs, doubts about demand for such housing, and loss of a downtown site that could have provided needed green space. In both cases, various means of enhancing the positive effects and mitigating the negative ones could also be considered, and each of them would involve some positives and some negatives. In the end, when the two options are compared, they represent two competing packages of overall trade-offs, and a multitude of particular ones related to mitigation and enhancement components – financial arrangements, design features, materials selection, implementation plans and so forth.

Substantive trade-offs therefore come in an almost infinite variety of forms. Arguably, however, they are most usefully viewed as involving two main aspects: first, the nature and appropriateness of particular compensations; and second, the determination of overall net effects – positive, neutral or negative.

Compensations

Proponents of assessed undertakings often propose direct and indirect compensation for negative effects. Indeed this may be the only evident option when the negative effects cannot be avoided or fully mitigated (or when the proponent concludes that the avoidance or mitigation costs would be too high). Such compensations can include substitutions in kind, place and time. A *substitution in time* would be involved, for example, if an aggregate mining operation were permitted on degraded agricultural lands, with a commitment to rehabilitate those lands to superior standards at the end of mining operations in 20 years. The immediate ecological effects and broad quality of life effects for the neighbours would be largely and perhaps seriously negative. However, the longer-term results could be at least as strongly positive, if the lands are rehabilitated sufficiently. Whether the substitution is suitable and fair, to the neighbours and other interests, is open to debate.

A *substitution in place* would be involved, for example, in a proposal to eliminate a more or less natural wetland and replace it with a constructed wetland elsewhere in the watershed. Here the considerations might include the extent to which the constructed wetland might be or become the equivalent of a natural wetland. But the central questions would surround the significance of the change of location. What are the livelihood, system integrity and other effects in the vicinity of the old wetland? Are these compensated adequately by the effects in the new wetland location? Is there reasonable equity in the new distribution of gains and losses, or winners and losers in this exchange?

Perhaps most dramatic, and potentially controversial, are *substitutions in kind*. A hydrocarbon exploration company operating on traditional aboriginal lands might, for example, offer to provide new community recreational facilities in a remote village to compensate for the risk of ecological, economic and cultural damage from company activities in areas long used for hunting, fishing, trapping and foraging. Equivalence in such cases is not less crucial but inevitably more difficult to judge.

Net effect determinations

When particular compensation options are evaluated, some possibilities may be rejected in principle. Others may simply be unacceptable in the circumstances, at least in the view of one or more of the relevant parties. Often, however, the essential issue is whether the overall advantages to be gained will exceed the damages and the sacrifices.

Net effect determinations underlie many assessment and planning decisions, including judgements on the overall acceptability of a proposal or the relative desirability of competing options. Such determinations are not always done explicitly or openly. Sometimes the decision makers are unwilling to have their preferences scrutinized and their assumptions questioned. Often the task appears to be too difficult, perhaps because it involves things that seem impossible to measure (beauty, for example) or that may be cheapened by calculation (loss of life), or that evidently defy reasonable comparison (jobs and traditions, or oil revenues and caribou). But decisions resting on such judgements are made nonetheless. They are unavoidable. Net effects judgements underlie the vast majority of deliberations on undertakings that might be subject to sustainability assessment. And the eventual decisions are typically accompanied by some form of claim that the best choice was made in the circumstances and the overall results will be positive.

Narrowly biophysical forms of environmental assessment do not deal with the most important trade-off and net effects deliberations. Social, economic and other matters are left to other deliberations and the eventual integration, such as it is, usually remains hidden. With proper sustainability assessment, in contrast, the full suite of relevant concerns is included in an integrated, open process. Here it is possible to address all of the key trade-off issues explicitly. Indeed one of the chief advantages of sustainability assessment is that it provides a forum and framework for explicit attention to the key trade-offs.

The great hope for sustainability assessment is that its more open, comprehensive, integrated and forward looking approach, along with its respect for context, will lead to decisions that are better supported and more consistently positive. But these decisions still involve some form of net gain judgement in assessing whether a positive contribution to sustainability is likely. In such determinations gains and losses are aggregated and the totals as well as the particulars are compared.

Adoption of a sustainability focus does help in these net effects determinations. Use of the requirements for sustainability as common core criteria for evaluations provides basic guidance for judgements about what gains are crucial and what sacrifices may be too great. But this does not make comparison of effects and determination of net results easy. For many effects, measurement and comparison remain difficult, if not objectionable. And like deliberations on compensation proposals, determination of net effects must often address the complexities of distribution in kind, place and time. For example:

- An assessment of options for management of high-level radioactive wastes would involve comparison of the positive effects of reducing near-term ecological damage risks from surface storage of the wastes against the smaller but very long-term risks from deep geological disposal (differences in time).
- A proposed new dam may threaten major damages to the interests of the tribal people it will displace but also promise some enhancement of material security for larger numbers of poor farmers downstream (differences in place).
- Industrial process improvements at a facility that is a major polluter and a major employer may require assessment of net effects from efficiency gains and emission reductions, on the one hand, and associated job losses, on the other (substitution in kind).

Even where sustainability objectives are widely understood and commonly accepted, different interests are likely to reach different conclusions about which of these trade-offs may be justified.

In these ways and others, the challenges and discomforts of measurement, aggregation and comparison remain. As a result, the substantive trade-off issues in sustainability assessment cannot be reduced to matters of technical analysis and expert ruling. They are matters of choice. While application of existing and adjusted tools for depiction and evaluation – including the cost-benefit, alternatives assessment, scenario building and other options listed above – can help, with them and with trade-off decision making, generally, the process matters. And here too there are trade-off issues.

Assessment process trade-offs

All institutional initiatives involve a long list of trade-offs. What portion of the available resources should be devoted to one activity as opposed to another? When should a priority action be pushed a little further despite the risk of offending an influential client? Which new alliances should be pursued when that means abandoning or weakening the old ones? When should the temporary safety of secrecy be abandoned for the harsh light but greater credibility of public openness? What new powers should be sought despite the additional tasks and expectations. And so on.

All of these are issues that institutions have addressed for millennia. The long history of making such judgements seems not to have illuminated a reliable path to wise decisions on process trade-offs, and given the diversity of institutional mandates and operating contexts, no single correct path is plausible. The rise of global sustainability concerns has changed the situation a little, however. Arguably, contribution to sustainability should now be accepted as a shared mandate of all institutions, and decision criteria based on sustainability requirements should be used to help guide the usual trade-off decisions.

The value of such an approach is even clearer for institutions that are responsible for designing and implementing assessment processes. Along with the usual institutional trade-off dilemmas, these bodies must deal with a particular set of process trade-off issues that are directly centred on the promotion of progress towards sustainability. These include trade-offs at every step in the assessment process – what kinds of undertaking to assess, with what level of rigour, scope, funding, time, public participation, information and review requirements, monitoring and enforcement (Wood, 2003)? As well, there are trade-offs in the allocation of roles and responsibilities – to proponents, government reviewers, public critics, public servants and elected officials, technical experts and local citizens, the courts and the media. There are tensions between the need to impose clear obligations and the importance of allowing flexibility and fostering creativity. And as assessment agendas become more ambitious, more emphasis is placed on efficiency initiatives, which may not have to conflict with broader application and higher standards, but in practice often do.

Here again, broad application of sustainability-based decision criteria should help by providing a clearer basic set of objectives, a more integrated approach to considering the relevant factors, and greater overall consistency. The emphasis on mutually reinforcing gains should encourage identification of means to promote improvements in both effectiveness and efficiency. And the sustainability criteria clearly favour some options in the usual institutional deliberations – for example, by clarifying the importance of public engagement, accepting uncertainty, guiding the proper setting and allocation of the burden of proof, and encouraging representation for the otherwise unrepresented.

But at best, application of the broad sustainability criteria can only clarify some process trade-off implications and provide some helpful direction for the tough choices. The process trade-off decisions, like the substantive ones, remain difficult. It is therefore worth considering whether we might be able to provide some guidance especially for trade-off decision making, perhaps even a set of broadly applicable general rules.

Trade-off rules

In sustainability-based assessments, some kinds of trade-offs are clearly unacceptable. Sacrificing an important long-term gain for a trivial and transitory benefit is no route to sustainability. We could state that as a firm rule. Moreover, we can surely identify other rules of similar reliability. But care is needed. As in the identification of core sustainability requirements, the search for trade-off rules must recognize that situations differ and general prescriptions must often bow to the particulars of context. Killing the goose that lays golden eggs is generally a bad idea for sustainability. But it may be justified if the eggs are contaminated with a persistent toxin or if we are starving and goose soup is the only option.

While it might be convenient to have a mighty collection of universally valid rules to guide choices among trade-off options – revealing which ones are reliably acceptable and which are always to be avoided – we will probably find only a few. And of these, some will be about *how* the trade-off options should be considered, rather than which option should be favoured. But even a short list of good rules, including decision process guides, should be useful.

Moreover, there are good reasons for avoiding a proliferation of rules. The pursuit of sustainability requires creativity as well as commitment and clarity of agenda. Rule-cluttered systems that discourage innovation are not desirable. Finding ways to encourage and reward better solutions to sustainability problems is an enormous challenge, and the value of additional rules must always be weighed against the perils of increased bureaucratization. Assessment regimes, like other institutionalized processes, are ill-served by obligations that foster more attention to the minutia of regulatory compliance than to ensuring significant improvements in the world.

The agenda here is therefore to identify a basic working list of rules to guide trade-off deliberations. These will include broad rules for general application and rules for developing more context-specific guidance for trade-off decisions when the general rules are not suitable or not sufficient.

Six basic rules

Maximum net gains

The starting point for trade-off rules is the same as the starting point for sustainability assessment generally. The objective is maximum progress towards sustainability, with mutually reinforcing gains all round. Even if negative effects must be accepted, the objective remains. Where trade-offs must be made, the decision making should still be guided by commitment to maximizing net gains.

The maximizing net gains test relies on comparative evaluation of options – from alternative designs, mitigation and enhancement features to alternative undertakings, even alternative purposes. The evaluations combine application of decision criteria based on sustainability requirements with examination of the various possibly feasible ways of providing the best sustainability results. Ideally, the process identifies an option that promises mutually reinforcing steps towards meeting all of the requirements for sustainability. But where such an option is not available, the best choice offers the most positive overall result that is feasible. This is the core difference between sustainability-centred assessment and assessments that are satisfied with mitigating significant adverse effects. Sustainability assessment requires a positive contribution to sustainability. The focus is on gains. If negative effects are unavoidable and trade-offs must be made, the net result must always be a positive overall contribution. And since the evaluation is comparative, the most positive option is to be favoured.

In some cases, there may be no feasible option that qualifies as positive, except that it is better than the others (including the status quo). Least-bad solution situations are common. In toxic site clean-up, for example, there may be no fully satisfactory way of treating and/or disposing of the contaminants, but if the existing situation is intolerable, there are likely to be less-bad options. While it may seem inappropriate to treat least-bad undertakings as positive contributions to sustainability, the test of progress is improvement relative to current or impending conditions. In areas where we are far from sustainability now, and where there is no feasible route to dramatic gains, an incremental move towards less irresponsible practice may be the best choice. It may offer the most positive feasible overall result in the circumstances, and be an achievement to celebrate.

The Voisey's Bay nickel mine case discussed in the opening chapter was not aimed explicitly at the most positive result for sustainability. But in effect, that is what it attempted. The panel began by setting out the basic sustainability test. In reviewing the proponent's environmental impact statement and other submissions on the case, the panel said it would consider 'the extent to which the Undertaking may make a positive overall contribution towards the attainment of ecological and community sustainability, both at the local and regional levels' (Voisey's Bay Panel, 1997). Then in its review of the mining proposal, the panel saw that a key determinant of any lasting positive overall contributions would be the rate of production and the consequent life expectancy of the mine. Finally, in its recommendations, the panel favoured the longer life option that, in its view, was likely to maximize the net positive effects (Voisey's Bay Panel, 1999).

The Voisey's Bay panel guidelines included only general requirements for the evaluation of alternatives and did not offer much elaboration of the contribution to sustainability test. The panel provided only a brief interpretation of the requirements for progress towards sustainability, along with some encouragement for attention to net sustainability contribution through all stages of the undertaking – from planning and design to management and monitoring. Other matters, including the weighing of possible trade-offs between the ecological and community aspects of sustainability, were left to the assessment review process. This was a pioneering sustainability assessment. As sustainability assessment matures, means of evaluating alternatives and associated trade-offs in light of the requirements for sustainability will no doubt become more sophisticated. But the Voisey's Bay panel's basic approach merits general adoption.

1   *Any acceptable trade-off or set of trade-offs must deliver net progress towards meeting the requirements for sustainability; it must seek mutually reinforcing,*

cumulative and lasting contributions and must favour achievement of the most positive feasible overall result, while avoiding significant adverse effects.

Burden of argument on trade-off proponent

The emphasis on maximum net progress suggests a bias against trade-offs, or at least against accommodating negative effects. The most positive route to substantial long-term improvement is to seek gains on all fronts in ways that link the gains together and build positive synergies. And, in principle, there is no necessary conflict between the requirements for sustainability. In practice, trade-offs may be unavoidable, but they are all about compromise. The substantive ones involve allowing some decline (or allowing less progress than would be feasible) in one or more of the areas required for progress towards sustainability. That, clearly, is undesirable.

Opposition to trade-offs can go too far. Some sacrifices may be necessary to permit more important gains elsewhere. Providing an opening for trade-offs in sustainability deliberations may also be a good way of fostering innovative thinking.[1] But no sacrifice should be made lightly. While trade-offs are often necessary, and may even be desirably creative, we do not want to encourage any easy acceptance of the associated negatives.

Perhaps the most widely accepted means of discouraging acceptance of negative effects centres on the placement of a burden of proof or justification. The burden of proof approach begins by assuming that the negative aspects of any proposed trade-off are unacceptable unless proven otherwise. This is roughly similar to the prosecutor's burden of proof, which is commonly applied in criminal law. In many legal regimes, a person alleged to have committed a crime is assumed to be innocent until proven guilty. The prosecutor must establish that the accused is guilty. In a sustainability assessment, the proponent of a trade-off would be obliged to provide persuasive evidence in support of the proposed trade-off. That would involve establishing that a trade-off of some sort is needed in the circumstances and that the one proposed would contribute to maximum net gains.

Burdens of proof are typically accompanied by some specification of the standard of proof. In criminal law the standard is often 'proof beyond a reasonable doubt'. In sustainability assessments this would not work. Because the evaluation of possible trade-offs involves comparison of multiple options and frequently relies on highly uncertain predictions of future effects, doubt is almost always reasonable. Sometimes there is good evidence from well monitored experience. More often the best that can be expected is a persuasive argument with a reasonable estimate of the likelihood of error. The standard of proof or persuasiveness will therefore have to be adjusted to fit the circumstance. Nonetheless, a general trade-off rule centred on the burden of argument is possible.

2   *Trade-off compromises that involve acceptance of adverse effects in sustainability-related areas are undesirable unless proven (or reasonably established) otherwise; the burden of justification falls on the proponent of the trade-off.*

Avoidance of significant adverse effects

In simple net gains calculations, the sum of the anticipated costs is subtracted from the sum of the benefits. Sustainability assessment deliberations are more complex. This is, in part, because many of the gains and losses are uncertain, non-quantified and perhaps not quantifiable. But a no less important factor is that movement towards sustainability depends on mutually reinforcing progress on all fronts. That is the chief grounds for the bias against trade-offs discussed above. It also suggests particular emphasis on avoiding significant adverse effects in any area.

Simple net gains calculations balance the gains against the losses, as if each category of gain and loss was independent, equivalent and substitutable. The pursuit of sustainability, in contrast, sees the relevant considerations to be interdependent, crucial and variable in weight from one context to the next. All guidance for sustainability assessments – including the basic trade-off rules – is meant to encourage proponents and other players to find ways of making positive contributions in all of the sustainability requirement areas.

The United Kingdom's Countryside Agency explains this well in a report on rural planning:

> *Decisions with the planning system have traditionally been based on the idea of 'balance'. The economic advantages of a particular proposal, for example, might be deemed to be more important than the local environment so the development goes ahead: in other words the balance of the argument favours the development even though there is an acknowledged loss. A balanced approach is widely used and easy to comprehend but the inevitable result is that there is a 'winner' and a 'loser'. For instance, major town expansion has meant that attractive countryside has been lost; while tight restraint on village development has meant that affordable homes for local people have often gone unprovided (UK, 2000).*

The appropriate corrective, the agency argues, is a two stage approach that begins by looking for solutions that serve all sustainability objectives and then ensuring that none of the losses is significant:

> *Integrate policies so that plans and the development plan process look first for solutions which bring social, economic, and environmental benefits, and then for solutions where unavoidable adverse impacts are mitigated or compensated; there should always be a net gain and no significant losses from development (ibid.).*

Trade-off rules should therefore encourage integrated benefit-seeking rather than narrow balancing. Perhaps the best way of facilitating this is by blocking any easy acceptance of significant adverse effects even when the overall net results are positive.

Requiring avoidance of significant adverse effects demands an ability to distinguish significant effects from insignificant ones. This is a familiar problem. 'Significance' decisions are common in environmental assessment work and we have had over three decades of experience developing protocols and processes for the necessary determinations. A host of research studies and deliberations at all levels from the local to global have identified priority concerns and vulnerabilities, thresholds of tolerance and criteria for case-specific applications. Significant judgements are still challenging (Chapter 8 is devoted to some of the complexities), but the challenges seem unavoidable and manageable.

3   *No trade-off that involves a significant adverse effect on any sustainability requirement area (for example, any effect that might undermine the integrity of a viable socio-ecological system) can be justified unless the alternative is acceptance of an even more significant adverse effect.*

   Generally, then, no compromise or trade-off is acceptable if it entails further decline or risk of decline in a major area of existing concern (for example, as set out in official international, national or other sustainability strategies or accords or as identified in open public processes at the local level), or if it endangers prospects for resolving problems properly identified as global, national and/or local priorities.

   Similarly, no trade-off is acceptable if it deepens problems in any requirement area (integrity, equity, etc.) where further decline in the existing situation may imperil the long-term viability of the whole, even if compensations of other kinds, or in other places are offered (for example, if inequities are already deep, there may be no ecological rehabilitation or efficiency compensation for introduction of significantly greater inequities).

   No enhancement can be permitted as an acceptable trade-off against incomplete mitigation of significant adverse effects if stronger mitigation efforts are feasible.

There is a possible second way of fostering attention to broadly integrated gains and discouraging crude balancing. This is by restricting cross-category trade-offs. Such trade-offs are common – for example, more efficient industrial processes that reduce pollution but also eliminate jobs, affordable housing projects that eat into parkland, and new hydro dams that displace traditional land users but also replace greenhouse gas emitting thermal power stations. Refusing to accept such trade-offs might push efforts to find alternatives that provide positive results in all categories – more jobs, housing, equity, security, eco-efficiency and socio-ecological system integrity, etc. But such options may not be available.

   Moreover, a cross-requirement trade-off that is clearly unacceptable in one circumstance may be well justified in another. Consider, for example, introduction of a new livelihoods opportunity that involves harvesting previously untapped forest resources and may bring some consequent risk of upsetting system integrity. If the forest is already heavily stressed and the opportunity benefits will be usurped by the already wealthy, the trade-off should be rejected. But if the ecological risk is small and the livelihoods opportunities will go to people who are now seriously disadvantaged, the trade-off may be easily justified. The key factors here are the significance of the effects, positive and negative, and the avoidance of serious losses of any kind, not whether changes in one area may be traded off against changes in another.

A universal rule against cross-requirement trade-offs is therefore unrealistic. Where problems and dangers are already severe, it would be appropriate to forbid cross-requirement trade-offs that will make things even worse. But any such trade-offs would be rejected in any event, because they involve clearly significant adverse effects, which are to be avoided.

Protection of the future

One requirement area does merit special attention, however. That is the need for intergenerational equity. Concern for future generations is a core aspect of applied sustainability. A fundamental rationale for sustainability assessment is recognition that continuation of current practices and trends will bring an increasingly dangerous and ugly world. But service to future interests is difficult to ensure. Most sustainability requirements are likely to be promoted by some existing interest, if a reasonably fair and open process is in place. Future generations are never themselves present, though some public interest bodies may attempt to speak on their behalf. For future generations, care in process design should be supplemented by a trade-off rule that precludes trade-offs that impose significant new disadvantages on future generations.

4   *No displacement of a significant adverse effect from the present to the future can be justified unless the alternative is displacement of an even more significant negative effect from the present to the future.*

Explicit justification

All of the rules outlined so far involve judgements of some sort. These judgements will be strengthened by application of the core requirements for sustainability, and by more specific elaboration of these requirements for particular places and cases. Together with the trade-off rules, these provide a comprehensive set of basic criteria for evaluations and decisions. But use of these criteria cannot eliminate the role of judgement, especially where the requirements conflict and trade-off choices must be made.

Most trade-off judgements will also benefit from the participation of experts with special knowledge of system functions, local conditions, analytical methods, alternative design options, conflict resolution mechanisms and other key matters. But few sustainability assessment decisions can rest entirely on such expertise. Inevitably, the decisions also involve values and preferences that are properly exercised in open public discussion.

This situation is not unique to sustainability assessment. Values and preferences play key roles in decision making about important undertakings whether or not sustainability assessment is involved. In the usual fragmented decision making processes that prevail today, however, the environmental, social, economic and technical evaluations are done more or less separately and the overall decisions, including trade-off judgements, are made with minimal guidance, transparency or explicit rationale. Sustainability assessment takes the opposite approach. Guided by the accepted decision criteria, core considerations are addressed together as interdependent factors; the unavoidable conflicts are identified and open evaluation of trade-off options is a central task. Sustainability assessment is, thus, the venue in which the big issues are identified, the options evaluated and the trade-offs assessed. One of its chief advantages is that it provides a foundation for integrated decision making where good judgements can be made.

Requiring explicit justification of proposed trade-offs is therefore realistic in sustainability assessments. It is also desirable as a way of encouraging careful attention to the general decision criteria and trade-off rules, and to how these criteria and rules are affected by particular local circumstances.

5 *All trade-offs must be accompanied by an explicit justification based on openly identified, context specific priorities as well as the sustainability decision criteria and the general trade-off rules.*

Justifications will be assisted by the presence of clarifying guides (sustainability policies, priority statements, plans based on analyses of existing stresses and desirable futures, guides to the evaluation of 'significance', etc.) that have been developed in processes as open and participative as those expected for sustainability assessments.

Open process

Merely requiring reasoning and justification is not enough. There can be better and worse arguments and rationales. Explicit, public arguments for proposed trade-offs are necessary so that the arguments can be examined. The expectation is that the prospect of rigorous testing will encourage proponents of trade-offs to do a better job. It is therefore crucial that the process be open and that it include and empower participants with sufficient commitment and capacity for effective engagement.

Sometimes, government or assessment agency bodies have demonstrated the skills, resources and independence necessary to guide assessment work and provide rigorous critical review. But decades of environmental assessment experience have taught that broader participation is indispensable. Open processes have the advantage of a diversity of stakeholder interests and experts who are committed to careful review (at least on matters touching their perceived interests) and typically familiar with key aspects of the relevant context. Specialized experts wielding sophisticated technical tools have often played valuable roles. So have individuals with a rich understanding of the local context. But these have typically been mobilized (or given less fettered critical opportunity) by interested stakeholders and the power of public expectations in open processes.

Open public deliberations are therefore needed not just to evaluate possible trade-offs but also to build an understanding of the context – the particular pressures, possibilities and preferences – in which the decisions about trade-offs and all the other planning, approval and implementation decisions must be made.

6   *Proposed compromises and trade-offs must be addressed and justified through
    processes that include open and effective involvement of all stakeholders.*

    *Relevant stakeholders include those representing sustainability-relevant posi-
tions (for example, community elders speaking for future generations) as well as
those directly affected.*

    *While application of specialized expertise and technical tools can be very
helpful, the decisions to be made are essentially and unavoidably value-laden
and a public role is crucial.*

Beyond the rules

The six rules set out above provide a useful beginning at the level of general
principles for handling trade-offs. They do not provide much substantive
guidance. They have little to say about what specific kinds of compromises
might be unacceptable in a sustainability assessment. But perhaps that is as it
should be.

    Specific circumstances differ. So do priorities. In some places the most
pressing threat to sustainability is over-exploitation of ecological resources and
degradation of associated ecosystems. In others, deepening inequities, pervasive insecurity and erosion of civility may be more desperate concerns. Because
of these differences, application of the same core sustainability criteria will not
always lead to the same conclusions about what trade-offs should be accepted
or rejected. In one set of circumstances, it will be reasonable to accept job
losses as the price for adopting a new productive process that is more energy
and materials efficient and reduces pressure on a declining resource base. In
another case such a trade-off might be repugnant because existing inequities
are severe, the most poorly paid workers will be losing their jobs and few other
livelihood opportunities are available. In yet other situations, the complexities
will be greater, the choices more difficult and the potential value of firmly
dictated general substantive rules even less.

    This is not the end of the road, however. Substantive rules are not the only
option. Even the short list of general trade-off rules above includes process
requirements. While we cannot say what trade-off maybe acceptable, we can
require that a justification always be provided and that the process of reaching
that justification be an open one.

    Reliance on process arrangements is the traditional strength of environ-
mental assessment law and policy. Unlike prescriptive regulation, which specifies what must be done or achieved, environmental assessment has focused on
how deliberations should proceed and how decisions should be made. In this
way environmental assessment has been adjustable to multiple and diverse
circumstances. Sustainability assessment is more ambitious in scope and objectives. But it too is essentially about informed deliberation and good decision
making, and it too must rely chiefly on process.

    Chapter 7 will therefore focus on the process of sustainability assessment,
drawing from the decades of experience with environmental assessment and

Box 6.1 General trade-off rules

Maximum net gains
Any acceptable trade-off or set of trade-offs must deliver net progress towards meeting the requirements for sustainability; it must seek mutually reinforcing, cumulative and lasting contributions, and must favour achievement of the most positive feasible overall result, while avoiding significant adverse effects.

Burden of argument on trade-off proponent
Trade-off compromises that involve acceptance of adverse effects in sustainability-related areas are undesirable unless proven (or reasonably established) otherwise; the burden of justification falls on the proponent of the trade-off.

Avoidance of significant adverse effects
No trade-off that involves a significant adverse effect on any sustainability requirement area (for example, any effect that might undermine the integrity of a viable socio-ecological system) can be justified unless the alternative is acceptance of an even more significant adverse effect.

Generally, then, no compromise or trade-off is acceptable if it entails further decline or risk of decline in a major area of existing concern (for example, as set out in official international, national or other sustainability strategies or accords, or as identified in open public processes at the local level), or if it endangers prospects for resolving problems properly identified as global, national and/or local priorities.

Similarly, no trade-off is acceptable if it deepens problems in any requirement area (integrity, equity, etc.) where further decline in the existing situation may imperil the long-term viability of the whole, even if compensations of other kinds, or in other places are offered (for example, if inequities are already deep, there may be no ecological rehabilitation or efficiency compensation for introduction of significantly greater inequities).

No enhancement can be permitted as an acceptable trade-off against incomplete mitigation of significant adverse effects if stronger mitigation efforts are feasible.

Protection of the future
No displacement of a significant adverse effect from the present to the future can be justified unless the alternative is displacement of an even more significant negative effect from the present to the future.

Explicit justification
All trade-offs must be accompanied by an explicit justification based on openly identified, context specific priorities as well as the sustainability decision criteria and the general trade-off rules.

Justifications will be assisted by the presence of clarifying guides (sustainability policies, priority statements, plans based on analyses of existing stresses and desirable futures, guides to the evaluation of 'significance', etc.) that have been developed in processes as open and participative as those expected for sustainability assessments.

Open process
Proposed compromises and trade-offs must be addressed and justified through processes that include open and effective involvement of all stakeholders.

Relevant stakeholders include those representing sustainability-relevant positions (for example, community elders speaking for future generations) as well as those directly affected.

While application of specialized expertise and technical tools can be very helpful, the decisions to be made are essentially and unavoidably value-laden and a public role is crucial.

related planning initiatives. However, it will raise a second consideration that emerges from this chapter's discussion of trade-offs. That is the test of significance, which will get its own careful treatment in Chapter 8.

Several of the general trade-off rules turn quietly on whether an effect, or a trade-off, is significant. The significance test is clearly crucial in these rules. It determines, for example, whether an anticipated adverse effect is bad enough to make a proposed trade-off unacceptable. It is therefore reasonable to demand some clarification of what qualifies as significant, or at least how proponents and other sustainability assessment participants should go about determining the significance of an effect or trade-off.

That matter is left for Chapter 8 for two reasons. First, as we will see in Chapter 7, significance decisions are pervasive throughout sustainability assessment process design and application, as they are in environmental assessment processes. Second, judgements about significance can themselves be guided only to a limited extent by substantive considerations. They too must vary according to circumstance and rely on proper process, to which we now turn.

Notes

1   Environmental assessment requirements have traditionally given proponents some incentive to mitigate negative environmental effects, but rarely any incentive to design for environmental enhancement. Willingness to permit certain compromises and trade-offs could spur greater interest in strengthening sustainability-enhancing effects. There are other means of

building such incentives, both in environmental assessment (for example, by requiring consideration of reasonable alternatives and selection of the most desirable) and through other policy initiatives (for example, ecological tax reform). But acceptance of certain compromises and trade-offs in environmental assessment could be useful as well.

Processes

Designing Sustainability Assessment Regimes

How versus what

There is very little rocket science in sustainability assessment. Sometimes it may be necessary to roll out complex equations for impact prediction and perhaps a few aspects of the desired trajectory for change can be illuminated through direct application of the laws of physics. But most of sustainability assessment is less precise and more difficult than rocket science calculations. As we have seen, there is a short list of common decision criteria and trade-off rules that can serve as the generally applicable laws of sustainability assessment physics. In the practical world of assessment, however, every case also faces multiplicities of factors, layers of uncertainty and realms of case-specific peculiarities. The pursuit of sustainability is therefore always as much about context as it is about common goals and guidance.

Sustainability assessment processes inherit from environmental assessment the great advantages as well as the bracing challenges of case-specific adjustment. Environmental assessment is an advance beyond conventional regulation in part because it provides a means of pushing better environmental behaviour through broader and more open decision making. Conventional environmental assessment imposes a standard substantive test centred on avoiding or mitigating significant adverse effects. But it is a test subject to interpretation given the particulars of the circumstances involved. Environmental assessment sets out a step-by-step process for identifying case-specific purposes and alternatives, describing the relevant environment, determining what is most important in the context, predicting the effects of particular options on particular environments, and so forth. The genius of environmental assessment lies mostly in how the decision making proceeds, not in what is decided (Farrell et al, 2001; Lawrence, 2003a).

Sustainability assessment just takes this further. The scope is broader, the hurdle is higher, and both of these are crucial. But the focus on process remains. Moving from theory to practice in sustainability assessment therefore depends heavily on designing assessment regimes that get the processes right. And there are multitudes of process components and applications to get right.

If sustainability assessment is essentially about adopting decision criteria based on the requirements for sustainability and being open and explicit in making trade-off choices, then sustainability assessment in some form – applied through some process – is needed wherever serious, future-affecting decisions are made. Municipalities deciding what to do with brownfield redevelopment sites, manufacturers choosing among competing suppliers, health authorities facing threats of new epidemics, bankers judging investment opportunities, educators designing new curricula, finance ministers drafting national budgets, even individual consumers deciding what groceries to buy – all of these and countless others should be paying attention to the implications for sustainability. All should be looking to make a positive overall contribution, to achieve multiple gains, and to minimize regrettable losses. All should be addressing the full suite of sustainability criteria, applying the basic trade-off rules with due sensitivity to their particular circumstances.

Some decision makers may already have more or less sufficient incentives and available capacity for sustainability assessment. But the practice is rare. As we saw in Chapter 2, the evolution of environmental assessment requirements is pushing some decision makers closer to sustainability-centred decision making. And as we saw in Chapter 4, a few exemplary innovators have found practical reasons and workable ways to apply admirably broad conceptions of sustainability. The vast bulk of decision makers and decision making processes, however, remain narrowly focused, secretive, myopic or otherwise deficient.

Correcting this is a task that demands much more than the delineation of workable sustainability assessment processes. Great sweeping issues of motivation and mandate are involved. New frames of understanding and rejuvenated capacities for innovation are required. All we hope to do here is sketch out an illustrative portion of the way forward.

The focus of this chapter is how to expand and redesign environmental assessment processes to establish an effective foundation for sustainability assessments. While sustainability requirements can and should be applied in many different ways, assessment processes that apply explicit evaluation criteria in the preparation, evaluation, approval and implementation of policies, plans, programmes and projects are particularly well suited as vehicles for the pursuit of sustainability. While that agenda falls well short of covering all the decision making that ought to be sustainability-centred, it does include a wide range of public and private sector undertakings, large and small. Moreover, the basics of transformed environmental assessment processes can be translated without much difficulty into other venues – land use planning processes, resource management decision making regimes, development aid programming, even corporate strategy development.

As we saw in Chapter 2, environmental assessment in various forms has already spread far beyond the confines of formal environmental assessment law. The reach of sustainability-based environmental assessment should be even greater, especially because it requires recognition of a larger context and greater attention to systemic linkages. Moreover, lessons from the adoption of 'contribution to sustainability' as the central test in environmental assessment can be expected to provide valuable guidance for applications beyond assessment regimes. So, while we should not imagine that a transformation of environmental assessment processes into sustainability assessment processes would be sufficient, we can expect it to illuminate much of the path.

Basic process principles

Rough versions of sustainability assessment can be built on the general model of advanced environmental assessment regimes without much difficulty. Indeed this has been done already. And as Chapter 1 illustrated, the starting point does not have to be particularly elaborate. We can get a long way simply by insisting on the basic sustainability test introduced by the Voisey's Bay mine panel – requiring that the undertaking being assessed will 'make a positive overall contribution towards the attainment of ecological and community sustainability, both at the local and regional levels' (Voisey's Bay Panel, 1997). The rest, arguably, is detail.

Unfortunately, the details are crucial if we wish to move from individual experiments to regular application. One of the firm lessons of environmental assessment experience has been that while flexibility is valuable, fuzziness about expectations and obligations is fatal. In advanced environmental assessments, the key details include matters of purpose, application, scope, streaming, transparency, participation, authority and follow-up. In sustainability assessment the list is just a little longer.

Specifying the sustainability test is especially important. A hefty portion of this book has been devoted to careful examination of the requirements for progress towards sustainability and the implications for decision criteria, including trade-off rules. The particular wording and categorizations of the criteria and trade-off rules are debatable and must in any event be adapted and elaborated for specific contexts. But effective sustainability assessment must have decision criteria based on a comprehensive and well integrated understanding of the key requirements for sustainability. It must have clear, sustainability-based rationales for trade-off choices. And it must include means of specifying and elaborating these decision guides for particular contexts and applications through informed choices by the relevant parties (stakeholders).

Sustainability assessment then applies these insights in the full set of process elements recognized in advanced environmental assessment processes, including:

- identifying appropriate purposes and options for new or continuing undertakings;
- assessing purposes, options, impacts, mitigation and enhancement possibilities, design implications, implementation plans, etc.;
- choosing (or advising decision makers on) what should (or should not) be approved and done, and under what conditions;
- monitoring, learning from the results and making suitable adjustments;
- integrating the whole package, including linked strategic and project level processes, into a broader regime that evaluates the status of efforts to move

towards sustainability, identifies emerging challenges and opportunities, sets priorities and reviews progress.

The main components of basic and advanced environmental assessment processes were identified in Chapter 2 (see Box 2.1). If we combine these and add clear commitment to sustainability objectives, elaboration and application of decision criteria based on sustainability requirements and attention to the rules for trade-off choices, the result is the basic set of design features presented in Box 7.1.

With some tweaking, these principles could be applied in a host of jurisdictions, for many kinds of undertakings at various levels of strategic breadth and project ambition. Differences in resource availability, institutional and public capacity, urgency, scale and significance would affect the nature of application. Some aspects – sophistication of criteria elaboration, range of alternatives, depth of analysis, extent of consultation, detail of design – might be constrained without serious loss in particular circumstances. But all of the principles should apply in all cases.

In the interests of broad application, the process design principles are necessarily general. For a clearer understanding of how actual process requirements might be specified, we could consider what would be involved in drafting a sustainability assessment law.

Components of a sustainability assessment law

Experience with conventional environmental assessment has taught that the process must be enshrined in law and compliance with requirements and decisions must be legally enforceable. Certainly some proponents do not need to be driven by law. They find sufficient motivation in commitment to public responsibility or enlightened self interest to embrace good assessment practice. But the demonstrated inclination of many proponents has been to avoid some or all assessment responsibilities. Sustainability assessment, at least in some of its forms, will need statutory foundations as well.

There can be no single correct model for sustainability assessment law. As we have seen, environmental assessment is now entrenched in laws of many kinds – covering review of capital projects, sectoral activities (mining, nuclear power generation, forest management, etc.), urban plans, development assistance, parks establishment and sensitive lands protection. Sustainability assessment, covering all these areas and more, might well need similarly diverse statutory foundations.

The following discussion imagines the construction of a generic sustainability assessment law. Only the main components are explored and these broadly. Actual laws would be much more detailed and would have special provisions designed to fit particular legal traditions, institutional structures, constitutional mandates, political possibilities and stakeholder expectations. Here the objective is merely to illustrate the process design principles in

Box 7.1   Best practice design principles for sustainability assessment processes

A best practice sustainability assessment process, built on the foundation of advanced environmental assessment regimes:

- begins with explicit commitment to sustainability objectives and to application of sustainability-based decision criteria and trade-off rules;
- incorporates means of specifying and integrating the general sustainability decision criteria and trade-off rules for local and broader context of particular cases;
- covers all potentially significant initiatives, at the strategic as well as project level, in a way that connects work at the two levels;
- ensures that proponents of undertakings and responsible authorities are aware of their assessment obligations before they begin planning and that they have effective motivations (legal requirements or the equivalent) to meet these obligations;
- focuses attention on the most significant undertakings or combinations of undertakings (at the strategic and project levels) and on work that will have the greatest beneficial influence;
- is transparent and ensures open and effective involvement of local residents, potentially affected communities, and other parties with important knowledge and concerns to consider and an interest in ensuring properly rigorous assessment;
- takes special steps to ensure representation of important interests and considerations not otherwise effectively included (for example, disadvantaged populations, future generations, broader socio-ecological relations);
- is initiated at the outset of policy, programme and project deliberations when problems and/or opportunities are identified;
- requires critical examination of purposes and comparative evaluation of alternatives in light of the sustainability-based decision criteria;
- addresses positive as well as negative, indirect as well as direct, and cumulative as well as immediate effects;
- recognizes uncertainties and requires estimates of confidence in effects predictions;
- seeks to identify alternatives that offer the greatest overall benefits and that avoid undesirable trade-offs;
- emphasizes enhancement of multiple, mutually reinforcing benefits as well as avoidance or mitigation of negative effects;
- specifies and applies explicit trade-off rules, including requirements for explicit rationales for trade-off decisions;
- favours options that reflect a precautionary approach to significant risks and incorporate adaptive design, and requires preparation for continuous learning and adaptive implementation;

- is enshrined in law, with effective means of ensuring compliance with process requirements and decisions;
- includes means of enforcing terms and conditions of approval, monitoring implementation and effects, and ensuring appropriate response to identified problems and opportunities through the full life-cycle of assessed undertakings;
- facilitates efficient implementation;
- is integrated into a more complete framework that links strategic and project level assessment and places both as contributors to and beneficiaries of a larger regime for the pursuit of durable and desirable futures.

application, to sketch out the nature and intent of the key provisions, and to note where significant choices emerge. As will be evident, there are devils even without many details in sustainability assessment process design.

Our generic sustainability assessment law has 12 main components: purposes, decision criteria, application rules, streams, hierarchies and tiers, scope, participation, evaluations, approvals, administration, linkages beyond assessment, and efficiencies. In practice such a law would also have sections on definitions and regulation-making powers. It would set out in some detail the requirements of and steps in different streams or levels of assessment, listing, for example, the expected points of notice, contents of reports and decision options in the identified assessment streams. It would make provision for reviews including hearings, conflict resolution mechanisms including mediation, and the appointment of authorities including hearing panel members. And it would be careful to define relations with other decisions and decision making authorities within and beyond the legislating jurisdiction. The following discussion of the 12 core components should, nevertheless, provide a good indication of what is involved.

Purposes

All laws have purposes and some of them, wisely, make these explicit. There are two standard options. Often the law will have a preface of some sort to explain the legislators' intent. Sometimes, however, the purposes are set out more authoritatively in the body of the law itself. This is preferable when there are disputes over interpretation and lawyers and/or the courts are drawn into the fray. Laws, like most things in life, are open to different readings. The details of assessment laws – content requirements, procedural fairness provisions, obligations to establish the 'significance' of things, and other such items – are especially vulnerable. Where different inclinations lead to different interpretations, it is often helpful to have the big picture of the legal intent clearly drawn and authoritatively included in the law.

Clarity of purpose does have drawbacks. Laws must evolve. They must reflect (and sometimes resist and other times foster) the shifts in understandings, priorities and tolerance that typify all modern cultures. Fuzzy goals may therefore be useful if they allow room for progressively sliding interpretation. Certainly this has been important in the history of sustainability where the 'creative ambiguity' of the concept has facilitated its spread into the mainstream of official commitments. However, the situation is different now that the commitments are largely in place. Vagueness and ambiguity are less valuable for the transition from commitments to applications. While legal flexibility remains important, sustainability assessment must now help us to move a few steps in the direction of firm obligations, clear criteria and practical tests.

In any event, there is little potential for precision in statements of legislative purpose. Like the laws themselves, the purposes mostly provide a framework upon which more specific guidance can be built through the more detailed provisions of the law and through accompanying regulations, guidance documents and precedents set through particular case decisions.

For sustainability assessment law, an appropriate general statement of purpose would include the following:

1   *The purposes of sustainability assessment are:*
   - *to improve decision making on all undertakings that may, individually or in combination, have a significant effect on progress towards sustainability;*
   - *to ensure comprehensive and integrated attention to all factors affecting long-term as well as immediate desirability and durability;*
   - *to provide the core framework (the main structure, criteria and process) for deliberations and decisions on significant undertakings (in contrast to environmental assessment's usual role as one among many contributions to a broader decision making process);*
   - *to encourage overall consistency and efficiency in decision making from policy and programme design to post-approval project implementation and monitoring (through application of a common set of fundamental requirements), while also favouring flexibility and decentralization by respecting uncertainty and context, working iteratively with the relevant stakeholders, and adapting to different ecosystems and communities, new understandings, and emerging challenges and opportunities;*
   - *to encourage effective public engagement in the conception, planning, approval and implementation of undertakings that may have a significant effect on progress towards sustainability;*
   - *to foster and facilitate creative innovation as well as just transitions to more sustainable practices.*

Decision criteria

Sustainability assessment is distinguished from conventional environmental assessment chiefly in its adoption of a broader purpose and a more ambitious basic test. Instead of aiming to avoid or mitigate significant adverse effects, it aims for durable gains. More than that, it seeks multiple, reinforcing benefits covering the full suite of requirements for progress towards sustainability, and it demands careful, open and explicit evaluation of unavoidable trade-offs.

As will be discussed below (in the section on evaluations), successful pursuit of reinforcing benefits requires good, sustainability-oriented decisions throughout the process from initial conception to final closure. A multitude of individual decisions is involved. Certainly a great deal depends on whether these decisions are guided by a consistent set of decision criteria, and whether the criteria are properly comprehensive, well integrated, and duly elaborated on for the case at hand.

The decision making provisions in a sustainability assessment law might set out the general criteria and trade-off rules as discussed in Chapters 5 and 6 and collected in Appendices 3 and 4 (or their equivalent adjusted for the particular jurisdiction). Alternatively, the law itself could just present the sustainability purposes to be served and leave presentation of the decision criteria to regulations.[1] The latter approach is suggested below. In either case, the general criteria and trade-off rules must be open for case specific elaboration and specification.

Broadly, then, the decision criteria requirements for sustainability assessment could be set out as follows:

2   *The evaluations, choices, trade-offs and other decisions made in the sustainability assessment process must:*
    – *focus on maximum gains for sustainability, aim for selection of the best option (rather than merely judge the 'acceptability' of proposed undertakings) and seek enhancement of multiple, reinforcing sustainability benefits in addition to avoidance or mitigation of significant negative effects;*
    – *apply the sustainability-based decision criteria (concerning socio-ecological system integrity, livelihood sufficiency and opportunity, intragenerational equity, intergenerational equity, efficiency, socio-ecological civility and democratic governance, precaution and adaptation, and immediate and long-term integration) and the trade-off rules (concerning net gains, burden of argument, avoidance of significant adverse effects, protection of the future, explicit justification and open process) set out in the regulations (as in Appendices 3 and 4);*
    – *also take into account any specification of these criteria and trade-off rules – and associated values, objectives and criteria – for particular undertakings in specific contexts, made through informed choices by the relevant parties (stakeholders);*
    – *maximize the transparency and accountability of the deliberations and facilitate open engagement of interested and affected parties.*

Application rules

The basic application rule for effective assessment regimes is self-evident. Suitably rigorous assessment requirements should apply to all undertakings that may have significant effects and implications for sustainability within the influence of the legislating jurisdiction. It should also be apparent that proponents of such undertakings must know about their assessment obligations from the very beginning of their deliberations. In environmental assessment regimes where the application decision comes only after an undertaking has been planned and proposed for approval, the key initial decisions on purposes and alternatives will already have been made and must be uncritically accepted or inefficiently revisited. Neither is acceptable in sustainability assessment.

Application determinations must therefore be clear and anticipatory. Pre-established assessment requirements must be in place for all predictable kinds of undertakings so that the potential proponents know to address their assessment obligations from the outset of planning. For uncertain cases in the grey zone between undertakings that clearly merit formal assessment and ones that clearly do not, it is much better to include them in the mandatory assessment list. That way, the proponents begin planning with sustainability in mind, at least to the extent necessary to prepare a persuasive request for exemption from assessment requirements. The alternative would let them steam along to a proposal in a narrowly focused way with the risk that a late screening decision will force them back to the beginning. Generally, the application rules should tend towards assumed inclusion (with provisions for exemptions and less onerous process application) rather than assumed exclusion (with provisions for designation or bump-up to more onerous process application).

The kinds of undertakings that deserve to be covered include strategic as well as project level initiatives, and private as well as public sector proponents. These involve intersecting complexities. Projects from public sector proponents are most familiar and least challenging. Compared with policies, plans and programmes, projects are quite well defined subjects for assessment. And compared with private companies, capable public governments typically have broader agendas, mandates and motivations. They are often, therefore, better equipped to consider and act on a range of alternatives for sustainability. However, the answer to private proponent limitations is not to sacrifice sustainability objectives, but to find other ways of ensuring properly broad assessment.

Often when project level proponents, public or private, are pushed to address options that are beyond their reasonable limits, it is time for strategic level assessment. This is the case, for example, when doubts about the desirability of a thermal power project suggest need for a policy level assessment of electricity demand and supply options. Or when questions about the cumulative effects of successive aquaculture projects suggest need for an assessment of aquaculture promotion policy or regional shoreline development planning. In both instances, a good strategic level assessment can examine the broad purposes and alternatives more effectively and help to streamline subsequent project level deliberations.

Assessments at the strategic level do present challenges. Because the need for them often emerges from problems encountered in project level assessments, as in the cases above, they are difficult to anticipate. They are also hard to pre-define, in part because there are so many strategic tools, forms and purposes in common use. For example, while policies on important issues may be generally worthy of assessment, not all government documents that are labelled as 'policies' are intended for serious application. Some are merely symbolic or cynically diversionary. Moreover, assessment obligations at the strategic level can be easy to avoid by simple re-labelling. For example, if policies and plans must be assessed, a government agency may choose to operate with draft policies or to substitute 'guidelines' for plans.

Sustainability assessment law must therefore be clear about what usual kinds of policies, programmes and plans are covered (for example, by requiring strategic level assessment of all ministerial or cabinet level strategic undertakings that may have significant sustainability effects), while being flexible enough to deal with legitimate secrecy needs (for example, in national budget preparations). And it must also provide means to encourage or require strategic level assessments where their desirability becomes evident (for example, where project level assessment has uncovered key issues that lie beyond the proper scope and authority of the project level participants, or where agencies are avoiding assessment of evidently significant strategic positions).

3a *Sustainability assessment requirements apply:*
  – *generally to all undertakings, including policies, programmes and plans as well as capital projects and physical activities, that might have significant effects on prospects for sustainability; and more specifically:*
  – *to undertakings in all categories identified in regulations made under the law;*
  – *to significant policies, programmes and plans that require ministerial approval;*
  – *to cases where need for strategic level initiatives has been identified in the course of a project level assessment and is recognized by the relevant authorities;*
  – *to any other cases where the government chooses to require an assessment in response to public concern or its own recognition of issues of significance for sustainability.*
3b *Requests for exemption from sustainability assessment requirements:*
  – *may be sought from the assessment authority;*
  – *must be accompanied by reasonable argument and evidence that the potential for sustainability effects has been carefully considered and no such effects are likely;*
  – *must be open for public review and comment before a decision is made.*

Hierarchies and tiers

An important advantage of an assessment regime that incorporates both strategic and project level applications is the opportunity for clarity and efficiency in a linked hierarchy of tiered assessments. As we have seen, deliberations at the project level can uncover needs for strategic level initiatives to address the broader issues. Similarly, strategic level assessments can provide guidance for project assessments, in part by resolving these broader issues. For example, a strategic assessment that leads to a well considered regional waste management master plan would provide the foundation for much more focused assessment of the desirable individual projects (landfill expansions, composting facilities, etc.) anticipated by the plan. In the same way, an assessed national policy on international trade liberalization could guide deliberations on options for a particular bilateral agreement, and an assessed provincial programme of support for domestic agriculture could guide design of particular initiatives to assist organic growers or to subsidize habitat preservation on small farms.

Linked hierarchies have long been used in urban and countryside planning where a comprehensive but minimally detailed regional plan sets out the framework for more specific local or community plans. If the plans at both tiers are developed through public processes and aim to serve sustainability objectives, these already represent a hierarchy of applied sustainability assessments. A roughly parallel approach is used in some environmental assessment regimes wherein a generic assessment, perhaps based on one typical case in a closely defined category, is used as a template for subsequent assessments of similar undertakings, with adjustments made for site specific differences.

In tiered assessments, there can be debate about whether the upper level conclusions should be imposed firmly or flexibly at the lower level. Since circumstances very, no single answer is likely to serve well. Flexibility will often be necessary to accommodate exceptional circumstances and recent changes in important factors. But permissive willingness to reopen broad scale debates at the project level will nullify the advantages of a linked hierarchy. Perhaps the best general solution is simply to shift the burden of argument to those who wish to reject some or all of the high level guidance.

4   *Strategic level policies, programmes and plans that have been approved after sustainability assessment:*
   – *may be used to guide the substantive scope of and/or the process for consequential assessments at the more specific programme, plan or project levels;*
   – *may, in particular, be used to focus the lower level assessment on a more limited range of options than would be required in the absence of the broader level assessment;*
   – *may be reconsidered at the more specific programme, plan or project levels only where the parties seeking reconsideration can justify this on the grounds of exceptional circumstances or recent changes in important factors.*

Streams

Even in the most advantaged jurisdictions, there will never be enough time, resources or human capacity to do carefully rigorous sustainability assessments of all undertakings that may deserve them. Inevitably, a sort of triage is needed. Efforts must be concentrated on the cases (or groups of cases where cumulative effects are involved) that threaten the worst losses if assessment is weak and promise the greatest gains if assessment is given full attention.

Less significant cases can be left to a generic process with less supervision, so long as someone is keeping a careful lookout for surprises. And the cases that appear to be inconsequential (or beyond positive influence) must be left largely to their own devices.

Some of this triage is properly achieved through judicious decisions about what undertakings should be subject to the application of the process. However, streaming is a no less important tool. In broadly applied conventional environmental assessments regimes, only a tiny minority of cases get the full treatment with detailed assessment requirements and public hearings. The rest follow a shorter, less rigorous and often less open path. Or perhaps they just take a first step into a screening mechanism and are excused from further obligations if no serious issues emerge.

In principle, most cases should be expeditious. The practice, however, is often undermined by administrative routinization, exclusion of the potentially affected public, unduly narrow scoping, and inadequate procedures for identifying and dealing with the significant exceptions. While none of these limitations is surprising, given the usual temptations of institutions seeking efficiencies, none is acceptable or necessary.

In best practice environmental assessments, it has been possible to combine breadth, openness and expeditious deliberation.[2] The quicker streams usually feature more concise documentation and a more modest level of public and institutional review, but they retain the full range of basic requirements (for example, to assess purposes and alternatives as well as the preferred option, in light of potential social, economic and cultural, as well as, biophysical effects), and ensure public notice and comment opportunities. To address exceptions, they usually also include a 'bump-up' mechanism for moving particularly difficult or controversial cases from the streamlined stream to the more intensive review category. Similar arrangements are desirable and realistic for effective sustainability assessment.

5   *Cases subject to sustainability assessment may be allocated to different, more or less demanding assessment streams, as set out in the law:*
   – *to ensure detailed, substantive evaluation and rigorous public and institutional review of the most significant and potentially worrisome undertakings;*
   – *to permit more expeditious assessment review of less significant and worrisome undertakings;*
   – *so long as in every case, the assessment provisions:*
      • *apply the full set of sustainability criteria and trade-off rules;*
      • *address the full range of basic requirements (see the provisions under 'scope', below), except where a narrowing has been justified by a higher tier assessment (see provisions under 'hierarchies and tiers', above);*
      • *include timely opportunities for public notice and comment;*
      • *include a mechanism for open consideration of applications (from a proponent, or the public or any other interested party) to bump-up an exceptionally significant or controversial case to more intensive review or to bump-down an exceptionally benign or insignificant case to less intensive review;*

- *with schedules providing, to the extent possible, clear early guidance and procedures for determining more specifically the stream of assessment and review required in all categories of reasonably anticipated undertakings.*

Scope

Because the objectives of sustainability assessment are ambitious, the proper general scope of the assessment process is very broad. The aim is undertakings that are, of all the practical options, the most positive responses to well considered problems or opportunities. The process, therefore, must ensure attention to the full set of intertwined factors affecting prospects for sustainability and the entire lifecycle of an undertaking – from the initial consideration of purposes and alternatives to eventual cancellation, replacement or decommissioning. This is crucial; indeed, it is a defining characteristic of sustainability assessment processes.

At the same time, no practical process can hope to cover everything that might be relevant. In usual environmental assessment parlance, scoping also includes setting boundaries for particular assessments and focusing attention on the most important issues and options. Both are also necessary in sustainability assessments, for effectiveness as much as for efficiency. But both are open to abuse. Proponents are generally inclined to limit their obligations and to exclude matters that may pose difficulties. In Canada, we have seen logging road assessment boundaries set to consider only the right of way and not the forest to be harvested, and mining assessment boundaries set as a tidy rectangle around a proposed mine site that is located in a sensitive watershed and in the migratory path of a large caribou herd. Scoping must therefore be an open, participative exercise that gives close attention to the complex systems in which assessments and undertakings proceed.

6a *The scope of all assessments must cover:*
- *the full suite of considerations relevant to specifying and applying the decision criteria including social, economic and biophysical aspects recognized as components of complex and dynamic systems;*
- *the full life-cycle of the undertakings;*
- *all key openings for critical examination and innovation, including requirements in every case:*
  - *to establish the need(s) and/or justify the purpose(s) to be served;*
  - *to identify the reasonable alternatives, including different general approaches as well as different designs, for serving the purpose;*
  - *to integrate consideration of related undertakings and cumulative effects of existing, proposed, consequential and reasonably anticipated undertakings, except insofar as these matters have been addressed at least as thoroughly and openly in a broader strategic assessment whose conclusions have not been superceded by subsequent developments.*
6b *The particular scope of an assessment must be specified through public process in ways that:*

- *focus attention on the most significant alternatives, socio-ecological system components and effects;*
- *match the level of assessment effort to the significance of the case, with significance in all cases determined through application of the sustainability-based decision criteria.*

Participation

Ensuring effective public involvement in sustainability assessment is crucial for at least four reasons. First, and perhaps most obvious, is the legitimate interest of local citizens as the most likely recipients of the resulting gains and losses. This is particularly significant because of the unavoidable importance of public choice. Especially in sustainability assessments, which accept complexity, uncertainty and value-laden preferences as unavoidable aspects of the decisions to be made, simple reliance on expertise cannot be justified.

Second, along with interest, many public participants bring valuable knowledge to the assessment table. In some places, especially where government authorities have very limited internal capacity and few resources for outside expertise, local knowledge can be the main source of key information. This was the case in the Lutsel K'e example discussed in Chapter 4 and has been well documented in a recent study in Ghana (Appiah-Opoku, 2005).

The third and, perhaps, most practically important reason for emphasis on public involvement combines balance and credibility. Public participants are the stakeholders with the most reliably broad and powerful motivations to counter the biases of proponents and to demand thorough assessment. Since assessment requirements are intended to force and facilitate the incorporation of sustainability factors in the planning of undertakings, those doing the planning must be given the main responsibility for assessment work. But most proponents have narrow interests, restricted mandates or dominant incentives that do not encourage devotion to the full set of sustainability requirements. Able critics are therefore indispensable. Government reviewers can serve well. Typically, however, they are too constrained by narrow mandates, competing demands and/or political delicacies to offer comprehensive and forthright comments. Public interest organizations, potentially affected residents and other civil society stakeholders also have limitations, but taken together and provided with timely information, early and repeated opportunities for engagement, modest support and complementary work by government experts, they can do much to raise the standard as well as the legitimacy of sustainability assessment.

Finally, sustainability assessment is not just about making better decisions. It is also about institutional and public learning (Parson and Clark, 1995; Diduck, 2001; Connor and Dovers, 2004). The sustainability-based decision criteria recognize the value of socio-ecological civility and the need to deepen its roots in shared understanding and enriched capacity for civic deliberation. Assessment processes, as much as the undertakings that result, should be designed to build this understanding and capacity.

7   *Transparency, accountability and effective engagement of participants must be provided throughout the sustainability assessment process, in all streams:*
    - *to mobilize public knowledge as well as specialized technical expertise;*
    - *to encourage all participants to look beyond their particular interests, mandates and expertise to recognize broader implications where trade-offs or positive reinforcements may be involved;*
    - *to ensure effective public as well as technical notification and consultation at key points throughout the proposal development and assessment process including:*
        - *the initial identification of need(s), purpose(s) and potential alternatives;*
        - *the scoping of an assessment and the identification of valued system components;*
        - *the selection of the preferred alternative;*
        - *the application for approval;*
        - *implementation monitoring and adaptation;*
    - *with support, including resources, for important participants who would not otherwise be able to play an effective role in key steps through the process, including early deliberations and post-approval monitoring;*
    - *with convenient and open access to assessment documentation;*
    - *with arrangements for public hearings on cases of particular public interest and significance for sustainability.*

Evaluations

Laws establishing processes for the assessment (or planning or management) of undertakings involve decisions of many kinds. The usual focus in conventional environmental assessments is on the approval (or rejection) decision – the ruling on whether the assessed undertaking should proceed and, if so, under what conditions. This is understandable, although in many assessment regimes these rulings are just recommendations for consideration by the actual approval authorities. Even recommendation making involves important choices and, in a properly open and credible process, the recommendations can be powerful. But these are not the only, or always the most influential decisions.

In many cases, the key decisions will be about the purposes to be served and the alternatives to be examined. We have, for example, seen many cases where a municipal landfill is reaching the limits of its capacity and the relevant authorities have proposed an assessment in which they define their purpose as finding a new dump site. Accordingly they frame their inquiry around the evaluation of alternative landfill technologies or perhaps alternative locations. Where assessment law has permitted participation in and critical review of such decisions, citizens groups have often forced a broader approach – defining the purpose as waste management and framing the assessment around evaluation of waste reduction, reuse and recycling opportunities, as well as disposal options. In these and other such cases, it is easy to see how initial conception decisions might be key determinants of prospects for sustainability-directed innovation.

Much the same can be said about the choices made at other steps in the process. Between initial conception and eventual approval (or rejection), and indeed on through implementation monitoring and final review, assessments involve multitudes of other decisions. Individually, many of these decisions will be unremarkable. Together, however, they can determine much of the assessment's direction and many of its conclusions. To ensure consistently guided and informed assessments and to maintain openings for iterative learning, sustainability-based decision criteria must be applied in evaluations and decisions throughout the full deliberative process.

8   *Open application of sustainability-based decision criteria (as specified for case-particular context) is required throughout the entire process, including in evaluations and other decision making in:*
   – *selecting appropriate purposes and reasonable options for consideration in particular cases;*
   – *scoping assessment work, including through the identification of valued system components by the stakeholders as well as relevant experts;*
   – *identifying means of enhancing positive effects as well as avoiding or mitigating negative effects;*
   – *judging the nature and significance of uncertainties (about effect predictions, mitigation and enhancement effectiveness, etc.) and associated risks;*
   – *determining the relative merits of the reasonable alternatives and justifying the selection of the preferred alternative as the proposed undertaking;*
   – *clarifying and, where possible, resolving conflicts;*
   – *approving (or rejecting) a proposed undertaking and identifying appropriate conditions of approval;*
   – *designing and implementing post-decision follow-up, including monitoring, adjustment and, where relevant, closure and/or replacement;*
   – *in tiered assessments, elaborating substantive and/or process guidance for subsequent undertakings.*

Approvals and authority

While decisions throughout the process are important, approval decisions retain their special place in sustainability assessment. Indeed, they become much more important insofar as sustainability assessment becomes the core framework for developing new undertakings.

Here the key process design issues centre on questions of authority. Do the sustainability assessment conclusions themselves become the go/no-go decision, or are they instead incorporated into some other decision vehicle? In either case, are there adequate tools and capacities for enforcement of the decision and the associated commitments and terms of approval? Who is to make the decision? Should it be the public officials who supervised the deliberations, or an independent body of government assigned to review the evidence, or elected and therefore more democratically accountable authorities, or perhaps even the relevant stakeholders who might, in some cases, reach a consensus agreement? And where should this authority be located? Is this a matter for an environment ministry, given the origins in environmental assessment; or a central agency, given the more comprehensive sustainability agenda; or a more independent authority reporting directly to the legislature?

There are few universally suitable answers to these questions. Arrangements that work well for one jurisdiction will fail in another with different governmental structures and traditions. Even within a single assessment regime, project and strategic assessment approvals, and major and minor cases may need to be handled differently. We can, nevertheless, set out some general requirements.

9 *Approval decisions must:*
   - *be explicitly and openly justified in light of the process purposes including case specific elaborations of the decision criteria and trade-off rules (see above);*
   - *include effectively enforceable obligations for implementation, based on assessment commitments and approval conditions (obligations for monitoring, review, adaptation, correction and, where appropriate, replacement or closure);*
   - *include requirements and provisions for comparing actual effects with predicted effects (to allow adaptive management and to enhance learning from experience) through the full life of the undertaking;*
   - *in the case of strategic level assessments, provide clear substantive and process guidance for subsequent undertakings covered by the assessed policy, plan or programme.*

Administration

Just as there are many possibilities for the assignment of final decision making authority, there are many ways of designing and locating process administration. Some of the desired characteristics are also similar. To the extent possible, both administration and final authority should be transparent, located at or near the centre of decision making, and minimally vulnerable to the pressures of immediate political expediency. In most cases, however, it will be best to separate the two functions.

The location of administration and decision making raises important questions about substantive emphasis. Most conventional environmental assessment processes have been attached to, or have reported through, resource and/or environmental management ministries with typically junior status in government. This has had the advantage of focus on environmental issues but the disadvantage of political marginalization. The broader integrative agenda of sustainability assessments is better suited to a position in, or reporting to, central authority. The risk, however, is dissipation of the hard-won and still limited attention to environmental issues that was built up over the past few decades. This issue will be examined further in the final section of this chapter. For now it is important just to recognize the problem and to recommend firm emphasis on application of the full set of sustainability criteria.

Assessment process administration typically also involves the development of guidance documents and regulations. Both of these can be powerfully influential and regulations, being enforceable in law, are of particular importance. When the basic assessment legislation provides few details about implementation, regulations often carry the main weight of clarifying what is required. While actual regulation making is typically the responsibility of elected officials, the development of regulatory proposals – the background research, evaluation of options and specification of contents – and the preparation of associated explanatory material may be left to the process administrators. Because the regulation and other guidance documents play key roles in assessment process elaboration and function, it is crucial that they be developed in a credible, open and consultative process.[3]

10 *Process administration must:*
   – *be directed by an impartial authority that serves, but is at arm's length from, the centre of decision making;*
   – *be responsible for ensuring fair process, including opportunity for effective public participation in, and critical review of, assessment work and of the development of regulations, policies and other process guidance;*
   – *insist on, and provide guidance for, full and fair application of all the core sustainability decision criteria and trade-off rules;*
   – *be subject to independent auditing with public reporting.*

Linkages beyond assessment

Sustainability assessment is just one tool. It will not deliver sustainability by itself, and it is much more likely to be effective within its own realm if it is linked into other complementary initiatives – that, for example, help to define and focus the task, clarify the criteria and monitor progress. Ideally, sustainability assessment would be just one contributor to (and beneficiary of) a larger complex system of sustainability-oriented activities. These include work to report current conditions and trends, identify priority concerns and opportunities, select useful indicators of change, delineate and debate future scenarios, plot alternative possible routes to desired futures, evaluate their feasibility, propose suitable strategies for change, monitor new and continuing activities, and propose adaptations and innovations, at every scale from the local to the global, all somehow linked and mutually responsive, flexible and adaptive, dynamic and open-ended.

We have many of the pieces now. Any capable internet search engine will find thousands of initiatives in most of these categories. In some areas (sustainability indicators, for example) there is an impressive array of near duplicates. Organization into firm links of communication and influence has been slower to emerge.

At the same time, sustainability assessment processes are entering a world already heavily populated by legislated planning, review and approval requirements. These requirements are evidently insufficient for essential sustainability purposes – they are generally too narrowly focused, too short term in vision and too fragmented in application to serve sustainability purposes effectively. Still, most if not all of them play some useful role. And few jurisdictions can manage addition of yet more requirements on top of the existing ones.

A sustainability assessment law must therefore both add and subtract. It must encourage the interweaving of innovative sustainability initiatives into more viable whole systems, and it must clarify, coordinate, harmonize and sometimes supplant relationships with existing regulatory and administrative requirements.

11 *To strengthen the effectiveness and efficiency of the larger set of policy making, planning, regulatory and reporting process in which it operates, the sustainability assessment process must:*
  – *make best use of credible broader sustainability initiatives (such as the development of national or regional sustainability strategies, indicator lists or monitoring protocols) where these can help clarify application of the sustainability decision criteria;*
  – *encourage and facilitate cooperative application with other affected jurisdictions, following the principle of upward harmonization to ensure application of the highest standard of sustainability assessment;*
  – *organize its decision making and reporting to facilitate subsequent regulatory deliberations;*
  – *facilitate other initiatives to situate sustainability assessment in a larger system in which:*
    • *broad sustainability needs, goals and indicators are identified, in part for sustainability assessment application;*
    • *sustainability assessment findings, including monitoring results, are used in continuous review and adjustment of the identified needs, goals and indicators.*

Efficiencies

Ensuring process efficiency is a major challenge for sustainability assessment. It is also an absolute requirement. Inefficiency is not just wasteful, it is also a gift to the opposition. Because sustainability assessment is a vehicle for substantial change, it will always have enemies and they will be pleased to complain of waste and delay, should the opportunity arise.

Confident authorities may be able to ignore such resistance, but it is a short-term strategy at best. The longer-term objective for sustainability assessment is proponents who automatically think, plan and act with sustainability imperatives in mind. This can only be achieved if proponents accept the process as legitimate, necessary and at least in some ways valuable. A process typified by unnecessary burdens, uncertainties, inconsistencies and delays cannot win such acceptance.

Assessment process efficiency relies as much on capable administration as on the design of the law. But the legal provisions can play a major role and make efficient administration much more likely. Much depends on the combination of firmness and flexibility. Clear application rules with provisions for exempting or bumping-up exceptional cases, basic content requirements with provisions for issue scoping, and standard decision criteria with provisions for local elaboration – all these establish certainty about the fundamentals while still allowing means of adjustment.

More specific openings for efficient administration include the application, streaming and scoping provisions that match assessment effort to case or issue significance. These are already common in advanced environmental assessments. Important additional efficiencies are promised by sustainability assessment processes that encourage the tiering of assessments so that strategic level work can streamline assessment at the more specific plan or project level.

Perhaps the most visible efficiencies emerge when properly designed and applied sustainability assessments replace and/or coordinate and guide the multiplicity of fragmentary and independent approval processes that proponents typically face. Because proper sustainability assessment should deliver better integrated and more broadly supported approvals, the results should also include greater legitimacy, less institutional resistance and quicker implementation.

Finally, though probably not immediately, broader efficiencies are promised if sustainability assessment fosters construction of a more coherent and adaptive larger system linking the setting of overall sustainability objectives to the management and monitoring of ongoing activities, as discussed above.

12 *Efficiencies in and beyond the sustainability assessment process must be facilitated by:*
   - *legal language that is firm on the application of fundamental components (including application of the general decision criteria, attention to purposes and alternatives, etc.) but flexible in case elaboration, and accompanied by clear procedures for seeking exceptions;*
   - *application, streaming and scoping provisions that match assessment effort with the significance of the cases and issues involved;*
   - *tiered assessment provisions that allow use of strategic assessment results to streamline subsequent assessments;*
   - *provisions that allow sustainability assessments and resulting approvals to replace less comprehensive and ill-coordinated existing process or permitting requirements, and to guide other more specific licensing processes;*
   - *linkages between the sustainability assessment process and a coherent larger system of sustainability analyses and initiatives.*

At best, this list of 12 components provides a rough guide for sustainability assessment process legislators. The drafting of specific provisions would have to take into account many more complex issues and options than have been recognized here. And the necessary adjustments to context and application would have significant effects on the resulting law. An actual statute for sustainability assessment in Namibia would be quite different from one designed for Norway. There would also be differences if we were instead drafting a sustainability-based urban planning statute or legislation governing fisheries management.

The core considerations would apply, nonetheless. Indeed, many of the core considerations would apply if the objective were a non-legislated process, meant for internal adoption by a development assistance bank evaluating funding proposals or a civil society organization engaged in fair trade certification. While the points here focus on sustainability assessment law, the main intent is to help frame the broader discussion.

Transitions

In the event that all this still seems simpler than rocket science, we should remember that there is no fixed target here. Nor is there a standard beginning point or an elegantly drawn arc for travel from start to finish. Therefore, we should not imagine that there is a single proper vehicle design that can be directly imposed. The design principles and illustrative legal components sketched out here are unavoidably general not just because they are meant for application to different kinds of undertakings in different jurisdictions, but because the situation everywhere is fluid.

Sustainability assessment is by its origins and intent part of a larger transition. As we saw in Chapter 2, environmental assessment has been evolving, erratically but visibly, in the direction of sustainability assessment for many years. Similarly in Chapters 3 and 5, we saw that debates about the concept of sustainability have been moving slowly towards common identification of key requirements. And these are just two topics among many of at least equal significance where things have been changing, though not always in a promising direction.

The core assumption behind sustainability assessment is that we can exert some intentional positive influence over the direction and character of change. There is little hubris involved. Complexity and uncertainty are respected. The rational and comprehensive structure of sustainability assessment process design is well battered and bent by participation, precaution, iteration and doubt. Still, the idea is to make the world a little better – to adopt some basic criteria, consider our purposes and options with care, and try to make a difference, through the cumulative effects of better decisions on projects and strategic undertakings.

That sounds innocent enough. But it means that we are planning to apply sustainability assessment in a world that we hope to change as we go. And that has some interesting implications for process design and application.

Consider, for example, what may be the biggest worry for advocates of sustainability assessment implementation today: what happens to the environment? The problem is that a poorly conceived shift to sustainability-based assessment could reduce the attention given to ecological considerations. Environmental assessment law, indeed environmental law generally, has struggled for decades to force serious attention to ecological concerns and that battle is not yet won. Even in the greenest jurisdictions there remain business, political and bureaucratic proponents of narrowly conceived economic development who would welcome an opening to slide back to the good old days of unfettered entrepreneurialism and environmental disregard.

Would it then be better to delay introduction of sustainability assessment process requirements? Would it be wise to spend a few more years (or decades) strengthening environmentally focused assessment, arguing for better appreciation of ecosystem services, educating people about health threats from environmental neglect?

We could reject that option on the grounds that environmental concerns may never be widely enough embraced so long as they are treated as an alternative to economic priorities. We could argue that integrated sustainability-based approaches promise more effective attention to the contributing causes of environmental degradation. Certainly, rigorous sustainability-based assessment would be no friend of narrow economic priorities. Moreover, its place is at the core of decision making. While the current forms of environmental assessment may give concentrated, public attention to ecological issues, they frequently play a marginal end role, making recommendations to closed, economically driven approval processes.

Proper sustainability-based assessment would force public attention to the full suite of social/economic/ecological interdependences. It would demand open evaluation of the trade-offs and compromises often proposed in conventional environmental assessment processes, and apply a higher test for identifying and measuring durable benefits. If such were achieved, the effective influence of ecological considerations would be considerably enhanced.

But while all this is well and fine, it depends on ensuring that sustainability assessment is designed well, implemented effectively and situated to be powerful. Weak sustainability assessment could be a step backward. It could undermine some of the limited environmental gains of the past 30 years, though perhaps not for long without stirring public disgust. In some circumstances, at least, it would be better to push the gradual evolution of advanced environmental assessment a little further.

The key lies in recognizing the place and role of sustainability assessment in a transition. As presented in this chapter, sustainability assessment design is general and in some ways primitive, but it is fully conceived. It is a complete, integrated package. And there may be few opportunities to apply that complete package in the near future. Often there will at least be pressures for compromise. Like the evolution of environmental assessment the transition to sustainability assessment may have to be gradual and hesitant in the face of resistance and confusion.

The matter of transitions moves us from desirable models to dirty-under-the-fingernails strategies for implementation. Sustainability assessment is a tool for change. But it is also at this stage mostly a possibility. It has been attempted in various forms and contexts, and its proper basic characteristics and design are easy to delineate. The tricky part is judging how best to push it forward and for that there are no simple solutions. What adoption and evolution strategies will work best will depend on the context, on the particular openings and perils that emerge in transitions that will be a little different from one jurisdiction and application to the next. The advantage of having a fully conceived sustainability assessment process in mind is that the various transitional paths may all be designed to point in roughly the same direction. That is as close to rocketry as we are likely to get.

Notes

1 One common model for the latter approach is represented by the *Ontario Planning Act* (1990), which is the key legal foundation for municipal planning in the Canadian province (Ontario, 2001). The Act requires municipal planning decisions to be 'consistent with' provincial policy statements. These statements must be prepared in a consultative manner but are issued, like regulations, without going through the full legislative process and therefore are more flexible tools.

2 An imperfect but illustrative example is the class environmental assessment process used under the Ontario provincial *Environmental Assessment Act*. See discussion in Byer et al (1992).

3 The Canadian federal government uses a multi-stakeholder Regulatory Advisory Committee to help guide and review the preparation of new or amended regulations under the *Canadian Environmental Assessment Act*. The committee includes representatives of other federal agencies, provincial authorities, Aboriginal organizations, industry associations and non-government public interest groups.

8

Decisions

Applying Sustainability-based Criteria in Significance Determinations and Other Common Assessment Judgements

Decisions and significance

Decisions, decisions, decisions. While the informed observer might be forgiven for thinking that assessment activities were mostly about deliberation and evaluation, decision making is even more pervasive. Everywhere in the assessment process there are potentially crucial decisions to be made – not just in the usual deliberations about purposes, alternatives and conditions of approval, or just in the common evaluations of anticipated effects, mitigation or enhancement options or monitoring plans, but throughout all of the many steps from process design to final decommissioning of assessed undertakings. The general list of the main decisions in Appendix 6 includes 20 categories and 35 subcategories without reaching the level of particular choices.

The defining characteristic of sustainability assessment is that all of these decisions are informed by sustainability-based criteria, and aim to deliver multiple, lasting, mutually reinforcing gains rather than just mitigation of environmental damage. Chapter 7 explored how commitment to sustainability ends and means would affect decisions about the design of the assessment process (or at least its generic statutory foundation). Here, we look more closely at sustainability-based decision making within the process, or at least within a few crucial components of the process.

This will have to be an illustrative rather than comprehensive discussion. The focus will be on decisions about the application of assessment requirements, about the importance and implications of predicted effects, and about the selection among alternatives and approval options, including decisions about trade-offs. These three – applications, effects and approvals – are commonly recognized as the most important assessment decision areas. They are also areas where decision making has traditionally relied on judgements about significance. Application decisions rest on judgements about the likely significance of proposed undertakings and whether they should be subject to assessment requirements. Effects evaluations turn on the significance of predicted effects and how this should influence subsequent decisions. And approvals involve conclusions about the significance of competing options' strengths, weaknesses and trade-offs, and the implications for what should be approved and under what conditions.

In each area, application of sustainability-based criteria has a substantial effect on the interpretation of significance, on the nature of decision making and on the character of the likely results.

Significance in context

Significance has been a subject of practical interest and professional enquiry throughout the history of environmental assessment and it is bound to be important in sustainability assessment as well. Significance is involved because at every step of the process there is too much to do. There are too many undertakings, too many possible alternatives, too many potentially relevant factors, too many conceivable effects, and too many options for mitigation, enhancement and adaptation. Not all of them can be considered, at least not thoroughly, and not all of the ones that are considered can be given much attention in the decisions on approval and implementation. Priorities must be set.

The challenge may seem to lie in defining 'significance' clearly and defensibly for each point in the process. For sustainability assessment administrators, proponents and other participants, it would be convenient to have tidy pre-set lists or guidelines for determining significance and priority at each major decision point. It would be most convenient to have accepted significance thresholds – clear dividing lines between what is and what is not significant for each key decision. But for better or worse the world is not designed for administrative convenience. Moreover, sustainability assessment is deeply interested in the interrelationships among factors, effects and choices. It could not rely just on individual significance rulings even if these could be guided by standard threshold rules and delivered in neat packages.

Significance decisions sit uncomfortably in the disputed no-man's land between tests that can be defined clearly and unambiguously, and context-sensitive choices that depend on fair process rather than any universally applicable definition or standard. Regulatory authorities in many fields impose controls based on standards that define the line between what is acceptable and what is illegal. Highway speed limits, building set-back requirements, food additive concentration maxima and effluent discharge thresholds all work this way. Some may be carefully based on the available scientific data and rigorously applied evaluative methodologies, but all involve choices that are, to some extent, arbitrary. Their main strengths are clarity of obligation and simplicity of application; their main limitations are insensitivity to context and an associated tendency to see the world as a set of separate concerns, each with its own identifiable boundary between what is and is not allowed.

In assessment decision making, including significance judgements, the attractions of the regulatory model are undermined by the especially central role of context. The significance of a possible new gravel pit or stone quarry, for example, will depend on many factors including whether there are already many similar activities in the vicinity, whether the proposed site is in an ecologically sensitive area or on already degraded lands, whether the excavation will go below the water table and require pumping, whether the new road building or other construction that it will facilitate is clearly desirable, and whether the assessment might reveal a materials recycling alternative that might bring less damage and more positive gains.

A similarly wide range of considerations influences the significance of particular potential effects. For example, removing a small dam and its large, shallow reservoir in an urban watershed might be expected to eliminate the reservoir's water heating effect and facilitate recovery of a cold water fishery in a more natural floodplain. But the extent, durability and appreciation of this effect will depend on whether there are competing hydrological changes from upstream developments, contaminant loadings from tributaries and storm sewer outfalls, complementary or damaging initiatives by adjoining landowners, climate change effects, acts of vandalism or successful engagement of local youth in restoration activities, and local extinctions or residual persistence of indigenous species to repopulate the re-naturalized stream.

In all such cases, the significance decision involves judgement in light of the context. Moreover, the context involves intertwined and dynamic systems of mutually influencing components that will be further influenced by any new undertaking and set of accompanying effects. In sustainability assessments, the whole is different from the sum of the parts as well as different from place to place. While it will be possible to identify some common thresholds that are suitable for application in many divergent cases, most evaluations of significance and most of the important assessment decisions will need to rely on methods and processes that take the specifics of the case into account.

Because they focus on case specific deliberations, assessment processes are well suited to context sensitive decision making. Sustainability-based assessments have additional advantages, including their comprehensive scope, emphasis on engagement of relevant stakeholders and efforts in each case to clarify how the basic decision criteria should be elaborated for application in the particular circumstances.

Significance and sustainability

Many jurisdictions with environmental assessment processes or the equivalent have attempted to assist significance interpretations by providing recommended methods and processes for screening decisions, effects evaluation and other common decisions. There is also useful academic and professional literature on factors to be considered, processes for engaging relevant experts and stakeholders, criteria to be applied, approaches to aggregation and weighting, means of comparing alternatives, and use of other tools and methodologies (Lawrence, 2000, 2003b).

Little of this guidance has been developed with sustainability criteria in mind. Most assessment processes focus on a limited range of relevant considerations, usually with most attention given to direct negative ecological effects. And even where a broad enough basic agenda may be in place, the significance judgements are made individually on particular effects and options, without much attention to their interrelations and without explicit sustainability-based criteria or any other common vision of the larger purposes to be served.

Adopting a sustainability-based approach to assessment entails attention to the full suite of sustainability requirements and the full range of effects, positive and negative. It aims not just to avoid serious adverse effects but also to identify the most positive ways of meeting sustainability criteria, preferably through multiple, mutually reinforcing gains. And the sustainability criteria – properly specified for the particular context – are to be the unifying foundation for all key assessment decisions. As we have seen, this is much more ambitious than environmental assessment as usually practised. Applying sustainability-based criteria will bring a bigger set of considerations, and a more coherent and better integrated overall agenda, into judgements about significance and into the development of significance guidelines, thresholds, processes and evaluative tools.

At least some of the implications of this more ambitious approach can be seen through an exploration of its effects on significance decisions on applications, effects and approvals.

Applying sustainability-based criteria in significance judgements

On the surface, decisions about what sorts of undertaking should be assessed, what effects are most important, and what options are worthy of approval have little in common. While all may turn on judgements about significance, they differ markedly in topic, scale, timing, required expertise and finality. In assessment practice, however, they have proven to be so deeply intertwined that they might be considered different aspects of the same basic choice.

In the early years of assessment, the biggest significance controversies swirled around the application decision. The environmental assessment obligations introduced by the *US National Environmental Policy Act of 1969* immediately spawned questions about which proponents and what undertakings would have to comply. The law was not much help. It merely set a significance test, requiring assessments of 'proposals for legislation and other major Federal actions significantly affecting the quality of the human environment' (US Congress, 1970). This clearly tied the significance of the undertaking to the significance of its potential effects. But no definition or test for significance was provided. The inevitable result, in a famously litigious culture, was years of legal disputation. Gradually some clarification emerged, and criteria for significance determinations were codified in regulations. Complexities remained, however, and debates about the significance of actions and effects spread throughout the world of environmental assessment application (Wood, 2003).

The drivers of these debates link application and effects significance to approval decisions. Proponents have tended to avoid assessments where possible because of the unfamiliar thinking, added burdens and possible delays involved. But they have often been most seriously unsettled by the prospect of rejection, the danger that in the end they would not get approval for their preferred approach. Critics (or at least parties not fully inclined to trust the proponent's judgement) have also tended to see the application decision as a major influence on the approval decision. The ruling on whether or not a proposed undertaking merits assessment is often a ruling on whether any serious attention will be paid to issues beyond the proponent's immediate mandate or to options beyond the proponent's usual practice. The application decision is often also a ruling on whether there will be any opportunity for effective public scrutiny and influence during the planning process. If the assessment process is powerful, if it can successfully impose a broader way of thinking, evaluating and choosing, then the application decision is typically a decision in favour of a different result than would have been reached otherwise.

For organizational simplicity, the following discussion will consider application, effects and approval decisions separately. In reality, however, they are closely connected.

Significance and sustainability in decisions on process application

All undertakings, or sets of undertakings, that may have significant implications for sustainability should be subject to assessment. But not all possibly relevant undertakings, effects and alternatives can be covered, at least not very thoroughly. Conventional means of addressing this problem include provisions for exemption of minor undertakings, provisions establishing more and less rigorous streams of assessment (basic screening, class review, more comprehensive study, full public hearing), and provisions for case specific scoping (boundary setting and focusing). Significance judgements are central in all of these matters.

Defining significance for the purposes of allocating certain types of undertaking to more and less demanding assessment streams is superficially simple. Take the eight sustainability criteria and assign greatest significance to the types of undertaking that are most likely to benefit from assessment because:

- they (alone or in combination with other existing and anticipated undertakings) seem most likely to threaten progress on one or more of the eight aspects of sustainability;
- careful attention to purposes and alternative approaches seems most likely to reveal much less risky or damaging and/or much more beneficial options;

- careful attention to the broadly environmental context seems most likely to reveal mitigation and enhancement possibilities, or adaptive design elements that would make the undertaking much less risky or damaging and/or much more beneficial.

Similarly, least significance would be assigned to those types of undertaking that are:

- most likely to have trivial or modestly beneficial effects on sustainability;
- clearly the best (or least bad) of potentially available options;
- least likely to have unanticipated effects influencing some aspect of sustainability;
- already well designed to be reversible or otherwise adaptive to surprise.

More detailed deliberations would consider the particular contexts of the undertakings involved and apply context-specified versions of the eight basic decision criteria. Simply examining 'types of undertaking' without attention to their specific ecological and socio-economic surroundings is likely to miss some of the most important factors affecting significance. And application decisions that focus only on types of individual undertakings will miss the significance of groups of undertakings that are individually inconsequential but collectively and cumulatively important.

Even without these details, however, applying sustainability-based significance criteria in process application decisions would entail substantial adjustments to the conventional approaches taken in most jurisdictions. The extent of these adjustments would depend mostly on the breadth of considerations now applied.

For example, a key initial question is how central ecological concerns should be in deciding what types of undertaking should be subject to assessment requirements. In many assessment regimes, the potential significance of ecological effects is the primary criterion in application decisions. Where the more comprehensive sustainability-based criteria are adopted, ecological considerations remain important – they are relevant to all of the criteria and central in the integrity, efficiency and precautionary ones. But sustainability assessments could also be triggered in cases where the main immediate concerns are social.

Use of quite comprehensive criteria in process application decisions is common now in the assessment processes of development agencies such as the World Bank, which are necessarily interested in social and economic as well as ecological effects, and are aware that these are interrelated. Broadly comprehensive approaches are also anticipated in some new processes, such as the *Yukon Environmental and Socio-economic Assessment Act* (Canada, 2003a). Older national and provincial/state regimes could, as an interim measure, continue to use ecological significance as a necessary criterion in basic process application decisions (only undertakings with some potential ecological significance would be assessed) but use the full set of sustainability criteria in other significance judgements, such as choosing the appropriate assessment stream.

For most existing regimes, the difficult step in the transition to sustainability-based application decisions will be ensuring integrated attention to the sustainability criteria. While many advanced environmental assessment processes and related planning and approval frameworks give at least some attention to social, ecological and economic effects, most do so in separate analyses that are weak on the links and difficult to merge. The sustainability decision criteria outlined in Chapter 5 should help. They are designed to cross the usual social, ecological and economic boundaries and to facilitate integrated consideration. But because of this they demand unfamiliar thinking. And while unfamiliar thinking may be exactly what is required here, it is not easily adopted.

A final broad point about significance in process application decisions concerns the relative weighting of strategic versus project-level assessments. Greater attention to strategic level assessment is already widely advocated for process efficiency and other reasons not directly tied to sustainability objectives (Partidário and Clarke, 2000). Serious application of sustainability criteria adds to these arguments. Comprehensive and integrated consideration of systemic effects and broad alternatives is typically easier and more timely in assessments of policies, programmes and plans than in project level assessments. As a result, significant sustainability gains (and avoidance of significant sustainability losses) can be considerably greater at the strategic level. In many jurisdictions, the main authorities responsible for policies, programmes and plans that are significant from a sustainability perspective are inclined to resist mandatory and open strategic assessment. However, these authorities have typically also expressed commitment to sustainability and assessment efficiencies.

At both the strategic and project levels, decisions about whether or not to require a sustainability assessment turn on judgements about the possible significance of the effects. The key question is not whether the undertaking itself will be significant, but whether the results may be better if assessment is required and sustainability considerations are incorporated in the planning, approval and implementation processes. It is therefore reasonable to expect that the role of sustainability criteria in application decisions will be illuminated by an examination of the role of these criteria in the evaluation of effects.

Significance and sustainability in effects evaluation

We have had decades of experience with efforts to define the significance of environmental (including social and economic as well as ecological) effects. David Lawrence's (2000, 2003b) reviews of the substantial literature and lessons from practice in this area show that practitioners have developed many frameworks, consultation approaches and analytical methodologies as well as detailed sets of significance criteria, benchmarks and checklists for a wide range of parameters: purposes, environmental components, proposal types, sectors and technologies, regions and sites, regulatory contexts and so forth. Some have served very well. But not many pay serious and careful attention to system realities and interrelationships, or to the combination of positive and negative effects that are central to sustainability-based assessment.

It is not possible here to survey the best of current practice in effects evaluation and specify adjustments and additions that would ensure adequate incorporation of sustainability considerations. For illustrative purposes it may be enough to set out a standard generic list of effects significance criteria and to show how a similarly generic sustainability-centred list would differ.

Box 8.1 presents a list of generic criteria for evaluating the significance of effects. The list, drawn largely from Lawrence's work, is not meant to be comprehensive. Moreover, in the literature many of the listed considerations are supported by clarifications and elaborations, including indicators of potential threats to certain kinds of sensitive ecosystems, criteria for judging riskiness, and means of judging the potential adequacy of mitigation measures. Still, the Box 8.1 list indicates the range and substance of the main significance considerations in current environmental assessment literature. Note that the criteria can be applied to individual effects or to sets of effects. Most could also be used in evaluating the overall significance of a proposed undertaking's positive and negative effects.

Box 8.1 Conventional criteria for evaluating the significance of effects

- Are the effects permanent or irreversible?
- Are the receptors highly sensitive, potentially unstable or at the limits of their resilience?
- Are the receptors highly valued?
- Is the intensity, magnitude, scale, extent, duration or frequency of the effects great?
- Are there potentially severe human health and/or ecological risks?
- Are the resources or features to be affected rare, scarce or unique?
- Is there a high level of public controversy?
- Are substantial cumulative effects likely?
- Are existing environmental quality standards likely to be contravened?
- Will the effects conflict with the intent of public policies, plans, programmes, guidelines, criteria or objectives?
- Are transboundary effects likely?
- Will assimilative or carrying capacity be jeopardized?
- Is a high level of resource or energy consumption or waste generation involved?
- Are major inequities in the distribution of effects likely?
- Are the anticipated effects likely?
- Are there important uncertainties about the effects and their context?
- Is the context complex and are unanticipated indirect effects likely?
- May important precedents be set?
- Can the adverse aspects be substantially mitigated?

For comparison and integration, Box 8.2 lists sustainability-based criteria directly related to the eight principles identified in this paper. Each of these considerations needs clarification and elaboration – for example, with indicators of potential threats to ecological integrity, key needs for material security gains and equity improvements, and characteristics of adaptive design. The generic list, nevertheless, illustrates the nature of the broad considerations involved.

Box 8.2 Generic sustainability-based criteria for evaluating the significance of effects

- Could the effects add to stresses that might undermine socio-ecological integrity at any scale, in ways or to an extent that could damage important life support functions?
- Could the effects contribute substantially to ecological rehabilitation and/or reduce stresses that might otherwise undermine socio-ecological integrity at any scale?
- Could the effects provide more economic and other opportunities for human well-being, especially for those now disadvantaged?
- Could the effects reduce economic or other opportunities for human well-being, especially for those now disadvantaged?
- Could the effects reduce material and energy demands and other stresses on socio-ecological systems?
- Could the effects increase material and energy demands and other stresses on socio-ecological systems?
- Could the effects increase equity in the provision of material security and effective choices for future as well as present generations?
- Could the effects reduce equity in the provision of material security and effective choices for future as well as present generations?
- Could the effects displace lasting negative effects from the present to the future?
- Could the effects build government, corporate and public incentives and capacities to apply sustainability principles?
- Could the effects undermine government, corporate or public incentives and capacities to apply sustainability principles?
- Can we expect effective provisions (for example, in the design of the undertaking) to permit effective corrective or adaptive response if unanticipated adverse effects emerge?
- Could the effects contribute to serious or irreversible damage to any of the foundations for sustainability?
- Could the effects contribute positively to several or all aspects of sustainability in a mutually supportive way?
- Could the (positive or negative) effects in any aspect of sustainability have consequences that might undermine prospects for improvement in another aspect?

The sustainability-based criteria complement the more conventional ones. Moreover, they do not introduce entirely new factors. Aspects of most of the Box 8.2 questions are addressed by items in Box 8.1 and have been considered at least to some extent, though often indirectly, in past assessments. This is particularly true of uncertainty, equity and consumption/waste considerations. But direct and explicit attention to sustainability-based criteria will change how significance evaluations are done and affect the resulting judgements.

Both lists refer to effects. While the criteria and underlying concerns are also relevant to the evaluation of individual effects, the focus is on groups of effects. Ultimately what matters is the full set of effects – of the assessed options when the task at hand is selection among alternatives, and of the proposed undertaking when the approval decision must be made. The effects questions are therefore also to be asked in deliberations leading to these decisions, though they are not the only considerations.

Significance and sustainability in decisions on proposals and approvals

The academic and professional literature quite properly insists that the assessment process should extend throughout the life-cycle of an undertaking – from initial conception through planning and implementation to the eventual end – and that all of the many decisions made along the path should be respected as influential contributions. However, as we have noted before, the common practice is to focus on the approval decision. Even when the process just leads to recommendations for those with actual approval authority, the 'approval' decision remains the centre of attention.

That focus is no great problem so long as it accepts that all recommendation and approval decisions depend heavily on the work that has gone before. Ideally, the role of approval stage deliberations is just to confirm the appropriateness of the early planning and analysis, accept the conclusions, and translate the implications into suitable terms and conditions for the go-ahead permitting. In the real world of assessment, this is seldom enough. Most actual assessments benefit from a thorough critical review at the approval stage. But either way, it is best to think of the approval decisions as a package, including review of the earlier judgements – especially about the desirability of the proposed activity in comparison to other alternatives and design options, the acceptability of trade-offs, and the adequacy of enhancement and mitigation measures – as well as the immediate decisions about acceptability, terms and conditions of approval, and monitoring and reporting requirements.

Significance issues arise in all these decisions. The appropriate thoroughness of review depends on the significance of the case, the significance of doubts about the assessment work, and the significance of the remaining controversies. The acceptability of the proposed undertaking depends on the significance of its trade-offs, on its avoidance of possibly significant risks and damages, and on its potential for delivering significant gains. The adequacy of mitigation commitments depends on their likely success in reducing the significance of anticipated risks and damages. The adequacy of proposed enhancements depends on their likely success in increasing the significance of mutually reinforcing gains. And so on.

In sustainability assessments the key considerations in all of these approval stage decisions centre on four realities:

1 Significance should be judged in light of the full set of sustainability criteria, as elaborated for the context of the case involved.
2 The major concerns are overall effects and the most important significance judgements involve overall comparisons. While assessing the significance of individual effects remains important, reviews and decisions at the approval level require the consolidation and aggregation of effects predictions and evaluations. This is a familiar problem in assessments and there are many available tools (frameworks, processes, even quantitative methods) designed to enhance the rigour and consistency of the work. Few of the established tools were designed for use in broad sustainability assessments and most will require considerable adjustment to ensure attention to all the criteria, to account for contextual variations in priorities and to recognize systemic behaviour. However, the proliferation of more comprehensive and better integrated planning and assessment processes is already spurring rapid advance in this area (Dalal-Clayton and Sadler, 2005).
3 Approval decisions turn on comparison of broad alternatives (incorporating mitigation and enhancement options) with particular emphasis on the comparative evaluation of trade-offs. In conventional environmental assessments, the approval recommendation may be based on the acceptability of the proposed undertaking, taking into consideration whether or not it seems likely to bring significant adverse effects. In sustainability assessments, the question is not whether a proposed undertaking is acceptable, but whether it is the best of the practical options available for serving the (critically examined) purposes, for meeting the sustainability criteria, for imposing the least regrettable trade-offs and for maximizing the prospects for mutually reinforcing sustainability gains. Similarly, the focus for terms and conditions of approval, including provisions covering implementation, monitoring and reporting, is maximization of net gains, while avoiding significant damage. This is, as we have seen, a higher test, promising much more positive results. But it also demands more complex evaluations, including attention to the comparative significance of the overall effects discussed above and the significance of trade-offs.
4 Finally, all of these significance decisions are essentially matters of public choice. Assessment is more about valuing than about calculating. The decisions may be guided by established rules, illuminated by expert knowledge, and facilitated by technical methodologies. In the end is it usually proper that the major decisions be made by constituted responsible authorities. Still, the decisions remain expressions of preference, values and understanding, and ought to be discussed, made and justified openly as public judgements. They should also be closely linked with broader deliberations

about current conditions and possibilities, desired sustainable futures, and ways of getting from here to there, which are also matters of preference, values and understanding.

Taken together, these four points suggest that it might be useful to look more closely at trade-off evaluations. Comparison of alternatives in light of their overall effects is clearly central to sustainability assessment. It is the route to the most positive option. But it is also difficult even with careful application of sustainability criteria. Trade-off evaluations that give particular attention to the significance of trade-offs offer a means of dealing with some of the difficulties. Moreover, as we saw in Chapter 6, explicit and open attention to trade-offs in sustainability assessments is an important vehicle for enhancing the transparently of decision making, opening the crucial choices to public scrutiny and engagement.

The particular problem of trade-offs

After sustainability criteria have been applied in the identification and evaluation of overall effects, the results can be used in comparative evaluation of the alternatives. Such evaluations can be done in many ways, but all of them face the dilemmas of choosing between apples and oranges (or, perhaps more often, between garlic and pickled herring). Typically, the competing sets of potential gains and losses differ in ways that frustrate easy comparison.

Examining the significance of the trade-offs involved cannot eliminate this difficulty. However, it does provide a common approach to the comparison. Essentially it centres on:

* identifying main anticipated positive and negative effects of the options under consideration, through application of the sustainability-based decision criteria;
* identifying the evident trade-offs:
* assessing their significance, again in light of the decision criteria (see Box 8.3) and with public and stakeholder participation;
* applying the trade off rules (see Chapter 6 and Appendix 4).

While the questions in Box 8.3 are generic, they respect differences in context. The significance of the positive and negative effects in proposed trade-offs clearly depends on the nature of existing conditions and dynamics, how well these are understood, what qualities are particularly valued, what concerns are most prominent, what other anticipated activities may contribute to cumulative effects, and a host of other factors that differ from one ecosystem and community to the next. All of these are matters that ought to have been raised and specified, at least roughly, in the assessment process long before the stage of trade-off evaluation. And all of them should be captured in the questions listed.

Box 8.3   Generic questions for evaluating the significance of trade-offs

1   Concerning the positive effects expected from a proposed trade-off:
  − Are the positive effects expected to:
    • reduce stresses on ecological integrity at any scale;
    • increase opportunities for more viable and fulfilling livelihoods;
    • reduce material and energy demands and other stresses on socio-ecological systems;
    • increase equity in the distribution of material security and effective choices;
    • maintain the foundations for well-being in future generations;
    • strengthen government, corporate and/or public incentives and capacities to apply sustainability principles;
    • avoid potentially dangerous uncertainties, enhance flexibility and/or strengthen capabilities for response to surprise;
    • foster or support complementary efforts to serve other aspects of sustainability?
  − Are the positive effects expected to:
    • be great in intensity, magnitude, scale, extent, duration or frequency;
    • be permanent and irreversible (or at least sustainable for the foreseeable future);
    • preserve or enhance highly valued ecological or socio-economic qualities;
    • combine with the effects of other undertakings for more positive cumulative results;
    • earn a high level of public approval;
    • encourage performance beyond levels anticipated in regulatory standards and/or public policies;
    • enhance international relations;
    • set important precedents?
  − Are these positive effects expected to reduce concerns that are particularly serious in the context of the case at hand?
  − What level of confidence should be placed on the prediction of these positive effects?
2   Concerning the negative effects expected in a proposed trade-off:
  − Are the adverse effects expected to:
    • damage ecological integrity at any scale in ways or to an extent that could damage important life support functions;
    • reduce economic opportunities for more viable and fulfilling livelihoods;
    • increase material and energy demands and other stresses on socio-ecological systems;
    • reduce equity in the distribution of material security and effective choices;

- displace burdens from present to future generations;
- involve or introduce important uncertainties and/or risks;
- undermine government, corporate or public incentives and capacities to apply sustainability principles;
- introduce or deepen potentially dangerous uncertainties, reduce flexibility and/or otherwise undermine capabilities for response to surprise;
- undermine prospects for improvement in other aspects of sustainability?
- Are the adverse effects expected to:
  - be severe in intensity, magnitude, scale, extent, duration or frequency;
  - be permanent or irreversible (at least for the foreseeable future);
  - involve rare, scarce, unique or otherwise highly valued ecological or socio-economic qualities;
  - combine with the effects of other undertakings for more adverse cumulative results;
  - stir a high level of public controversy;
  - contravene established regulatory standards and/or public policy positions;
  - damage international relations;
  - set important precedents?
- Are these negative effects expected to worsen concerns that are already particularly serious in the context of the case at hand?
- What level of confidence should be placed on the prediction of these negative effects?

Often in comparative assessments involving many relevant factors, some form of weighting is used. This too is a way of taking the context into account. The extent to which weighting is typically necessary for sustainability assessment trade-off evaluations can be debated. As listed here, each question and more specific consideration is as important as the next, but some questions place special emphasis on matters that are 'particularly serious in the context'. Perhaps in most cases, answering these questions will be enough to distinguish the relatively acceptable trade-offs from the relatively intolerable ones. In closer judgements a weighting scheme, properly based on the particular circumstances and preferences, will provide a more clearly defined and transparent basis for the crucial approval decision.

In all cases, however, the general trade-off rules apply. And these include not just substantive requirements (to ensure net gains, to avoid significant adverse effects, to reject displacement of burdens to the future) but also process obligations. All proposed trade-offs must be justified explicitly, with the burden of justifying a trade-off falling on its proponent, in an open process (see Chapter 6 and Appendix 4).

Significance of effort

All of the decisions discussed above – on application, effects and approvals including trade-off evaluations – involve potentially paralyzing complexities. They must address the full suite of sustainability considerations, the great intricacy of interacting human and ecological factors in dynamic complex systems, debatable purposes, competing alternatives, multiple effects, persistent uncertainties and murky futures. Facing this, every assessment will be partial and incomplete. And at every assessment step there will be judgements about how far to go.

This problem is addressed most directly at the application stage of decisions on what undertakings merit assessment and on allocation of various kinds of undertaking to more and less demanding assessment streams. But the issue is revisited throughout the processes and always the question of significance enters. In trade-off evaluations, for example, reasonable expectations for rigour, detail and stakeholder engagement must rest on judgements about the significance of the undertaking, the stream of assessment, the potential importance of the effects and the weightiness of the approval. While these judgements can be well supported by research and analytical tools, they are unavoidably debatable judgements that ought always to be open to scrutiny and challenge.

Decision making about the appropriate level of effort is also affected by factors beyond the character of the undertaking and its effects. It must respect the capacities of the jurisdiction applying the assessment requirements and of the proponent and other participants in the process. As well it must take into account the current place of sustainability assessment in the larger framework of deliberation and decision. The focus, as well as level of effort, that is needed for a sustainability assessment that merely contributes to decisions by mostly economically driven authorities will be very different from what is suitable for sustainability assessment as the core deliberative focus for planning, approval and implementation.

Because of the great variations in undertakings, contexts, capacities and larger decision frameworks, the design and application sustainability assessment must be highly flexible. At the same time, if the various forms and practices are to move decision making towards more consistent and effective attention to sustainability requirements, the fundamentals must be respected wherever the results may be significant.

9

Continuations

The Way Ahead

Proliferation

Today's morning's mail included an announcement from the transportation planners in our regional municipality. They are beginning work on a rapid transit initiative that will link the core areas of the region's three cities and they have proposed a set of terms of reference for the assessment required under provincial and federal law. On the surface the document is unremarkable. It outlines the general boundaries of the anticipated corridor, promises to describe the existing environment and to examine broad alternatives as well as alternative technologies and routes, and anticipates extensive consultation with potentially affected citizens and other interested parties (RMW, 2005). All of these are standard contents. But on page 25 the ground shifts. Exhibit 10 sets out the core decision criteria – the ones to be used in assessing the alternatives (see Appendix 2, final entry) – and none of them are about merely mitigating the most significant negative effects. Instead, there are 6 goals and 15 criteria drawn largely from the region's broader Growth Management Strategy exercise. While the goals and criteria are not categorized or organized in the way favoured in this book, they are nearly as comprehensive. Most of them are about positive contributions and they are clearly intended to cover the full range of considerations that should matter in the choices to be made. The region's planners are undertaking a sustainability assessment.

This is not yet a conventional approach, but it is no longer surprising. The region's earlier efforts to develop a growth management strategy also had amounted to a sustainability assessment of sorts, and the region's innovations are far from peculiar. Last week a consulting firm called about a possible new iron mining project in Labrador. The proponents, looking back at the Voisey's Bay case, were anticipating sustainability assessment obligations. That week also brought a copy of new federal–provincial hearing panel guidelines – for a quarry and marine terminal assessment in Nova Scotia – repeating the increasingly common commitment to examine whether the project would make 'a positive overall contribution towards the attainment of ecological and community sustainability, both at the local and regional levels' (WPQP, 2005).

As well there were emails from a colleague in Western Australia hoping to use the sustainability assessment trade-off rules, and from another in Namibia working on a sustainability-based decision support tool for development assistance applications.

Sustainability assessment initiatives are proliferating quickly around the world. At the April 2004 annual conference of the International Association for Impact Assessment, dozens of presentations described efforts to apply some form of sustainability-based analysis or other adoption of sustainability objectives as core guides for evaluations and decisions. In a recent global survey, Barry Dalal-Clayton and Barry Sadler (2005) seem to have found sustainability assessment (they call it 'sustainability appraisal') initiatives virtually everywhere they looked. Any capable internet search engine will now uncover hundreds of government, corporate, academic, civil society, even personal websites presenting work labelled as sustainability assessment or the equivalent. And these assessment efforts are accompanied by a much more extensive set of evidently serious attempts to define sustainability objectives, identify appropriate indicators, and apply sustainability criteria in important decision making, public and private, at all levels from the local to the global.

The vast diversity of sustainability assessment experiments includes many with tenuous claims to the category. As in the larger realm of asserted commitments to sustainable development, conceptual rigour and effective action are much less common than cheerful visions and passionate endorsement. We should not be surprised. A transition to sustainability-based decisions and practices is no small undertaking. It is complex, demanding and, to many established interests, at least vaguely threatening. As we have seen, the concept of sustainability may be pleasant-sounding, but it stands as a profound critique of business-as-usual. It is a response to evidence that current conditions and trends – social and economic as well as biophysical or ecological – are simply not viable in the long run. It suggests that serious change is required. Resistance, avoidance and hiding behind fuzzy verbiage may be futile, but they are understandable and the concerns involved must be respected.

If our 30-some years of experience with environmental assessment are any guide, the foreseeable future of sustainability assessment will include a good deal more avoidance, fuzziness and overt resistance. Even in the most positive initiatives, we will more often be stumbling towards sustainability than striding with deserved confidence. At the same time, we have learned a good deal over the years of deliberation and experience. We now know enough from the evolution of environmental assessment, enough from the debates about the essential requirements for sustainability, and enough from the common lessons of practice, to identify the common core components of effective sustainability assessment.

The fundamentals and the variations

The fundamentals of sustainability assessment rest on a combination of process and substance. Assessment is the mostly process part. As we have seen, environmental assessment was introduced and has advanced as an attempt to expand the list of what is considered seriously in the conception, planning, approval and implementation of undertakings. It aims to foster (and, if necessary, to force) attention to key public interest factors – environmental concerns, more or less broadly defined – in the decision making processes leading to significant projects, programmes, plans and policies.

There are important substantive elements here too. Defining the 'environment' to include socio-economic and cultural as well as biophysical and ecological factors and their interrelations, affects the substance of deliberations. So do requirements to defend purposes, evaluate alternatives, predict effects, mitigate anticipated damages and prepare for monitoring. But the key contribution of assessment is the process for applying these requirements. And perhaps the most crucial characteristic of the process is that although it imposes the substantial requirements in a more or less standard format, each application is centred on the particulars of the case and its context.

Sustainability brings mostly substance, although it too has process implications. As a concept and a popular term, sustainability has been much maligned, abused and debated. But it has retained an extraordinary level of official commitment from a great diversity of authorities. This adoption, even where it is superficial, is especially remarkable considering that the notion of sustainability represents a critique of the prevailing practices of those authorities. If nothing else, the term sustainability stands in contrast to unsustainability. Its acceptance signals awareness, however muddled and ill-formed, that current conditions and trends are not viable in the long run, and that the reasons for this are as much social and economic as they are biophysical. And this is just the start. Nearly 20 years of sustainability explorations, in application as well as deliberation, now point to important areas of broad agreement on the essentials of sustainability.

The following seven points are now safe assertions about the basic considerations, at least for the purposes of sustainability assessment. Notice that implications of the first five are mostly about the substance of sustainability assessments, but the final two are about the process:

1 Sustainability considerations are comprehensive, including socio-economic as well as biophysical matters, and the interrelations between and interdependency of the two over the long term as well as the short.
2 Precaution is needed because human and ecological effects must be addressed as factors in open, dynamic, multi-scalar systems, which are so complex that full description is impossible, prediction of changes uncertain, and surprise likely.
3 Minimization of negative effects is not enough; assessment requirements must encourage positive steps – towards greater community and ecological sustainability, towards a future that is more viable, pleasant and secure.
4 Corrective actions must be woven together – to serve multiple objectives and to seek positive feedback in complex systems.

5 Sustainability recognizes both inviolable limits and endless opportunities for creative innovation.
6 The notion and pursuit of sustainability are both universal and context dependent; while a limited set of fundamental, broadly applicable requirements for progress towards sustainability may be identified, many key considerations will be location specific – dependent on the particulars of local ecosystems, institutional capacities, socio-economic circumstances and public preferences.
7 In the pursuit of sustainability the means and ends are intertwined and the process is open-ended; there is no end state to be achieved.

Building sustainability assessment

Environmental assessment practice is still highly uneven and the substance and process implications of sustainability still inspire lively debate. But there is now enough experience and understanding to support a broadly applicable generic approach to sustainability assessment. Though it may involve pushing the 'building sustainability assessment' metaphor a little too far, we could say that the seven points above provide the bedrock for construction, and the foundation combines the three components discussed in the preceding chapters: the basic sustainability assessment decision criteria that were presented in Chapter 5 and in Appendix 3; the basic rules for dealing with trade-offs discussed in Chapter 6 and Appendix 4; and the basic principles and structure for process design set out in Chapter 7 and Appendix 5.

This foundation is an early design. The components have been carefully considered and some have been well tested in sustainability initiatives and advanced environmental assessments. But for the foreseeable future of sustainability assessment, everything will be a learning experience. Even if the foundational components in this book prove to have been well conceived, they should be subject to continuing review, reconsideration and improvement.

And like any foundation, this one is just a beginning. It is a base that does not entail a single architecture. For different kinds of undertakings, in different social and ecological places and under different jurisdictions, the generic decision criteria, trade-off rules and process components will need to be elaborated, adjusted and assembled in different ways to suit the context. Sustainability assessment in urban planning should not be the same as sustainability assessment of poverty reduction strategies or community scale biogas projects or policies for regulating food biotechnology applications. Processes for modest undertakings and struggling authorities should not be identical to those for major initiatives and well-resourced participants.

At the same time, serious respect for the foundations is crucial. The predictable temptations in sustainability assessment, as in so much else, will be to focus on immediate demands, to avoid difficult issues, and to make exaggerated claims about comprehensiveness, rigour, innovation and commitment. If sustainability assessment is to be effective, we will have to insist on all of the fundamental components.

The basic decision criteria set out in this book are broad and generic, but they are not optional. Each of them rests on something that is *required* for progress towards sustainability. The eight requirements discussed in Chapter 5 are for gains in:

1   socio-ecological integrity;
2   livelihood sufficiency and opportunity;
3   intragenerational equity;
4   intergenerational equity;
5   resource maintenance and efficiency;
6   socio-ecological civility and democratic governance;
7   precaution and adaptation;
8   immediate and long-term integration.

All of them are crucial and positive steps towards meeting sustainability objectives, and every one of them is needed. Certainly the requirements can be categorized, organized and specified differently. To facilitate effective integration and deal more directly with core sustainability concerns, this list avoids the usual social, ecological and economic 'pillars'. But even pillar-based criteria may serve well enough in many cases, so long as all the core considerations are included and special efforts are made to address the interconnections and interdependencies.

The trade-off rules presented in Chapter 6 are similarly general but indispensable. Most initiatives will involve trade-offs within or between sustainability requirements and how these decisions are made will often be a key determinant of assessment effectiveness and credibility. Here too a variety of formulations can work, and contextual factors (case specific needs, possibilities and limitations) will always be important. But the basic thrust of core trade-off rules needs to be respected wherever trade-offs are to be made:

* Trade-offs must deliver net gains (overall progress towards meeting the requirements for sustainability).
* The burden of justification falls on the proponent of the trade-off.
* No trade-off that involves a significant adverse effect on any sustainability requirement area can be justified (unless the alternative is acceptance of an even more significant adverse effect).
* No displacement of a significant adverse effect from the present to the future can be justified (unless the alternative is displacement of an even more significant negative effect from the present to the future).
* All trade-offs must be accompanied by an explicit sustainability-based justification.
* Proposed compromises and trade-offs must be addressed and justified through processes that include open and effective involvement of all stakeholders.

Finally, all sustainability assessment regimes must respect the core principles of appropriate process design. The crucial process components are a little more difficult to specify than the basic decision criteria and trade-off rules. Not all sustainability assessments will or should be initiated under the formal requirements of a legislated process. Some of the components discussed in Chapter 7 and summarized in Appendix 5 will be irrelevant in informal or ad hoc assessments. Others will have to be adjusted significantly for jurisdictions with few resources and limited administrative capacity. And as with the decision criteria and trade-off rules, the specifics of application may vary greatly from one context to another. Nevertheless, the basics remain. The 19 best practice design principles for sustainability assessment processes set out in Box 7.1 are universally applicable for formal regimes and only the principles referring to legal obligations would be safely ignored in less formal applications.

Together these three – the decision criteria, trade-off rules and process design principles – are the fundamentals of sustainability assessment, and the foundation upon which a colourful and innovative diversity of particular forms can be built. They do not represent a distant ideal. While very elaborate and demanding versions will be needed for some jurisdictions and categories of undertaking, simple and quick versions are no less possible. Applying these fundamentals should be within the grasp of any proponent, any authority, any stakeholder.

Unfortunately, that does not mean that a transition to regular application of the sustainability assessment fundamentals will be easy.

Getting there

The good news is that the current proliferation of sustainability assessment explorations and applications is likely to continue. Some initiatives will be incremental expansions of already advanced environmental assessment or planning processes. Others will focus on the efficiencies to be gained by replacing the ill-organized snarl of existing planning, review and approval processes. Yet others will be the grudging responses of jurisdictions that have long trumpeted their commitment to sustainability and are now facing pressures to act accordingly. But most simply, sustainability assessment will continue to spread because there are so many real problems that demand credibly open public attention, involve intertwined socio-economic/political and biophysical/ecological considerations, and require a long-term perspective.

The difficulty is that taking sustainability assessment seriously and doing it properly entail substantial changes in ways of thinking and in institutional structures as well as in particular criteria and processes. And like all such changes, the transition requires renovation of the house we are living in. The normal and, perhaps, the only realistic response is to favour a gradual, incremental approach.

Incremental change can be effective. Insofar as sustainability assessment is essentially a matter of learning about complex interrelationships, local

priorities and possibilities, mutually reinforcing gains, trade-off comparisons and other such matters, gradual steps are the only means to the desired
ends. Moreover, most sustainability assessment applications so far have been
particular initiatives undertaken in more or less special circumstances. Often
this has involved the creation of ad hoc processes (as, for example, in the
Madhya Pradesh and Tahltan cases discussed in Chapter 4). And even when it
has been possible to use existing legislated regimes (as in the Voisey's Bay environmental assessment case discussed in Chapter 1 and the Greater Victoria
growth management strategy case in Chapter 4), the sustainability assessment
characteristics have usually been introduced by special innovation using an
available opening rather than a clear reflection of conscious legislative intent.

Such ad hocery can be pushed further and both facilitated and complemented by legislative reform. Expanded versions of existing strategic and
project level environmental assessment processes have great potential as
vehicles for sustainability assessment. As we have seen, they have, for some
time, been evolving in the direction of sustainability assessment, and most
environmental assessment processes today incorporate more of the basic
design features of best practice sustainability assessment processes than they
did 10 and 20 years ago. The most advanced of current environmental assessment processes apply explicit evaluation criteria in the preparation, evaluation,
approval and implementation of policies, programmes, plans and projects.
They are also characteristically anticipatory and forward looking, integrative, flexible enough for application to very different cases in very different
circumstances, generally intended to force attention to otherwise neglected
considerations, open to public involvement, and adaptable in ways that suggest
capacity for progressive evolution.

At the same time, few environmental assessment processes today are well
designed for addressing human and ecological effects within complex systems.
Few emphasize attention to maximizing positive long-term improvements.
Most environmental assessment processes fail to ensure effective integration of environmental considerations in the key early decisions on purposes
and preferred options. Too often the results are merely advisory, have little
influence in final decisions, or are incorporated with compromises and trade-
offs that are reached through separate, non-transparent negotiations wherein
environmental matters are still treated as constraints, in conflict with priority
objectives.

Correcting these deficiencies through further gradual progress in the
direction of sustainability assessment is both plausible and desirable. It is not
entirely risk free, however. As we saw in the discussion of transition issues in
Chapter 7, one of the great challenges of environmental assessment processes
has been to force attention to factors that had been generally neglected in
conventional decision making. Effects on ecosystems and communities are
now much more likely to be noted and taken seriously than they were in the
years before environmental assessment. But the gains so far have been limited
and remain fragile in many jurisdictions. Steps to introduce broader sustainability assessment should root environmental considerations more deeply

in the core of deliberations and decisions at the strategic as well as project levels. But because sustainability assessment integrates the ecological and community concerns with other social, economic and political factors, badly designed sustainability assessment processes could reduce direct attention to environmental issues and reverse some of the hard won gains of the past three decades.

New or adjusted assessment processes that ensure attention to the full suite of sustainability requirements, and incorporate all of the basic process characteristics listed above, are unlikely to threaten any past gains. But putting such processes in place is not likely to be achieved in one step. The risk lies in ill-conceived or poorly implemented incremental changes.

Three complementary solutions are available. The first is to continue efforts to clarify sustainability assessment aims and requirements. The better we understand the objectives and their implications, the less likely we are to go astray in implementation efforts. The second is to insist on treating the foundational components – the decision criteria, trade-off rules and process design principles – as an integrated package, subject to adjustment but not compromise. The third is to accept the precautionary reliance on diversity. Experiments with sustainability assessment or its equivalent have been and are being undertaken not just in environmental assessment regimes but also in land use planning, site restoration, infrastructure development, corporate greening, community level development assistance, trade option evaluation and a host of other fields. Moreover, they are using not just conventional law and policy tools but also certification schemes, corporate behaviour codes, ethical investment criteria, sustainable livelihood analyses, multi-stakeholder collaborations and a long list of other mechanisms. Errors and missteps in any one of these areas will be minimally dangerous so long as the same basic agenda is being pursued on many other fronts.

Sustainability assessment is no magic solution. As with the notion of sustainability itself, there is no grand plan, no state to be reached, no blueprint. On the contrary, sustainability assessment accepts that life on Earth is and must be dynamic and diverse, that it is lived in large and intersecting complex systems in which full description is impossible, prediction uncertain, and surprise likely. Accordingly, sustainability assessment is mostly about how decisions are made, not about what conclusions are reached, and even the decision making is messy. While the conceptual basics, as discussed in this book, are not very difficult, they depend on processes and case specific applications of potentially infinite variety and face the additional challenges of incremental implementation. The precautionary principle applies *to* sustainability assessment as well as *in* it.

At the same time, business-as-usual decision making is not a viable option. We live in a world of serious change and significant peril in any event. Determined efforts to build greater sustainability merely aim to bring us a more attractive future than the one we will get otherwise. Sustainability assessment is one tool among many to be used, thoughtfully and carefully, in these efforts. It aims high. Its objective is to make decision making more effectively comprehensive, far-sighted, critical and integrated, while remaining context sensitive and happy with incremental gains. And it responds to global needs for change. But its application is to specific cases and particular decisions. Sustainability assessment is focused on the day to day work of conceiving, selecting, designing and implementing individual policies, programmes, plans and projects. It is about making the world better, one undertaking at a time.

References

Aalborg Charter (1994) *Charter of European Cities and Towns Towards Sustainability*, as approved by the participants at the European Conference on Sustainable Cities and Towns in Aalborg, Denmark, 27 May 1994, www.iclei.org/ICLEI/la21. htm#la21dec

AEUB/CEAA, Alberta Energy and Utilities Board and Canadian Environmental Assessment Agency (1997) *Report of the Joint Panel on Cardinal River Coals Ltd, TransAlta Utilities Corporation – Cheviot Coal Project*, Calgary, AECB

Alexander, D. (2002) 'The resurgence of place', *Alternatives Journal*, vol 28, no 3, 17–20

Anderson, R. C. (1998) *Mid-course Correction: Toward a Sustainable Enterprise – the Interface Model*, Atlanta, Peregrinzilla Press

Appiah-Opoku, S. (2005) *Indigenous Knowledge and Environmental Impact Assessment in Developing Countries: An African Example*, Lewiston, Edwin Mellen Press

Arendt, H. (1958) *The Human Condition*, Chicago, University of Chicago Press

Aristotle (1998) *Nicomachean Ethics*, Ross, W. D., Ackrill, J. L. and Urmson, J. O., (trans), Oxford, Oxford University Press

Arrow, K., Daily, G., Dasgupta, P., Ehrlich, P., Goulder, L., Heal, G., Levin, L., Mäler, K. G., Schneider, S., Starrett, D., Walker, B. (2003) *Are We Consuming too Much?*, Beijer International Institute of Ecological Economics, Stockholm, www.beijer.kva. se/publications/pdf-archive/Disc151.pdf

Athanasiou, T. (1996) *Divided Planet: The Ecology of Rich and Poor*, Boston, Little, Brown and Co

Australia, Commonwealth of (1992) *National Strategy for Ecologically Sustainable Development*, Canberra, Australian Government Publishing Service

Ayres, R., Castaneda, B., Cleveland, C. J., Constanza, R., Daly, H., Folke, C., Hannon, B., Harris, J., Kaufmann, R., Lin, X. Norgaard, R., Ruth, M., Spreng, D., Stern, D. I., van den Bergh, J. C. J. M. (1997) *Natural Capital, Human Capital and Sustainable Economic Growth*, Boston University Center for Energy and Environmental Studies working paper 9702, Boston, CEES, www.bu.edu/cees/research/workingp/9702. html

Beanlands, G. and Duinker, P. (1983) *An Ecological Framework for Environmental Impact Assessment in Canada*, Institute for Resource and Environmental Studies, Halifax, Dalhousie University

Beck, U. (1999) *World Risk Society*, Malden, Polity Press

Becker, B. (1997) *Sustainability Assessment: A Review of Values, Concepts and Methodological Approaches*, Issues in Agriculture 10, Washington, DC, Consultative Group on International Agricultural Research/World Bank

Beetham, D. (1999) *Democracy and Human Rights*, Cambridge, Polity

Bendell, J. (ed) (2000) *Terms for Endearment: Business, NGOs and Sustainable Development*, Sheffield, Greenleaf Publishing

Benería, L. and Bisnath, S. (1996) *Gender and Poverty: An Analysis for Action*, New York, UNDP

Bentham, J. (1834) *Deonthology or the Science of Morality*, Bowring, J. (ed), London, Rees, Orme, Green and Longman

Berger, P. L. and Luckmann, T. (1967) *The Social Construction of Reality: A Treatise in the Sociology of Knowledge*, New York, Anchor Press

Berger, T. R. (1977) *Northern Frontier, Northern Homeland: The Report of the Mackenzie Valley Pipeline Inquiry*, vol 1, Ottawa, Supply and Services Canada

Berkes, F. (1999) *Sacred Ecology: Traditional Ecological Knowledge and Resource Management*, Philadelphia, Taylor and Francis

Berkes, F., Colding, J. and Folke, C. (eds) (2003) *Navigating Social-ecological Systems: Building Resilience for Complexity and Change*, New York, Cambridge University Press

Bertalanffy, L. von (1968) *General System Theory*, New York, George Braziller

Biosphärenreservat Rhön (2004) *Rhön Biosphere Reserve*, www.biosphaerenreservat-rhoen.de/englisch/indexengl.html

Black, M. (2002) *The No-Nonsense Guide to International Development*, Oxford, New Internationalist

Bolin, B., Clark, W., Corell, R., Dickson, N., Faucheux, S., Gallopin, G., Gruebler, A., Hall, M., Huntley, B., Jager, J., Jaeger, C., Jodha, N., Kasperson, R., Kates, R., Lowe, I., Mabogunje, A., Matson, P., McCarthy, J., Mooney H., Moore, B., O'Riordan, T., Schellnhuber, J., Svedin, U. (2000) 'Sustainability Science', statement of the Friibergh workshop on sustainability science, Friibergh, Sweden, 11–14 October 2000, http://sustsci.harvard.edu/keydocs/fulltext/FW_statement.pdf

Bonilla, J. A. et al (78 signatories) (2001) 'Lowell Statement on Science and the Precautionary Principle', statement from the International Summit on Science and the Precautionary Principle hosted by the Lowell Center for Sustainable Production, University of Massachusetts, Lowell, 20–22 September 2001, http://sustainableproduction.org/precaution/

Borgmann, A. (1984) *Technology and the Character of Contemporary Life: A Philosophical Inquiry*, Chicago, University of Chicago Press

Boulding, K. (1966) 'The economics of the coming spaceship earth', in Jarrett, H. (ed) *Environmental Quality in a Growing Economy*, Baltimore, John Hopkins University Press, 3–14

Boyle, M., Gibson, R. B. and Curran, D. (2004) 'If not here, then perhaps not anywhere: Urban growth management as a tool for sustainability planning in British Columbia's Capital Regional District', *Local Environment*, vol 9, no 1, 21–43

Boyle, M., Gibson, R. B., Curran, D. and Foreman, K. (2003) *The Capital Regional District Growth Strategy: Herding Cats onto the Road to Sustainability*, The Assessment and Planning Project, British Columbia Case Report No 6, Integrating the Environment into Planning for Growth Study, ERS, University of Waterloo, www.fes.uwaterloo.ca/research/asmtplan

Bradley, B., Daigger, G.T., Rubin, R. and Tchobanoglous, G. (2002) 'Evaluation of onsite wastewater treatment technologies using sustainable development criteria', *Clean Technologies and Environmental Policy*, vol 4, no 2, 87–99

Brekke, K. A. and Howarth, R. B. (2002) *Status, Growth and Environment: Goods as Symbols in Applied Welfare Economics*, Cheltenham, Edward Elgar

British Columbia, Government of (1996) *Revised Statutes of British Columbia, Chapter 323 Municipal Act, Part 25 – Regional Growth Strategies*, Victoria, Government of British Columbia

Brody, H. (2000) *The Other Side of Eden: Hunters, Farmers and the Shaping of the World*, Vancouver, Douglas & McIntyre

Brunk, C., Haworth, L. and Lee, B. (1991) *Value Assumptions in Risk Assessment: A Case Study of the Alachlor Controversy*, Waterloo, Wilfrid Laurier University Press

Bury, J. B. (1955) *The Idea of Progress*, New York, Dover

Byer, P., Gibson, R. and Lucyk, C. (1992) *Report to the Minister on Reforms to the Environmental Assessment Program* (Environmental Assessment Advisory Committee Referral No 47, Part 2), 27 January 1992

Cairns, J. (1995) 'Ecosocietal restoration: Reestablishing humanity's relationship with natural systems', *Environment*, vol 37, 4–33

Camus, A (1956) *The Rebel: An Essay on Man in Revolt*, New York, Vintage

Canada, Government of (2003a) *Yukon Environmental and Socio-economic Assessment Act*, SC 2003, c7, Bill C-2, assented to 13 May 2003, http://laws.justice.gc.ca/en/Y-2.2/107968.html

Canada, Government of (2003b) *Canadian Environmental Assessment Act*, SC 2003, c9, http://laws.justice.gc.ca/en/c-15.2/text.html, incorporating Government of Canada, *An Act to Amend the Canadian Environmental Assessment Act*, Bill C-9, assented to 11 June 2003

Cardoso, F. H. (2004) *Civil Society and Global Governance*, New York/Geneva, United Nations High Level Panel on UN-Civil Society, www.un.org/reform/pdfs/cardosopaper13june.htm

Carson, R. (1962) *Silent Spring*, Boston, Houghton Mifflin

Checkland, P. (1981) *Systems Thinking, Systems Practice*, Chichester, John Wiley & Sons

CID, The Commission on International Development, Lester B. Pearson, chair (1969) *Partners in Development*, New York, Praeger

CIDA, Canadian International Development Agency (1996) *Human Rights, Democratization and Good Governance: Policy and Objectives for CIDA*, Ottawa/Hull, CIDA, www.acdi-cida.gc.ca/cida_ind.nsf/852562900065549c8525624c0055bafb/498e7f0a30827528852563ff00611f10?OpenDocument

CIDA, Canadian International Development Agency (1997a) *Our Commitment to Sustainable Development*, Ottawa/Hull, CIDA

CIDA, Canadian International Development Agency (1997b) *CIDA'S Policy on Meeting Basic Human Needs*, Ottawa/Hull, CIDA, www.acdi-cida.gc.ca/cida_ind.nsf/0/57BCC6A3A52B339B85256484006187C5?OpenDocument

CIDA, Canadian International Development Agency (2002) *Canada Making a Difference in the World: Strengthening Aid Effectiveness*, Ottawa/Hull, CIDA, www.acdi-cida.gc.ca/aideffectiveness

CIDA, Canadian International Development Agency (2003) *Expanding Opportunities through Private Sector Development*, Ottawa/Hull, CIDA, www.acdi-cida.gc.ca/cida_ind.nsf/AllDocIds/C21E4EA87075A4CE05256CC2006FE2F3?OpenDocument

Clark, N., Perez-Trejo, F. and Allen, P. M. (1995) *Evolutionary Dynamics and Sustainable Development: A Systems Approach*, Aldershot, Edward Elgar

Colborn, T., Dumanoski, D. and Myers, J. P. (1996) *Our Stolen Future*, New York, Dutton

Commoner, B. (1972) *The Closing Circle*, New York, Bantam

Connor, R. and Dovers, S. (2004) *Institutional Changes for Sustainable Development*, Cheltenham, Edward Elgar

Costanza, R., d'Arge, R., de Groot, R., Farber, S., Grasso, M., Hannon, B., Limburg, K., Naeem, S., O'Neill, R. V., Paruelo, J., Raskin, R. G., Sutton, P. and van den Belt, M. (1997) 'The value of the world's ecosystem services and natural capital', *Nature*, vol 387, 253–260

Costanza, R., Low, B., Ostrom, E. and Wilson, J. (eds) (2001) *Institutions, Ecosystems, and Sustainability*, Boca Raton, Lewis Publishers

Counsell, D. and Haughton, G. (undated) *Sustainability Appraisal of Regional Planning Guidance: Final Report*, London, Office of the Deputy Prime Minister, www.odpm. gov.uk/stellent/groups/odpm_planning/documents/page/odpm_plan_607860.hcsp

CRD, Capital Regional District (2003) *Bylaw 2952 – The CRD Regional Growth Strategy*, www.crd.bc.ca/regplan/rgs/whatsnew.htm

Cribb, J. (2003) 'Listening to the community', *CSIRO Sustainability Network Update*, vol 21E, 23 January, 2–8

Crocker, D. (1990) 'Principles of just, participatory, ecodevelopment', in Engels, J. R. and Engels, J. G. (eds) *Ethics of Environment and Development*, Tuscon, University of Arizona Press

CSA, Canadian Standards Association, Working Group of the EIA Technical Committee (1999), *Preliminary Draft Standard: Environmental Assessment*, Draft #14 CSA, Toronto, 26 July

Dalal-Clayton, D. B. and Sadler, B. (2005) *Sustainability Appraisal: A Review of International Experience and Practice*, first draft of work in progress, January, www.iied. org/spa/sa.html

Dalby, S. (2002) *Environmental Security*, Minneapolis, University of Minnesota Press

Daly, H. E. (1977) *Steady-state Economics*, San Francisco, W. H. Freeman

Daly, H. E. (1996) *Beyond Growth: The Economics of Sustainable Development*, Boston, Beacon Press

Daly, H. E. (2002) 'Five policy recommendations for a sustainable economy', in Schor J. B. and Taylor, B. (eds) *Sustainable Planet: Solutions for the Twenty-First Century*, Boston, Beacon Press, 209–221

Daly, H. E. and Cobb, J. B. (1989) *For the Common Good: Directing the Economy Towards Community, the Environment and a Sustainable Future*, Boston, Beacon Press

Dearden, P. and Mitchell, B. (1998) *Environmental Change and Challenge: A Canadian Perspective*, Toronto, Oxford University Press

DeSimone, L. D., Popoff, F. and World Business Council for Sustainable Development (1997) *Eco-efficiency: The Business Link to Sustainable Development*, Cambridge, MIT Press

de Soto, H. (2000) *Mystery of Capital: Why Capitalism Triumphs in the West and Fails Everywhere Else*, New York, Basic Books

Devuyst, D. (1999) 'Sustainability assessment: The application of a methodological framework', *Journal of Environmental Assessment Policy and Management*, vol 1, no 4, 459–487

Devuyst, D. with Hens, L. and De Lannoy, W. (eds) (2001) *How Green Is the City: Sustainability Assessment and the Management of Urban Environments*, New York, Columbia University Press

DFO, Department of Fisheries and Oceans, Canada (1999) Government of Canada response to the Environmental Assessment Panel Report of the proposed Voisey's Bay Mine and Mill Project, August 1999, www.dfo-mpo.gc.ca/COMMUNIC/ Reports/Voisey_e.htm

Diduck, A. (2001) *Learning through Public Involvement in Environmental Assessment: A Transformative Perspective*, PhD Thesis, Waterloo, University of Waterloo

Diduck, A. (2004) 'Incorporating participatory approaches and social learning', in Mitchell, B. (ed) *Resource and Environmental Management in Canada: Addressing Conflict and Uncertainty,* Toronto, Oxford University Press, 497–527

Donnelly, A., Dalal-Clayton, B. and Hughes, R. (1998) *A Directory of Impact Assessment Guidelines,* second edition, London, International Institute for Environment and Development

Dovers, S. (2001) 'Informing institutions and policies', in Venning, J. and Higgins, J. (eds) *Towards Sustainability: Emerging Systems for Informing Sustainable Development,* Sydney, UNSW Press

Douthwaite, R. (1996*) Short Circuit: Strengthening Local Economies for Security in an Unstable World,* Dublin, Lilliput Press

Dryzek, J. S. (1987) *Rational Ecology: Environment and Political Economy,* London, Basil Blackwell

Dryzek, J. S. (1992) 'Ecology and discursive democracy: Beyond liberal capitalism and the administrative state', *Capitalism, Nature and Socialism,* vol 3, no 2, 18–42

Durning, A. (1992*) How Much is Enough? The Consumer Society and the Future of the Earth,* New York, Norton

Easterlin, R. (1974) 'Does economic growth improve the human lot?', in David, P. and Reder, M. (eds) *Nations and Households in Economic Growth,* New York, Academic Press, 89–125

EFTA, European Fair Trade Association (2002) *Challenges of Fair Trade 2001–2003,* European Fair Trade Association, www.eftafairtrade.org/yearbook.asp

Ekins, P. (1992) *A New World Order: Grassroots Movements for Global Change,* London, Routledge

Elliott, L. (2002) 'Global environmental (in)equity and the cosmopolitan project', *CSGR Working Paper No 95/02,* Centre for the Study of Globalisation and Regionalisation (CSGR), Coventry, University of Warwick, www2.warwick.ac.uk/fac/soc/ csgr/ research/workingpapers/2002/wp9502.pdf/

Ellis, S. C. (2005) 'Meaningful consideration? A review of traditional knowledge in environmental decision making', *Arctic,* vol 58, no 1, 66–77

EMCBC, Environmental Mining Council of British Columbia (1999) *The Stikine: A Regional Profile of Mining and Land Use,* www.embc.miningwatch.org/emcbc/ publications/profiles/stikine/

Emond, D. P. (1978) *Environmental Assessment Law,* Toronto, Emond-Montgomery

Epstein, S. (1978) *The Politics of Cancer,* San Francisco, Sierra Club Books

Equator Principles (2003) *The Equator Principles: An Industry Approach for Financial Institutions in Determining, Assessing and Managing Environmental & Social Risk in Project Financing,* www.equator-principles.com/principles.shtml

Esty, D. C. and Porter M. C. (2001) 'Ranking national environmental regulation and performance: A leading indicator of future competitiveness?', in Schwab, K., Porter, M. E. and Sachs, J. (eds) *The Global Competitiveness Report 2001–2002,* New York, Oxford University Press, 78–100

FAO, Food and Agriculture Organization of the United Nations (2002) *Crops and Drops: Making the Best Use of Water for Agriculture,* Rome, FAO

FAO, Food and Agriculture Organization of the United Nations (2003) *The State of Food Insecurity in the World 2003,* Rome, FAO, www.fao.org/docrep/006/j0083e/ j0083e00.htm

Farrell, A., VanDeever, S. D. and Jaeger, J. (2001) 'Environmental assessment: Four under-appreciated elements of design', *Global Environmental Change,* vol 11, 311–333

Flood, R. and Carson, E. (1988) *Dealing with Complexity: An Introduction to the Theory and Application of Systems Science*, New York, Plenum

Franceschi, D. and Kahn, J. (2003) 'Beyond strong sustainability', *International Journal of Sustainable Development and World Ecology*, vol 10, 211–220

Frankfort, H. and Frankfort, H. A. (1949) 'The emancipation of thought from myth', in Frankfort, H., Frankfort, H. A., Wilson, J. and Jacobsen, T. (eds) *Before Philosophy: The Intellectual Adventure of Ancient Man*, Harmondsworth, Penguin, 237–263

Freire, P. (1970) *Pedagogy of the Oppressed*, New York, The Seabury Press

Friedmann, J. (1973) *Retracking America: A Theory of Transactive Planning*, Garden City, Anchor Press/Doubleday

FSC, Forest Stewardship Council (2004a) *FSC Principles and Criteria for Forest Stewardship*, www.fsc.org/fsc/how_fsc_works/policy_standards/princ_criteria

FSC, Forest Stewardship Council (2004b) *About FSC*, www.fsc.org/fsc/about

Funtowicz, S. O. and Ravetz, J. R. (1993) 'Science for a post-normal age', *Futures*, vol 25, 735–755

Gallopín, G. C., Funtowicz, S., O'Connor, M. and Ravetz, J. (2001) 'Science for the twenty-first century: From social contract to the scientific core', *International Journal of Social Science*, vol 168, 219–229

Galtung, J. (1975) *Essays in Peace Research*, Copenhagen, Ejlers

Gardner, G. and Sampat, P. (1998) *Mind Over Matter: Recasting the Role of Materials in Our Lives*, Worldwatch Paper 144, Washington, DC, Worldwatch Institute, www.worldwatch.org/pubs/paper/144/

Gardner, J. E. (1989) 'Decisions making for sustainable development: Selected approaches to environmental assessment and management', *Environmental Impact Assessment Review*, vol 9, 337–366

George, C. (1999) 'Testing for sustainable development through environmental assessment', *Environmental Impact Assessment Review*, vol 19, no 2, 175–200

Gibson, R. B. (1993) 'Environmental assessment design: Lessons from the Canadian experience', *The Environmental Professional*, vol 15, no 1, 12–24

Gibson, R. B. (2000) 'Favouring the higher test: Contribution of sustainability as the central criterion for reviews and decisions under the Canadian Environmental Assessment Act', *Journal of Environmental Law and Practice*, vol 10, no 1, 39–54

Gibson, R. B. (2002) *Specification of Sustainability-based Environmental Assessment Decision Criteria and Implications for Determining 'Significance' in Environmental Assessment*, Ottawa/Gatineau, Canadian Environmental Assessment Agency, www.ceaa-acee.gc.ca/015/0002/0009/index_e.htm

Gibson, R. B. and Hanna, K. S. (2005) 'Progress and uncertainty: The evolution of federal environmental assessment in Canada', in Hanna, K. S. (ed) *Environmental Impact Assessment: Participation and Practice in Canada*, Toronto, Oxford University Press, 16–32

Giri, C. P., Shrestha, S., Foresman, T. W., and Singh, A. (2001) *Global Biodiversity Data and Information*, UN Economic and Social Commission for Asia and the Pacific, www.unescap.org/stat/envstat/stwes-26.pdf

Global Ecovillage Network (undated) *Community Sustainability Assessment (CSA)*, http://gen.ecovillage.org/activities/csa/English/

Goodland, R. (1995) 'The concept of environmental sustainability', *Annual Review of Ecology and Systematics*, vol 26, 1–24

Green, T. L. (1998) *Lasting Benefits from Beneath the Earth: Mining Nickel for Voisey's Bay in a Manner Compatible with the Requirements of Sustainable Development*, report for the environmental assessment hearings into the proposed Voisey's Bay nickel mine, prepared for Innu Nation

GRI, Global Reporting Initiative (2002) *Sustainability Reporting Guidelines*, Boston, GRI, www.globalreporting.org/guidelines/2002.asp

Grossman, G. M. and Krueger, A. B. (1995) 'Economic growth and the environment', *Quarterly Journal of Economics*, vol 110, 353–357

Guijt, I., Moiseev, A. and Prescott-Allen, R. (2001) *IUCN Resource Kit for Sustainability Assessment*, Geneva, IUCN Monitoring and Evaluation Initiative

Gunderson, L. H., Holling, C. S. and Light, S. S. (eds) (1995) *Barriers and Bridges to the Renewal of Ecosystems and Institutions*, New York, Columbia University Press

Gunderson, L. H. and Holling, C. S. (2002) *Panarchy: Understanding Transformations in Human and Natural Systems*, Washington, DC, Island

Harrernoës, P., Gee, D., MacGarvin, M., Stirling A., Keys, J., Wynne, B., Guedes Vaz, S. (2001) *Late Lessons from Early Warnings: The Precautionary Principle 1986–2000*, European Environment Agency, Environmental Issue Report 22, http://reports.eea. eu.int/environmental_issue_report_2001_22/en

Hawken, P., Lovins A. B. and Lovins, L. H. (1999) *Natural Capitalism: Creating the Next Industrial Revolution*, Boston, Little, Brown

Hertwich, E. G. (2005) 'Consumption and the rebound effect: An industrial ecology perspective', *Journal of Industrial Ecology*, vol 9, no 1–2, 85–98

Higgs, E. S. (1997) 'What is good ecological restoration?', *Conservation Biology*, vol 11, no 2, 338–348

Hinterberger, F., Giljum, S., Manner, M., Lorek, S., Luks, F., Omann, I., Stewen, M., Stocker, A., Hutterer, H., Schmidt-Bleek, F. and Strigh, A. (2004) 'Eco-efficient innovation: state of the art and policy recommendations', paper prepared for the *EU Regional Stakeholder Workshop on Eco-efficiency*, Paris, 28 May, www.seri.at/eco-innovation

Hirsh, F. (1976) *Social Limits to Growth*, Cambridge, Harvard University Press

HKPD, Hong Kong Planning Department, Government of (2000) *The Study on Sustainable Development for the 21st Century in Hong Kong*, www.info.gov.hk/ planning/p_study/comp_s/susdev/index_e.htm

HKSDU, Hong Kong Sustainable Development Unit (2002) *Sustainability Assessment*, www.susdev.gov.hk/text/en/su/sus.htm

Hodge, R. A. (2004) 'Mining's seven questions to sustainability: from mitigating impacts to encouraging contribution', *Episodes: Journal of International Geoscience*, vol 27, no 3, 177–185

Hodge, T., Holtz, S., Smith, C. and Hawke Baxter, K. (eds) (1995) *Pathways to Sustainability: Assessing Our Progress*, Ottawa, National Round Table on Environment and Economy

Holling, C. S. (1978) *Adaptive Environmental Assessment and Management*, London, John Wiley and Sons

Holling, C. S. (1986) 'The resilience of terrestrial ecosystems: Local surprise and global change', in Clark, W. C. and Munn, R. E. (eds) *Sustainable Development of the Biosphere*, Cambridge, Cambridge University Press

Homer-Dixon, T. F. (1999) *Environment, Scarcity and Violence*, Princeton, Princeton University Press

Hoon, P., Singh, N. C. and Wanmali, S. (1997) *Sustainable Livelihoods: Concepts, Principles and Approaches to Indicator Development*, New York, UNDP, www.undp.org/sl/ publication/ind2.htm

Hunsberger, C., Gibson, R. B. and Wismer, S. K. (2004) *Increasing Citizen Participation in Sustainability-centred Environmental Assessment Follow-up: Lessons from Citizen Monitoring, Traditional Ecological Knowledge, and Sustainable Livelihood*

Initiatives, Gatineau, Canadian Environmental Assessment Agency, www.ceaa. gc.ca/015/0002/0031/index_e.htm

IAIA, International Association for Impact Assessment (2002) *Strategic Environmental Assessment Performance Criteria*, IAIA special publication series No.1, www.iaia.org/ Non_Members/Pubs_Ref_Material/pubs_ref_material_index.htm

ICLEI, International Council for Local Environmental Initiatives (1996) *Local Agenda 21 Planning Guide: An Introduction to Sustainable Development Planning*, Ottawa, International Development Research Council

ICLEI, International Council for Local Environmental Initiatives (2004) Local Agenda 21 Campaign, www.iclei.org/ICLEI/la21.htm

ICLEI-Europe, International Council for Local Environmental Initiatives, Europe (1997) *Briefing Sheets on Local Agency 21 – Performance Criteria*, Freiburg, ICLEI, www.iclei.org/europe/la21/support/perfcrt.htm

Illich, I. (1978) *Towards a History of Needs*, New York, Pantheon Books

INAC, Indian and Northern Affairs Canada (1996a) *Comprehensive Claims (modern treaties) in Canada*, March, www.ainc-inac.gc.ca/pr/info/trty_e.html

INAC, Indian and Northern Affairs Canada (1996b) *Innu Nation Claim*, May, www. ainc-inac.gc.ca/pr/info/info71_e.html

INAC, Indian and Northern Affairs Canada (2001) *Labrador Inuit Land Claims Agreement-in-Principle Signed*, news release, 25 June, www.ainc-inac.gc.ca/nr/prs/m-a2001/2-01169_e.html

Inco Ltd (2002a) *Inco Limited Agrees on Statement of Principles with Province of Newfoundland and Labrador for Development of Voisey's Bay Deposits*, news release, 11 June, www.incoltd.com/mediacentre/news/default.asp?posting_id=1269

Innu Nation (1996) *Mineral Exploration at Emish (Voisey's Bay)*, updated April, www. innu.ca/voisey1.html

Inuit Tapiriit Kanatami (2004) *Seal Is Good for Us*,www.itk.ca/english/itk/departments/ enviro/wildlife/seal_n.htm

IUCN, UNEP and WWF, International Union for the Conservation of Nature and Natural Resources, United Nations Environment Programme and World Wildlife Fund (1980a) *World Conservation Strategy: Living Resource Conservation for Sustainable Development*, Geneva, IUCN

IUCN, UNEP and WWF, International Union for the Conservation of Nature and Natural Resources, United Nations Environment Programme and World Wildlife Fund (1980b) *Caring for the Earth: A Strategy for Sustainable Living*, Geneva, IUCN

IUCN, International Union for the Conservation of Nature and Natural Resources (undated) *Sustainability Assessment*, www.iucn.org/wssd/themes/eval/search/iucn/ sustassess.htm

Jackson, J. (1993) 'Postscript from an organizer's notebook', in Lerner, S. (ed) *Environmental Stewardship: Studies in Active Earthkeeping*, Waterloo, University of Waterloo Department of Geography Publications, 399–409

Jacobs, M. (1991) *The Green Economy: Environment, Sustainable Development and the Politics of the Future*, London, Pluto Press

Jacobs, P., Gardner, J. and Munro, D. (1987) 'Sustainable and equitable development: an emerging paradigm', in Jacobs, P. and Munro, D. (eds) *Conservation with Equity: Strategies for Sustainable Development*, Cambridge, International Union for the Conservation of Nature

James, J. (1993) *Consumption and Development*, New York, St Martin's Press

Jasanoff, S. and Wynne, B. (1998) 'Science and decision making', in Rayner, S. and Malone, E. (eds) *Human Choice and Climate Change*, vol 1, Columbus, Battelle Press, 1–87

Jenkins, B., Annandale, D. and Morrison-Saunders, A. (2003) 'The evolution of a sustainability assessment strategy for Western Australia', *Environmental and Planning Law Journal*, vol 20, no 1, 56–65

Jevons, W. S. (1865) *The Coal Question: An Inquiry Concerning the Progress of the Nation and the Probable Exhaustion of our Coal Mines*, London, Macmillan

Johnston, T. and Battaile, W. (2001) *2000 Annual Review of Development Effectiveness: From Strategy to Results*, Operations Evaluation Department, Washington, DC, World Bank

Jonaitis, A. (ed) (1991) *Chiefly Feasts: The Enduring Kwakiutl Potlach*, Vancouver, Douglas and McIntyre

Joy, B. (2000) 'Why the future doesn't need us', *Wired*, April, www.wired.com/wired/archive/8.04/joy.html

Karl, M. (1995) *Women and Empowerment: Participation and Decision Making*, London, Zed Books

Kay, J. J. and Schneider, E. (1994) 'Embracing complexity: The challenge of the ecosystem approach', *Alternatives Journal*, vol 20, no 3, 32–39

Kay, J. J., Boyle, M., Regier, H. A. and Francis, G. (1999) 'An ecosystem approach for sustainability: Addressing the challenge of complexity', *Futures*, vol 31, no 7, 721–742

Kerr, M. G. (1999) 'Environment and value at Nortel Networks', in Gibson, R. B. (ed) *Voluntary Initiatives and the New Politics of Corporate Greening*, Peterborough, Broadview Press, 176–181

Kotler, P., Roberto, N. and Lee, N. (2002) *Social Marketing: Improving the Quality of Life*, Thousand Oaks, Sage Publications

Lafferty, W. M. and Langhelle, O. (1999) *Towards Sustainable Development: On the Goals of Development – and the Conditions of Sustainability*, Basingstoke, Macmillan, Houndmills

Lao-Tse (1979) *Tao Te Ching*, Lau, D. C. (ed), Harmondsworth, Penguin

Lappé, A. and Lappé, F. M. (2004) 'The genius of Wangari Maathai', *Alternatives Journal*, vol 30, no 5, 30–31

Lawrence, D. (1997) 'Integrating sustainability and environmental impact assessment', *Environmental Management*, vol 21, no 1, 23–42

Lawrence, D. (2000) *Significance in Environmental Assessment*, Ottawa/Gatineau, Canadian Environmental Assessment Agency, www.ceaa.gc.ca/015/0002/0011/index_e.htm

Lawrence, D. (2003a) *Environmental Impact Assessment: Practical Solutions to Recurrent Problems*, Hoboken, New Jersey, John Wiley and Sons

Lawrence, D. (2003b) *The Significance of Social and Economic Impacts in Environmental Assessment*, Ottawa/Gatineau, Canadian Environmental Assessment Agency, www.ceaa.gc.ca/015/0002/0023/index_e.htm

Leach, M., Mearns, R., and Scoones, I. (1998) 'The institutional dynamics of community-based natural resource management: An entitlements approach', presented at *Crossing Boundaries*, the seventh annual conference of the International Association for the Study of Common Property, Vancouver, British Columbia, Canada, June 10–14, http://dlc.dlib.indiana.edu/archive/00000092/

Lee, K. N. (1993) *Compass and Gyroscope: Integrating Science and Politics for the Environment*, Washington, DC, Island Press

Leiss, W. (1976) *The Limits to Satisfaction: An Essay on the Problem of Needs and Commodities*, Toronto, University of Toronto Press

Leopold, A. (1970) 'The land ethic', in Leopold, A. (ed) *A Sand County Almanac*, New York, Ballantine

Lifton, R. J. (1969) *Boundaries*, Toronto, Canadian Broadcasting Corporation

Lindblom, C. E. (1959) 'The science of muddling through', *Public Administration Review*, vol 19, no 2, 79–88

Linder, S. B. (1970) *The Harried Leisure Class*, New York, Columbia University Press

Lister, N. M. and Kay, J. J. (2000) 'Celebrating diversity: Adaptive planning and biodiversity conservation', in Bocking, S. (ed) *Biodiversity in Canada: Ecology, Ideas and Action*, Peterborough, Broadview Press, 189–218

LKDFN, Lutsel K'e Dene First Nation and Ellis, S. (2004) *Ni hat'ni – Watching the Land: Results and Implications of 2002–2003 Monitoring Activities in the Traditional Territory of the Lutsel K'e Denesoline*, final report to the West Kitikmeot Slave Study Society and the Walter and Duncan Gordon Foundation, October 2003, updated February 2004, Lutsel K'e, NWT, LKDFN

Lomborg, B. (2001) *The Skeptical Environmentalist: Measuring the Real State of the World*, Cambridge, Cambridge University Press

Ludwig, D. (2001) 'The era of management is over', *Ecosystems*, vol 4, 758–764

Macpherson, C. B. (1973) *Democratic Theory: Essays in Retrieval*, Oxford, Clarendon Press

Maltais, A., Nilsson, M. and Persson, A. (2002) *Sustainability Impact Assessment of WTO Negotiations in the Major Food Crops Sector*, Stockholm, Stockholm Environment Institute

Martinez-Alier, J. (2002) *The Environmentalism of the Poor: A Study of Ecological Conflicts and Valuation*, Cheltenham, Edward Elgar

Maslow, A. (1970) *Motivation and Personality*, New York, Harper and Row

May, R. (1972) *Power and Innocence: A Search for the Sources of Violence*, New York, Norton

McCormick, J. (1989) *Reclaiming Paradise: The Global Environmental Movement*, Bloomington, Indiana University Press

McDonough, W. and Braungart, M. (1992) *The Hannover Principles: Design for Sustainability*, New York, W. McDonough Architects

McDonough, W. and Braungart, M. (2002) *Cradle to Cradle: Remaking the Way We Make Things*, New York, North Point Press

McHarg, I. (1998) 'Architecture in an ecological view of the world (1970)', in McHarg, I. L. and Steiner, F. R. (eds) *To Heal the Earth: Selected Writings of Ian McHarg*, Washington, DC, Island Press

McKenzie-Mohr, D. (1999) *Fostering Sustainable Behavior: An Introduction to Community-based Social Marketing*, Gabriola Island, New Society Publishers

McQuaig, L. (1998) *The Cult of Impotence: Selling the Myth of Powerlessness in the Global Economy*, Toronto, Viking

MEA, Millennium Ecosystem Assessment (2005) *Living Beyond Our Means: Natural Assets and Human Well-being, Statement from the Board*, World Resources Institute, March, www.millenniumassessment.org/en/products.aspx

Meadows, D. H., Meadows, D. L., Randers, J. and Behrens, W. W. (1972) *The Limits to Growth: A Report for the Club of Rome's Project on the Predicament of Mankind*, New York, Potomac Associates

Mebratu, D. (1998) 'Sustainability and sustainable development: Historical and conceptual review', *Environmental Impact Assessment Review*, vol 18, 493–520

Midgley, G. (2003) 'Science as systemic intervention: Some implications of systems thinking and complexity for the philosophy of science', *Systemic Practice and Action Research*, vol 16, no 2, 77–97

Milbrath, L. (1989) *Envisioning a Sustainable Society: Learning Our Way Out*, Albany, State University of New York Press

Mishan, E. J. (1967) *The Costs of Economic Growth*, London, Pelican

MMSD, Mining, Minerals and Sustainable Development Project (2002) *Breaking New Ground: The Report of the MMSD Project*, London, Earthscan, www.iied.org/mmsd/finalreport

MMSD-NA, Mining, Minerals and Sustainable Development Project North America, Task 2 Work Group (2002) *Seven Questions to Sustainability: How to Assess the Contribution of Mining and Minerals Activities*, Winnipeg, IISD

Moffat, I. (1995) *Sustainable Development: Principles, Analysis and Policies*, New York, Parthenon

Narayan, D., Patel, R., Schafft, K., Rademacher, A. and Koch-Schulte, S. (2000a) *Voices of the Poor: Can Anyone Hear Us?*, Washington, DC, The World Bank, www.worldbank.org/poverty/voices/reports.htm#cananyone

Narayan, D., Chambers, R., Shah, M. K. and Petesch, P. (2000b) *Voices of the Poor: Crying Out for Change*, Washington, DC, The World Bank, www.worldbank.org/poverty/voices/reports.htm#crying

NASA, Earth Observation Laboratory (2004) *The Carbon Cycle: The Human Role*, http://earthobservatory.nasa.gov/Library/CarbonCycle/carbon_cycle4.html

Nelson, P., Azare, C., Sampong E., Yeboah, B., Fosu, A., Tagu, P., Dare, O. and Darko-Mensah, E. (2004) *SEA and the Ghana Poverty Reduction Strategy*, paper presented at the International Association for Impact Assessment 2004 Conference, Vancouver, Canada, 28 April

Newfoundland and Labrador, Government of (1999) *The Response of the Government of Newfoundland and Labrador to the Voisey's Bay Environmental Assessment Panel Recommendations*, news release, August 1999, www.gov.nf.ca/releases/1999/envlab/Vbay-sum.htm

Newfoundland and Labrador, Government of (2002a) *Voisey's Bay Project Statement of Principles*, 11 June 2002, www.gov.nf.ca/releases/2002/exec/0611n03.htm

Newfoundland and Labrador, Government of (2002b) Voisey's Bay Project: Backgrounder – Aboriginal Involvement in Voisey's Bay, 11 June 2002, www.gov.nf.ca/voiseys/news/backgrounder9.htm

Nicolis, G., and Prigogine, I. (1977) *Self-organization in Non-equilibrium Systems*, New York, J. Wiley and Sons

Nicolis, G., and Prigogine, I. (1989) *Exploring Complexity*, New York, Freeman

Nilsson, H. (2005) *The State of Demand-Side Management and Energy Efficiency in the World*, International Energy Agency Demand-Side Management Programme, http://dsm.iea.org

Norgaard, R. B. (1995) 'Intergenerational commons, globalization, economism, and unsustainable development', in Freese, L. (ed) *Advances in Human Ecology*, vol 4, Greenwich, JAI Press

Nozick, M. (1992) *No Place Like Home: Building Sustainable Communities*, Ottawa, Canadian Council on Social Development

Nussbaum, M. C. and Sen, A. K. (1993) *The Quality of Life*, Oxford, Clarendon Press

Oakes, J. (1987) 'Raw seal and the spirit of plenty', *Alternatives Journal*, vol 15, no 1, 79

O'Brien, M. (2000) *Making Better Environmental Decisions: An Alternative to Risk Assessment*, Cambridge, MIT Press

O'Brien, M. (2003) 'Critiques of the precautionary principle', *Rachel's Environment and Health News*, no 781, www.rachel.org/bulletin/index.cfm?St=4

OECD (Organisation for Economic Co-operation and Development) (1996) *Shaping the 21st Century: The Contribution of Development Co-operation*, Paris, OECD Development Assistance Committee

OECD (1997a) *Towards a New Global Age: Challenges and Opportunities*, policy report, Paris, OECD

OECD (1997b) *The World in 2020: Towards a New Global Age*, Paris, OECD

OECD (1997c) *Sustainable Consumption and Production*, Paris, OECD

Ontario, Province of (2001) *Planning Act*, Revised Statutes of Ontario 1990, chap P13, www.e-laws.gov.on.ca/DBLaws/Statutes/English/90p13_e.htm#BK4

O'Riordan, T. (1996) 'Democracy and the sustainability transition', in Lafferty, W. M. and Meadowcroft, J. (eds) *Democracy and the Environment*, Cheltenham, Edward Elgar

Orr, D. W. (1994) *Earth in Mind: On Education, Environment and the Human Prospect*, Washington, DC, Island

Östensson, O. and Uwizeye-Mapendano, A. (2000) 'Macro-economic considerations and linkages', paper for the *Growth and Diversification in Mineral Economies: Regional Workshop for Mineral Economies in Africa*, Cape Town, South Africa, 7–9 November 2000, http://r0.unctad.org/infocomm/Diversification/cape/word/ostensson.doc

Paehlke, R. and Torgerson D. (eds) (1990) *Managing Leviathan: Environmental Politics and the Administrative State*, Peterborough, Broadview Press

Paehlke, R. (2003) *Democracy's Dilemma: Environment, Social Equity and the Global Economy*, Cambridge, MIT Press

Panday, D. R. and Mishra, C. (1998) *Nepal Human Development Report 1998*, Kathmandu, Nepal South Asia Centre

Parson, E. and Clark, W. (1995) 'Sustainable development as social learning: theoretical perspectives and practical challenges for the design of a research program', in Gunderson, L. H., Holling, C. S. and Light, S. S. (eds) *Barriers and Bridges to the Renewal of Ecosystems and Institutions*, New York, Columbia University Press, 428–460

Partidário, M. R. and Clarke, R. (eds) (2000) *Perspectives on Strategic Environmental Assessment*, Boca Raton, Lewis Publishers

Pateman, C. (1970) *Participation and Democratic Theory*, Cambridge, Cambridge University Press

Patterson, M. J. (2000) 'Natural capitalism', *New Internationalist*, vol 329, November, 14–15

Pauly, D., Christensen. V., Guénette, S., Pitcher, T. J., Sumaila, U. R., Walters, C. J., Watson, R. and Zeller, D. (2002) 'Towards sustainability in world fisheries', *Nature*, vol 418, 689–695

Pearce, D. W. (1988) 'Economics, equity, and sustainable development', *Futures*, vol 20, no 6, 598–605

Pearce, D. W., Barbier, E. and Markandya, A. (1990) *Sustainable Development: Economics and Environment in the Third World*, Aldershot, Edward Elgar

Pearce, D. W. and Turner, R. K. (1990) *Economics of Natural Resources and the Environment*, Baltimore, Johns Hopkins University Press

Pezzey, J. (1989) *Economic Analysis of Sustainable Growth and Sustainable Development*, Working Paper 15, Environment Department, Washington, DC, World Bank

Pezzoli, K. (1997) 'Sustainable development: A transdisciplinary overview of the literature', *Journal of Environmental Planning and Management*, vol 40, 549–574

Pimbert, M. (2000) *Transforming Bureaucracies: Institutional Participation and People-centred Process in Natural Resource Management – An Annotated Bibliography*, London, International Institute for Environment and Development

Pokorny, D. (1999a) 'Summary of activities at the Rhön Biosphere Reserve, Germany', *Biosphere Reserves in Canada Newsletter*, vol 11, article 20, www.biosphere-canada.ca/publications/newsletters-bulletins/11/newsletter11.pdf

Pokorny, D. (1999b) 'A window on Germany's Biosphere Reserves', *Proceedings of Leading Edge '99: Making Connections*, Georgetown, Ontario, Niagara Escarpment Commission/Niagara Escarpment World Biosphere Reserve, CD ROM

Pokorny, D. (2001a) 'Examples of the Rhön Biosphere Reserve, Germany', in UNESCO, *Seville +5 International Meeting of Experts, Pamplona, Spain, Proceedings*, MAB Report Series no 69, Paris, UNESCO, 123–125, http://unesdoc.unesco.org/images/0012/001236/123605m.pdf

Pokorny, D. (2001b) 'Biosphere reserves for developing quality economies: examples from the Rhön Biosphere Reserve, Germany', *Parks*, vol 11, no 1, 15–17

Polanyi, K. (1957) *The Great Transformation*, Boston, Beacon

Popp, D. (1997) Biosphere Reserve Rhön: A Model for Rural Regional Development, www.mluri.sari.ac.uk/livestocksystems/faunus/faunus2/rhon.htm

Porter, M. E. and van der Linde, C. (1995) 'Green and competitive: Ending the stalemate', *Harvard Business Review*, vol 73, no 5, September–October, 120–155

Ravetz, J. (2000) 'Integrated assessment for sustainability appraisal in cities and regions', *Environmental Impact Assessment Review*, vol 20, 31–64

Redclift, M. (1987) *Sustainable Development: Exploring the Contradictions*, London, Methuen

Rees, W. (1999) 'Consuming the Earth: The biophysics of sustainability', *Ecological Economics*, vol 29, 23–27

Rees, W. (2001) 'Ecological footprint, concept of', in Levin, S. A. (ed) *Encyclopedia of Biodiversity*, vol 2, San Diego, Academic Press

Reid, W. V. et al (2005) *Millennium Ecosystem Assessment Synthesis Report*, pre-publication final draft approved by the Millennium Assessment Board 23 March 2005,www.millenniumassessment.org/en/index.aspx

Relph, E. (1992) 'Modernity and the reclamation of place', in Seamon, D. (ed) *Dwelling, Seeing and Designing: Toward a Phenomenological Ecology*, New York, State University of New York Press

Renner, M. (1996) *Fighting for Survival: Environmental Decline, Social Conflict and the New Age of Insecurity*, New York, Norton

Riddell, R. (1981) *Ecodevelopment*, Westmead, Gower

RMW, Regional Municipality of Waterloo (2005) *Individual Environmental Assessment Terms of Reference: Rapid Transit Initiative*, Kitchener, RMW, 18 April

Robèrt, K. H. (2000) 'Tools and concepts for sustainable development, how do they relate to a general framework for sustainable development and to each other?', *Journal of Cleaner Production*, vol 8, 243–254

Robinson, A. (1999) 'Native groups want ruling overturned: Taking Ottawa to court over decision to allow Voisey's Bay to go ahead without settlements', Toronto *Globe and Mail*, 8 September 1999, B6

Robinson, J. and Tinker, J. (1997) 'Reconciling ecological, economic and social imperatives: A new conceptual framework', in Schrecker, T. (ed) *Surviving Globalism: Social and Environmental Dimensions*, New York, St Martin's Press, 71–94

Robinson, J. and Tinker, J. (1998) 'Reconciling ecological, economic and social imperatives', in Schnurr, J. and Holtz, S. (eds) *The Cornerstone of Development: Integrating Environmental, Social and Economic Policies*, Ottawa, International Development Research Centre, Boca Raton, Lewis Publishers, 9–43

Robinson, J. B., Francis G., Legge, R. and Lerner, S. (1990) 'Defining a sustainable society: values, principles and definitions', *Alternatives*, vol 17, no 2, 36–46

Robinson, N. A. (ed) (1993) *Agenda 21: Earth's Action Plan – Annotated*, New York, Oceana

Roue, M. and Nakashima, D. (2002) 'Knowledge and foresight: The predictive capacity of traditional knowledge applied to environmental assessment', *International Social Science Journal*, vol 54, no 3, 337–347

Runyan, C. (1999) 'Action on the front lines', *WorldWatch*, November/December, 12–21

Sachs, J. D. (2001) 'The strategic significance of global inequality', *The Washington Quarterly*, vol 24, no 3, 187–198

Sachs, W. (1999) *Planet Dialectics: Explorations in Environment and Development*, London, Zed Books

Sadler, B. (1996) *Environmental Assessment in a Changing World: Evaluating Practice to Improve Performance*, International Study on the Effectiveness of Environmental Assessment, Final Report, Canadian Environmental Assessment Agency and the International Association for Impact Assessment, www.ceaa.gc.ca/017/012/iaia8_e.pdf

Sainath, P. (1996) *Everybody Loves a Good Drought*, New Delhi, Penguin

Schama, S. (1996) *Landscape and Memory*, Toronto, Vintage

Schmidt-Bleek, F. B. (2000) *Factor 10 Manifesto*, Carnoules, Factor 10 Institute, www.factor10-institute.org/pdf/F10Manif.pdf

Schrecker, T. F. (1984) *Political Economy of Environmental Hazards*, Law Reform Commission, Ottawa, Law Reform Commission of Canada

Seattle, City of, Office of Sustainability and Environment (2001) *Sustaining Seattle: Our Defining Challenge*, Seattle, OSE, www.ci.seattle.wa.us/environment/About_OSE.htm

Sen, A. (1985) *Commodities and Capabilities*, Amsterdam, North-Holland

Senécal, P., Sadler, B., Goldsmith, B., Brown, K. and Conover, S. (1999) *Principles of Environmental Impact Assessment Best Practice*, International Association for Impact Assessment and Institute of Environmental Assessment, www.iaia.org/Non_Members/Pubs_Ref_Material/pubs_ref_material_index.htm

Sharma, B. D. (1994) 'On sustainability', in Tobias, M. and Cowan, G. (eds) *The Soul of Nature*, New York, Continuum, 271–278

Shiva, V. (ed) (1994) *Close to Home: Women Reconnect Ecology, Health and Development*, Gabriola Island, New Society Publishers

SIDA, Swedish International Development Agency (2003a) *Policy Guidelines for SIDA's Support to Private Sector Development*, www.sida.se/Sida/jsp/polopoly.jsp?d=171&a=5184

SIDA, Swedish International Development Agency (2003b) *Making Markets Work for the Poor: Challenges to SIDA's Support to Private Sector Development*, www.sida.se/Sida/jsp/polopoly.jsp?d=1265&a=22425

Simon, J. and Kahn, H. (1984) *The Resourceful Earth: A Response to Global 2000*, Oxford, Blackwell

Sinclair, J. and Diduck, A. (1995) 'Public education: An undervalued component of the environmental assessment public involvement process', *Environmental Impact Assessment Review*, vol 15, 219–240

Singh, N. and Ham, L. (eds) (1995) *Community-based Resources Management and Sustainable Livelihoods: The Grass-roots of Sustainable Development*, Winnipeg, International Institute for Sustainable Development

Singh, N. and Titi, V. (1994) *In Search of Sustainable Livelihoods: Adaptive Strategies of the Poor in Arid and Semi-arid Lands*, Winnipeg, International Institute for Sustainable Development

Singh, N. and Titi, V. (eds) (1995) *Empowerment for Sustainable Development: Towards Operational Strategies*, London, Zed Books

Stirling, A. (2000) *On Science and Precaution in the Management of Technological Risk*, vol 1, a synthesis report of case studies, a European Science and Technology Observatory project report prepared for the European Commission Joint Research Centre Institute for Prospective Technological Studies, Seville, http://esto.jrc.es/detailshort.cfm?ID_report=289

Stirling, A. (ed) (2001) *On Science and Precaution in the Management of Technological Risk*, vol 2, case studies, a European Science and Technology Observatory project report prepared for the European Commission Joint Research Centre Institute for Prospective Technological Studies, Seville, http://esto.jrc.es/detailshort.cfm?ID_report=809

Swift, J. (1999) *Civil Society in Question*, Toronto, Between the Lines

Tahltan First Nation and IISD, International Institute for Sustainable Development (2004) *Out of Respect: The Tahltan, Mining, and the Seven Questions to Sustainability Report of the Tahltan Mining Symposium*, 4–6 April 2003, Dease Lake, British Columbia, Winnipeg, IISD

Thompson, J (2003) 'Intergenerational equity: Issues of principle in the allocation of social resources between this generation and the next', *Research Paper no 7 2002–03*, Parliamentary Library, Information and Research Services, Canberra, Commonwealth of Australia

Tobias, M. and Cowan, G. (eds) (1994) *The Soul of Nature*, New York, Continuum

Torrie, R. and Parfett, R. (2000) 'Mind the Gap', *Alternatives Journal*, vol 26, no 2, 22–29

Truman, H. S. (1949) *Inaugural Address, 20 January 1949*, www.usembassy.de/usa/etexts/speeches/pres53.htm

UK, Government of the United Kingdom (1999a) *A Better Quality of Life: A Strategy for Sustainable Development for the United Kingdom*, www.sustainable-development.gov.uk/uk_strategy/index.htm

UK, Government of the United Kingdom (1999b) *Quality of Life Counts*, www.sustainable-development.gov.uk/sustainable/quality99/index.htm

UK, Countryside Agency (2000) *Planning Tomorrow's Countryside*, www.countryside.gov.uk/Publications/articles/Publication_tcm2-4220.asp

UK DETR (United Kingdom Department of the Environment, Transport and the Regions) (2000a) *Sustainability Appraisal of Regional Planning Guidance: Good Practice Guide*, www.odpm.gov.uk/stellent/groups/odpm_planning/documents/page/odpm_plan_606126.hcsp

UK DETR (2000b) *Guidance on Preparing Regional Sustainable Development Frameworks*, www.odpm.gov.uk/stellent/groups/odpm_planning/documents/page/odpm_plan_606126.hcsp

UN (United Nations) (1992) *Report of the United Nations Conference on Environment and Development* , Annex I, Rio Declaration on Environment and Development, A/CONF.151/26 (vol 1), www.un.org/documents/ga/conf151/aconf15126-1annex1.htm

UNDP (United Nations Development Programme) (1993) *Human Development Report 1993*, Oxford, Oxford University Press
UNDP (1994) *Human Development Report 1994*, Oxford, Oxford University Press
UNDP (1997) *Governance for Sustainable Human Development*, http://mirror.undp.org/magnet/Docs/guidepol.htm
UNDP (1998) *Human Development Report 1998*, Oxford, Oxford University Press
UNDP (2001) *Human Development Report 2001*, Oxford, Oxford University Press
UNDP (2002) 'Civic engagement', *Essentials*, no 8, UNDP, Evaluation Office, www.undp.org/eo/documents/essentials/CivicEngagement-Final31October2002.pdf
UNEP (United Nations Environment Programme) (2002) *Global Environmental Outlook 3*, London, Earthscan
UNFPA (United Nations Population Fund) (2002) *State of World Population 2002:People, Poverty and Possibilities – Making Development Work for the Poor*, New York, UNFPA
UNICEF (United Nations Children's Fund) (1999) *Children in Jeopardy:The Challenge of Freeing Poor Nations from the Shackles of Debt*, New York, UNICEF
UNPD (United Nations Population Division) (2003) *World Population Prospects: The 2002 Revision – Highlights*, www.un.org/esa/population/publications/wpp2002/WPP2002-HIGHLIGHTSrev1.PDF
US Congress (1970) *The National Environmental Policy Act of 1969*, Pub L 91-190, 42 USC 4321-4347, 1 January
Vaidyanathan, G. (2002) 'In Gandhi's footsteps: Two unusual development organizations foster sustainable livelihoods in the villages of India', *Alternatives Journal*, vol 28, no 2, 32–37
van der Laar, E. and Vreuls, H. (2004) *International Database on Demand-Side Management Technologies and Programmes (INDEEP) Analysis Report 2004*, International Energy Agency Demand-Side Management Programme, http://dsm.iea.org/
Viederman, S. (1994) *Five Capitals and Three Pillars of Sustainability*, New York, Jessie Smith Noyes Foundation
Vitousek, P., Ehrlich, P. R., Ehrlich, A. H. and Matson, P. (1986) 'Human appropriation of the products of photosynthesis', *BioScience*, vol 36, no 6, 368–373
Vitousek, P. M., Mooney, H. A., Lubchenco, J. and Melillo, J. M. (1997) 'Human domination of Earth's ecosystems', *Science*, vol 277, 494–499
Voisey's Bay Mine and Mill Environmental Assessment Panel (1997) *Environmental Impact Statement Guidelines for the Review of the Voisey's Bay Mine and Mill Undertaking*, 20 June
Voisey's Bay Mine and Mill Environmental Assessment Panel (1999) *Report on the Proposed Voisey's Bay Mine and Mill Project*, March, www.ceaa-acee.gc.ca/0009/0001/0001/0011/0002/contents_e.htm
Wackernagel, M. and Rees, W. R. (1996) *Our Ecological Footprint*, Gabriola Island, New Society Press
Walters, C. J. and Holling, C. S. (1990) 'Large-scale management experiments and learning by doing', *Ecology*, vol 71, no 6, 2060–2068
Waltner-Toews, D. and Lang, T. (2000) 'A new conceptual base for food and agricultural policy: The emerging links between agriculture, food, health, environment and society', *Global Change and Human Health*, vol 1, 116–130
Waltner-Toews, D. (2004) *Ecosystem Sustainability and Health: A Practical Approach*, New York, Cambridge University Press
Wanmali, S. (1998) *Participatory Assessment and Planning for Sustainable Livelihoods*, New York, United Nations Development Programme, www.undp.org/sl/Documents/documents.htm

Ward, B. and Dubos, R. (1972) *Only One Earth: The Care and Maintenance of a Small Planet*, London, Deutsch

Washington State, Department of Ecology (2003) *A Field Guide to Sustainability*, www. ecy.wa.gov/biblio/0304005.html

Watson, B. (2001) *The Carbon Cycle*, IPCC Briefings at the Conference of the Parties to the UNFCCC, Sixth Session part two, www.ipcc.ch/present/presentations.htm

WBCSD, World Business Council for Sustainable Development (2000) *Eco-efficiency: Creating More Value with Less Impact*, Geneva, WBCSD, www.wbcsd.org/ (go to eco-efficiency > publications)

WBCSD, World Business Council for Sustainable Development (2002) *Walking the Talk: The Business Case for Sustainable Development*, Sheffield, Greenleaf

WCED, World Commission on Environment and Development, G. H. Brundtland, chair (1987) *Our Common Future*, Oxford/New York, Oxford University Press

Weber, E. P. (2003) *Bringing Society Back In: Grassroots Ecosystem Management, Accountability and Sustainable Communities*, Cambridge, MIT

Weizsacker, E. von, Lovins, A. B. and Lovins, L. H. (1997) *Factor Four: Doubling Wealth, Halving Resource Use*, London, Earthscan

Western Australia, Government of (2003) *Hope for the Future: The Western Australian State Sustainability Strategy – A Vision for Quality of Life in Western Australia*, Perth, Department of the Premier and Cabinet

WHO, World Health Organization (2000) *Nutrition for Health and Development: A Global Agenda for Combating Malnutrition*, Geneva, WHO, www.who.int/nut/ publications.htm#pem

WHO (2004) *Meeting the Millennium Development Goals Drinking-water and Sanitation Target: A Mid-term Assessment of Progress*, Geneva, WHO/UNICEF, www.who. int/water_sanitation_health/monitoring/jmp2004/en/

Wignaraja, P. (1996) 'Towards an empowering model of macro/micro policy adjustment', in Singn, N. C. and Strickland, R. (1995) *From Vision to Legacy: Sustainability, Poverty and Policy Adjustment*, Winnipeg, International Institute for Sustainable Development, 111–142

Wood, C. (2003) *Environmental Impact Assessment: A Comparative Review*, second edition, Harlow, Essex, Pearson Education

WPQP, Whites Point Quarry and Marine Terminal Project Joint Review Panel (2005) *Environmental Impact Statement Guidelines for the Review of the Whites Point Quarry and Marine Terminal Project*, March, www.ceaa.gc.ca/010/0001/0001/0023/ nr050331_e.htm

Wright, R. (2004) *A Short History of Progress*, Toronto, House of Anansi Press

WSSD, World Summit on Sustainable Development (2002) *The Road from Johannesburg: What was Achieved and the Way Forward*, New York, United Nations, WSSD, www. johannesburgsummit.org/

WWF (Worldwide Fund for Nature) (2002) *Living Planet Report 2002*, Gland, WWF International, www.wwf.org.uk/filelibrary/pdf/livingplanet2002.pdf

WWF (2004) *Living Planet Report 2004*, Gland, WWF International, www.wwf.org. uk/livingplanet

Young, R. A. (2001) *Uncertainty and the Environment*, Cheltenham, Edward Elgar

Zarsky, L. (1999) *Civil Society and Clean Shared Growth in Asia: Towards a Stakeholder Model of Environmental Governance*, paper presented at the Outlook for Environmentally Sound Development Policies workshop organized by the US–Asia Environmental Partnership and the Asian Development Bank, Manila, Philippines, 2–3 August, www.nautilus.org/archives/papers/enviro/zarsky-usaep.html

Appendix 1

Selected Conceptions of Sustainability

Source	Components, principles, core objectives
Stockholm conference, 1972, five category grouping of the 26 conference principles, as summarized by McCormick (1989)	• Natural resources should be safeguarded and conserved, the Earth's capacity to produce renewable resources should be maintained and non-renewable resources should be shared. • Development and environmental concern should go together, and less developed countries should be given every assistance and incentive to promote rational management. • Each country should establish its own international standards of environmental management and exploit resources as they wish, but should not endanger other states. There should be international cooperation aimed at improving the environment. • Pollution should not exceed the capacity of the environment to clean itself and oceanic pollution should be prevented. • Science, technology, education and research should all be used to promote environmental protection.
Caring for the Earth: A Strategy for Sustainable Living (IUCN, UNEP and WWF, 1980b).	• Respect and care for the community of life. • Improve the quality of human life. • Conserve the Earth's vitality and diversity. • Minimize the depletion of non-renewable resources. • Keep within the Earth's carrying capacity. • Change personal attitudes and practices. • Enable communities to care for their own environments. • Provide a national framework for integrating environment and conservation. • Create a global alliance.

Source	Components, principles, core objectives
Eco-development, 11 macro-principles (Riddell, 1981)	• Establish an ideological commitment to eco-development. • Increase social equity. • Attain international parity. • Alleviate hunger and poverty. • Eradicate disease and misery. • Reduce arms. • Move closer towards self-sufficiency. • Clean up urban squalor. • Balance human numbers with resources. • Conserve resources. • Protect the environment.
World Commission on Environment and Development (Brundtland), fundamental objectives of sustainable development (WCED, 1987)	The critical objectives that follow from the concept of sustainable development are: • reviving growth; • changing the quality of growth; • meeting essential needs for jobs, food, energy, water and sanitation; • ensuring a sustainable level of production; • conserving and enhancing the resource base; • reorienting technology and managing risk; • merging environment and economics in decision making; • reorienting international economic relations.
IUCN, UNEP, WWF 1986 Conservation and Development Conference in Ottawa, summary of discussions (Jacobs et al, 1987)	Sustainable development seeks to respond to five broad requirements: • integration of conservation and development; • satisfaction of basic human needs; • achievement of equity and social justice; • provision of social self-determination and cultural diversity; • maintenance of ecological integrity.
Pearce (1988) sustainable development goals with broad support	Sustainable development is consistent with: • justice in respect of the socially disadvantaged; • justice to future generations; • justice to nature; • aversion to risk arising from: – our ignorance about the nature of the interactions between the environment, economy and society; – the social and economic damage arising from low margins of resilience to external 'shock'.

Source	Components, principles, core objectives
Pearce et al (1990) development elements that should be sustained over time	Development elements include: • increases in real income per capita; • improvements in health and nutritional status; • educational achievement; • access to resources; • 'fairer' distribution of income; • increases in basic freedoms.
Sustainability as justice and participation (Crocker, 1990)	Four key components are: • satisfaction of basic human needs; • democratic self-determination; • environmental respect; • equal opportunity for personal self-realization.
Robinson et al (1990) basic value principles plus principles of environmental/ ecological sustainability and principles of socio-political sustainability	Basic value principles: • The continued existence of the natural world is inherently good. • Cultural stability depends on the ability of a society to claim the loyalty of its adherents through the propagation of a set of values that are acceptable to the populace and through the provision of socio-political institutions that make realization of those values possible. Principles of environmental/ecological sustainability: • Life-support systems must be protected. This requires decontamination of air, water and soil, and reduction in waste flows. • Biotic diversity must be protected and enhanced. • We must maintain or enhance the integrity of ecosystems through careful management of soils and nutrient cycles, and we must develop and implement rehabilitative measures for badly degraded ecosystems. • Preventive and adaptive strategies for responding to the threat of global ecological change are needed. Principles of socio-political sustainability: • The physical scale of human activity must be kept below the total carrying capacity of the planetary biosphere.

Source	Components, principles, core objectives
	• We must recognize the environmental costs of human activities and develop methods to minimize energy and material use per unit of economic activity, reduce noxious emissions, and permit the decontamination and rehabilitation of degraded ecosystems. • Socio-political and economic equity must be ensured in the transition to a more sustainable society. • Environmental concerns need to be incorporated more directly and extensively into the political decision making process through such mechanisms as improved environmental assessment and an environmental bill of rights. • There is a need for increased public involvement in the development, interpretation and implementation of concepts of sustainability. • Political activity must be linked more directly to actual environmentally meaningful jurisdictions and the promotion of greater local and regional self-reliance. • A sustainable society requires an open, accessible political process that puts effective decision making power at the level of government closest to the situation and lives of the people affected by a decision. • All persons should have freedom from extreme want and from vulnerability to economic coercion, as well as the positive ability to participate creatively and self-directly in the political and economic system. • There should exist at least a minimum level of equality and social justice, including equality of opportunity to realize one's full human potential, recourse to an open and just legal system, freedom from political repression, access to high quality education, effective assess to information, and freedom of religion, speech and assembly.
Australia's *National Strategy for Ecologically Sustainable Development* (Australia, 1992)	The guiding principles: • Intergenerational equity: the present generation should ensure that the next generation is left an environment that is at least as healthy, diverse and productive as the one we enjoy. Owing to the massive and irreversible rate of loss of species and habitats at present, we have an additional responsibility to give the highest priority to conserving the world's natural environment and species.

Source	Components, principles, core objectives
	• Conservation of biodiversity and ecological integrity: conservation of biodiversity and the protection of ecological integrity should be a fundamental constraint on all economic activity. The non-evolutionary loss of species and genetic diversity needs to be halted and the future of evolutionary processes secured.
	• Constant natural capital and 'sustainable income': natural capital (e.g. biological diversity, healthy environments, freshwater supplies and productive soils) must be maintained or enhanced from one generation to the next. Only that income which can be sustained indefinitely, taking account of the biodiversity conservation principle, should be taken.
	• Anticipatory and precautionary policy approach: policy decisions should err on the side of caution, placing the burden of proof on technological and industrial developments to demonstrate that they are ecologically sustainable.
	• Social equity: social equity must be a key principle to be applied in developing economic and social policies as part of an ecologically sustainable society.
	• Limits on natural resource use: the scale and throughput of material resources will need to be limited by the capacity of the environment to both supply renewable resources and to assimilate wastes.
	• Qualitative development: increases in the qualitative dimension of human welfare and not quantitative growth in resource throughput is a key objective.
	• Pricing environmental values and natural resources: prices for natural resources should be set to recover the full social and environmental costs of their use and extraction. Many environmental values cannot be priced in monetary terms and, hence, pricing policies will form part of a broader framework of decision making.
	• Global perspective: a global perspective is needed to ensure that Australia does not simply move its environmental problems elsewhere.
	• Efficiency: efficiency of resource use must become a major objective in economic policy.
	• Resilience: economic policy needs to focus on developing a resilience to external economic or ecological shocks. A resource-driven economy is unlikely to be resilient.

Source	Components, principles, core objectives
	• External balance: Australia's economy needs to be brought into balance. External imbalance creates pressure to deplete natural capital and could undermine the prospect for an ecologically sustainable economy.
	• Community participation: strong community participation will be a vital prerequisite for affecting a smooth transition to an ecologically sustainable society.
Hannover Principles of design for sustainability, prepared for planning the 2000 World's Fair (McDonough and Braungart, 1992)	• Insist on right of humanity and nature to co-exist. • Recognize interdependence. • Respect relationships between spirit and matter. • Accept responsibility for the consequences of design. • Create safe objects of long-term value. • Eliminate the concept of waste. • Rely on natural energy flows. • Understand the limitations of design. • Seek constant improvement by the sharing of knowledge.
Aalborg Charter of European Cities and Towns towards Sustainability (1994)	'We seek to achieve social justice, sustainable economies, and environmental sustainability. Social justice will necessarily have to be based on economic sustainability and equity, which require environmental sustainability.'
Sustainability as community control of multiple forms of capital (Viederman, 1994)	Community control over: • nature's capital; • human capital; • human-created capital; • social capital; • cultural capital; to ensure that present and future generations can attain a high degree of economic security and achieve democracy while maintaining the integrity of ecological systems.
Systems approach with related imperatives (Robinson and Tinker, 1997)	Imperatives: • The ecological imperative is to remain within planetary biophysical carrying capacity. • The economic imperative is to ensure and maintain adequate material standards of living.

Source	Components, principles, core objectives
	• The social imperative is to provide social structures, including systems of governance that effectively propagate and sustain the values that people wish to live by.

Ecological, economic and social system characteristics:

• They are composed of complex sub-systems and are becoming increasingly globalized.
• The systems can be conceived of as self-organizing, though the extent to which scientific enterprise is able to reveal these mechanisms of self-organization is often limited.
• They change in response to 'stress' with consequences that may be both positive and negative to human society.
• They may have limits beyond which they may 'collapse'.

Source	Components, principles, core objectives
Pezzoli's summary of key challenges from a review of the political ecology of sustainable development (Pezzoli, 1997)	• Holism and co-evolution are needed in order to understand how environment and development interrelate. • Empowerment and community-building: each community of people has a right to a familiar habitat, like creatures in the natural world. New approaches are required that challenge economic and bureaucratic rationality and encourage political pluralism and participation by civil society. • Social justice and equity: require attention to ethics and moral philosophies. We need to know what ecological, social, political and personal values sustainable development serves, and how it reconciles the moral claims of human freedom, equality and community with our obligations to individual plants and animals. • Sustainable production and reproduction: how can we promote technology, together with social learning and social change, necessary to bring our patterns of production, reproduction and consumption in concert with the capacity of the ecosystem to perform life-giving functions in the long run?

Source	Components, principles, core objectives
Lafferty and Langhelle (1999) list of various ways in which the term 'sustainable' has been used	Sustainability used: • as a physical concept describing a stock of resources; • as a physical concept applied to ecosystem limits; • as reflecting social and economic concerns regarding the satisfaction of basic needs, equity and welfare.
George's (1999) twin pillars of sustainable development, with elaborations based on Rio UNCED commitments	• Intergenerational equity is a necessary condition for sustainability (the principle of conservation of capital). • Intergenerational equity is a necessary condition for development.
The Natural Step Framework developed for business and public-sector application (Robèrt, 2000)	For society to be sustainable, nature's functions and diversity must not be systematically: • subject to increasing concentrations of substances extracted from the Earth's crust; or • subject to increasing concentrations of substances produced by society; or • impoverished by physical displacement, over-harvesting or other forms of ecosystem manipulation; and • resources must be used fairly and efficiently in order to meet human needs globally.
City of Seattle, Office of Sustainability and Environment (2001), answer to 'what is sustainability?'	Sustainability 'for our city ... boils down to these six concepts': • saving what's special (the things that bring us pride and joy, the thing we want to hand down to our children and grandchildren); • maintaining our edge (our natural setting's sheer beauty and the economic, recreational and spiritual benefits we derive from it); • doing the right thing (sustainability is about fairness over time); • making connections (economic prosperity, environmental quality and social justice are inextricably intertwined); • saving money (by applying new technologies and designing new processes that use our resources more efficiently, eliminate waste and prevent pollution); • saving ourselves (nature is our life-support system).

Source	Components, principles, core objectives
MMSD (2002) broad set of goals for sustainability initiatives of the mining industry, integrated as a single sentence	Material and other needs for a better quality of life have to be fulfilled for people of this generation: • as equitably as possible; • while respecting ecosystem limits; and • building the basis on which future generations can meet their own needs.
Washington State Department of Ecology (2003) field guide to sustainability	Key principles of sustainability: • whole-systems thinking; • long-term thinking; • recognizing limits; • improved livelihoods.
Western Australia (2003) sustainability strategy list of seven foundation principles and four process principles based on the core values of sustainability	Foundation principles: • long-term economic health; • equity and human rights; • biodiversity and ecological integrity; • settlement efficiency and quality of life; • community, regions, 'sense of place' and heritage; • net benefit from development; • common good from planning. Process principles: • integration of the triple bottom line; • accountability, transparency and engagement; • precaution; • hope, vision, symbolic and iterative change.
Forest Stewardship Council (FSC, 2004a) revised list of objectives for forestry operations	• Forest management shall respect all applicable laws of the country in which they occur, and international treaties and agreements to which the country is a signatory, and comply with all FSC Principles and Criteria. • Long-term tenure and use rights to the land and forest resources shall be clearly defined, documented and legally established. • The legal and customary rights of indigenous peoples to own, use and manage their lands, territories and resources shall be recognized and respected. • Forest management operations shall maintain or enhance the long-term social and economic well-being of forest workers and local communities.

Source	Components, principles, core objectives
	• Forest management operations shall encourage the efficient use of the forest's multiple products and services to ensure economic viability and a wide range of environmental and social benefits.
	• Forest management shall conserve biological diversity and its associated values, water resources, soils and unique and fragile ecosystems and landscapes, and, by so doing, maintain the ecological functions and the integrity of the forest.
	• A management plan – appropriate to the scale and intensity of the operations – shall be written, implemented and kept up to date. The long-term objectives of management, and the means of achieving them, shall be clearly stated.
	• Monitoring shall be conducted – appropriate to the scale and intensity of forest management – to assess the condition of the forest, yields of forest products, chain of custody, management activities and their social and environmental impacts.
	• Management activities in high conservation value forests shall maintain or enhance the attributes that define such forests. Decisions regarding high conservation value forests shall always be considered in the context of a precautionary approach.
	• Plantations shall be planned and managed in accordance with Principles and Criteria 1–9, and Principle 10 and its Criteria. While plantations can provide an array of social and economic benefits, and can contribute to satisfying the world's needs for forest products, they should complement the management of, reduce pressures on, and promote the restoration and conservation of natural forests.
Millennium Ecosystems Assessment (Reid et al, 2005) depiction of 'linkages between ecosystem services and human well-being'	Conceptual framework of interactions involving four core categories, all interrelated, acting over the short and long term at local, regional and global levels: • ecosystem services (provisioning, regulating, cultural and supporting services); • human well-being and poverty reduction (basic material for a good life, health, good social relations, security, freedom of choice and action); • indirect drivers of change (demographic, economic, socio-political, science and technology, cultural and religious);

Source	Components, principles, core objectives
	• direct drivers of change (changes in local land use and cover, species introduction or removal, technology adaptation and use, external inputs, harvest and resource consumption, climate change, natural, physical and biological drivers).

Selected Sustainability Assessment Approaches, Criteria and Processes

Source	Assessment approach characteristics
International Council for Local Environmental Initiatives (ICLEI, 1996, 2004) and ICLEI-Europe (1997), Local Agenda 21 (LA21) campaign, various versions of a participatory planning process for communities, applied to over 6000 cities globally	In the current version, municipal councils commit to reaching five milestones: • Establish a multi-sector stakeholder group to oversee the LA21 process, consisting of representatives from all sectors of the community, that will be formally involved in the development and implementation of all actions aimed at the achievement of the LA21 Campaign milestones. • With the active participation of the LA21 stakeholder group, complete a sustainability audit considering social, economic and environmental conditions and trends in the community. • Complete a sustainable community vision for the future, based on community review of the audit and assessment of priorities. • Implement an LA21 action plan, identifying clear goals, priorities, measurable targets, roles and responsibilities, funding sources and work activities. • Establish community-based monitoring and annual evaluation and community progress reporting on performance in achieving the LA21 action plan, using locally appropriate indicators. ICLEI-Europe (1997) sets out performance criteria based on ten steps: • set-up of a stakeholder group or 'Local Agenda 21 Forum'; • community consultation; • agreement on a vision for the sustainable development of the community; • review of existing plans and strategies concerning the future development of the community;

Source	Assessment approach characteristics
	• development of sustainability indicators; • sustainable development/management audits; • definition of targets and priority setting; • reporting and controlling mechanisms; • linking the local perspective to the global dimension; • adopting the LA21 by the city council.

British Columbia's (1996) Growth Management Strategies law and process for pursuit of sustainability through preparation of planning strategies by municipalities in expanding urban regions	Process for establishing and implementing regional growth strategies in areas facing significant growth pressures:
	
	• Each regional growth strategy to act as a planning framework for growth management by municipalities within the region following a 20- (or more) year vision.
	• Fourteen legislated objectives for all growth strategies, setting out an implicit sustainability agenda for:
	  – avoiding urban sprawl and ensuring that development takes place where adequate facilities exist or can be provided in a timely, economic and efficient manner;
	  – settlement patterns that minimize the use of automobiles and encourage walking, bicycling and the efficient use of public transit;
	  – the efficient movement of goods and people while making effective use of transportation and utility corridors;
	  – protecting environmentally sensitive areas;
	  – maintaining the integrity of a secure and productive resource base, including the agricultural and forest land reserves;
	  – economic development that supports the unique character of communities;
	  – reducing and preventing air, land and water pollution;
	  – adequate, affordable and appropriate housing;
	  – adequate inventories of suitable land and resources for future settlement;
	  – protecting the quality and quantity of groundwater and surface water;
	  – settlement patterns that minimize the risks associated with natural hazards;
	  – preserving, creating and linking urban and rural open space including parks and recreation areas;

Source	Assessment approach characteristics
	– planning for energy supply and promoting efficient use, conservation and alternative forms of energy; – good stewardship of land, sites and structures with cultural heritage value. • Specification of more particular goals and priorities to fit local circumstances and objectives through the strategy development process. • Process centred on discussions, analyses and negotiations among participating municipalities to reach agreement on the contents of a regional growth management strategy that will provide the basis for subsequent adjustment of more specific municipal plans. • Formal requirements for public consultation plans and for public hearings on draft regional growth strategies. • Common use of alternative growth management option scenarios, impact analyses, sectoral studies and multi-stakeholder consultations (Boyle et al, 2003). • Legislated provision of a series of increasingly firm means of resolving conflicts between participating municipalities concerning contents of the regional growth strategy. • Application through provincial–regional implementation agreements and requirements for compliance by municipal official community plans.
Sadler's (1996) approach to sustainability assessment as next generation environmental assessment	Evolution of environmental assessment in jurisdictions with broadly scoped strategic and project-level assessment, established framework of sustainability policy commitments and application of other integrated policy tools: • focus on sustainability assurance rather than impact minimization; • application of six key sustainability principles: – precautionary principle (err on the side of conservation as a hedge against irreversible or highly damaging changes); – anticipate and prevent rather than react and cure; – stay within source and sink constraints (resource use/harvest with regenerative capacity; pollution/waste output within assimilative capacity); – maintain natural capital at or near current levels (no aggregate/net loss or drawdown of resource stocks or ecological diversity);

Source	Assessment approach characteristics
	– avoid conversion of land use from less intensive to more intensive uses; – polluter-pays principle (full costs for environmental damage must be borne by users, e.g. industry and consumers); • explicit attention to trade-offs and compensation issues, with emphasis on overall maintenance of natural capital; • centred on environmental sustainability, but with recognition of economic and social equity dimensions.
Becker's (1997) review of sustainability assessment values, concepts and methodological approaches	Generic sustainability assessment process (though designed with agricultural undertakings in mind): • initial process focuses on the value of the environment (recognizing debates about the monetization of nature), intergenerational equity and intragenerational equity; • next step: measurement (recognizing complex system context, risk, uncertainty and ignorance) with indicators either measuring single factors and combining them or representing complex processes, trends or states; • application of explicit criteria for selection of sustainability indicators; • selection among possible approaches (use of economic, social, ecological and composite indicators in lists without aggregation use of scoring system approaches; focus on system properties; focus on ecosystem health); • identification of short and long term, and local and global goals; • consideration of process options (use of expert opinion, participative/discursive approaches, etc.).
Basic approach to integration of sustainability into assessment requirements, proposed by Lawrence (1997)	Basic elements for design/application of a sustainability assessment process or specific sustainability assessments: • generic sustainability principles for general direction (e.g. identification of undertakings worthy of assessment); • more specific objectives or sustainability imperatives, including examination of alternative scenarios, adapted to different activity and environment types; • explicit consideration of sustainability in purpose, principles and priorities;

Source	Assessment approach characteristics
	• provisions for application to various types, scales, combinations of undertakings; • application of sustainability considerations in examination of broadly defined environmental conditions, effects, effects management options (mitigation and enhancement); • effective public involvement, including in conflict resolution; • coordination with deliberations of related stakeholders and authorities; • integration with other related processes (planning, management etc.).

Assessing the Sustainability of Societal Initiatives and Proposing Agendas for Change (ASSIPAC) method for sustainability assessment, designed chiefly for urban planning uses, but broadly applicable (Devuyst, 1999)	Two-stage sustainability-centred process for review of proposed initiatives: an initial screening or 'check' and a more detailed examination in cases where the screening uncovers possible conflicts with established sustainability objectives:
	
	• Initial checklist includes attention to existing sustainability policies or strategies, any identified alternatives, best international practice for initiatives of the sort proposed, public/stakeholder views, barriers to more sustainable design in the case, integrated attention to sustainability in design of the initiative, linkages between the proposed initiative and other activities and opportunities, precautionary characteristics, empowerment of the local community, and attention to a set of environmental, socio-cultural and economic considerations.
	• Environmental considerations:
	  – relation to carrying capacity of the region;
	  – inclusion of an environmental case system in the initiative;
	  – limited use of natural resources;
	  – limited use of materials and production of waste;
	  – protection of biodiversity;
	  – limited pollution;
	  – restoration and maintenance of ecological cycles;
	  – greenhouse gas implications;
	  – influence on population growth.
	• Social and cultural considerations:
	  – empowerment of groups in the community;
	  – limitation of social polarization;
	  – strengthening local cultural identity and diversity;
	  – protection and improvement of health;

Source	Assessment approach characteristics
	– improvement of possibilities for education and training; – improvement of possibilities for local employment; – increase in possibilities for socio-cultural/recreational exchanges; – encouragement of sustainable lifestyle; – strengthening of democratic community values; – strengthening of local community independence. • Economic considerations: – strengthening and diversifying local economy; – encouraging and supporting private entrepreneurship; – supporting environmentally conscious and ethically responsible trade. • Planning and design considerations: – promotion of development patterns that reduce material/energy demands; – promotion of development patterns that respect ecosystem functions. • Reliance on general sustainability principles and objectives if specific ones not available. • Report on application of checklist to inform decision makers and stakeholders. • More detailed ASSIPAC study local/regional vision must be prepared for case if not available already as baseline for analysis. • Both screening and detailed reviews require expert and independent assessors. • Strong emphasis on a sustainability vision/strategy as a foundation for judgements, plus larger context of indicator development, auditing and reporting (Devuyst et al, 2001). • General considerations do not all fit comfortably in the three main categories. • Appears designed to apply after an initiative has been prepared and proposed, but could influence earlier conceptualization and planning if established as a regular process requirement for approvals.
UK (UK, 1999a) strategy for sustainable development	Four objectives: • social progress that recognizes the needs of everyone; • effective protection of the environment; • prudent use of natural resources; • maintenance of high and stable levels of economic growth and employment.

Source	Assessment approach characteristics
	Ten guiding principles/approaches:

- putting people at the centre;
- taking a long-term perspective;
- taking account of costs and benefits;
- creating an open and supportive economic system;
- combating poverty and social exclusion;
- respecting environmental limits;
- the precautionary principle;
- using scientific knowledge;
- transparency, information participation and access to justice;
- making the polluter pay.

Implementation through:

- new bodies (cabinet committee, House of Commons environmental audit committee, Sustainable Development Commission);
- more integrated appraisal system covering environmental, economic, safety and other factors;
- initiatives in health, transportation, aggregates mining, regional development, etc.;
- use of broader range of instruments, including ecological tax reform;
- regional sustainable development frameworks, Local Agenda 21 strategies and planning system reform;
- annual reporting of progress in light of 15 headline indicators and full set of 147 indicators (UK, 1999b).

Integrated sustainable cities assessment method (ISCAM), proposed in light of case review of integrated planning for sustainability for Greater Manchester (Ravetz, 2000)

An integrated complex systems framework approach to urban and regional planning centred on the use of an accounting tool providing a means of examining trends, targets and alternative scenarios:

- respects technical indeterminacy and value multiplicity;
- focuses on upstream and downstream flows (e.g. from drivers such as values and needs through various activities, products and services, to outcomes and externalities), including information as well as materials and recognizing feedback and other linkages as well as linear phenomena, plus attention to system influences from the national and global to the local and back;
- presumes value of core accounts, but also need for deliberation on more complex factors and relationships;

Source	Assessment approach characteristics
	• requires, even for the core accounts, selection of values, key baselines and trends, scenario alternatives to business as usual, and anticipated change factors; • presumes use as a tool as a contribution to the larger context of initiatives to clarify visions, scenarios and options for action (including examination of barriers and constraints, responses in strategies, policies, programmes and projects); • presumes continued evaluation and adjustment.
UK approach to sustainability appraisal, chiefly used by planning authorities in the preparation of regional plans, but also used to inform decisions on other initiatives and to guide performance reviews of existing policies, activities and projects (UK DETR, 2000a; Counsell and Haughton, undated)	Broadly applicable general assessment process, used in the UK since 1998 for sustainability-centred appraisals of work done in successive steps of regional planning: • Evolved from strategic environmental assessment/appraisal in the development planning process. • Implemented through guidance documents rather than specified mandatory obligations. • Adopts general sustainability principles and related indicators from UK sustainability strategy (UK, 1999a), but relies heavily on efforts to characterize the particular region's current conditions and set region-specific sustainability objectives (UK DETR, 2000b). • Appraisals done in parallel with, and to inform, the typical steps in regional plan preparation: setting planning objectives, identifying and evaluating development options, drafting development policies and the regional development plan. • These steps followed by reviews by senior government, public and hearing panel and decision by senior government. • Appraisal may also be done of the final plan and is meant to continue during plan implementation with contributions of indicators for auditing of monitoring results. • Common use of scoring methods including identification of anticipated positive, negative or uncertain effects on achievement of selected objectives. • Important roles in fostering policy integration (ensuring attention to economic, social and environmental policy concerns) and linking regional and national strategies.

Source	Assessment approach characteristics
	• Reported challenges in encouraging enough commonality of objectives and indicators to permit inter-regional comparisons, in ensuring evaluation of alternative development options, in integrating attention to different sustainability considerations and dealing with conflicts and trade-offs, in ensuring sustainability appraisals are influential in planning decision making, in ensuring timely public access to appraisal documents and more generally in opening up the planning and appraisal process to more effective scrutiny (Counsell and Haughton, undated).
IUCN (World Conservation Union) sustainability assessment method for evaluating human and environmental conditions progress towards sustainability (Guijt et al, 2001)	Two pillar approach centred on ecosystem well-being and human well-being, applied to sustainability evaluation: • focus on evaluation of conditions and progress; • intended also to complement strategic and project-level decision making by providing a framework for information gathering and interpretation; • human well-being distinguished from wealth and defined as 'a condition in which all members of society can determine and meet their needs, from a range of choices'; • ecosystem well-being defined as 'a condition in which the ecosystem maintains diversity and quality, its capacity to support all life, and its potential to adapt to change to provide future options'; • 'egg of well-being' depiction of people as yolk within the ecosystem; • seven-stage process with initial work to develop a shared vision of sustainability, leading to more specified objectives, indicators and performance criteria, followed by assessment using and combining the indicators, and considering implications; • standard suggested indicators but context-specific emphasis and reliance on a participatory process involving relevant stakeholders; • human and ecosystem well-being factors measured separately to allow 'progress in human development and ecosystem conservation to be compared'; • indicators jointly presented on two axes of matrix (barometer of sustainability); • tested in case applications, including ones in Zimbabwe and India;

Source	Assessment approach characteristics

	• apparently not strong on system interactions; • offers contextual information for trade-off decisions but no assessment process guidance; • not sustainability assessment as an approach to strategic or project decision making.
Mining, Minerals and Sustainable Development project (MMSD, 2002) outline of basic components of integrated impact assessment (itself to be integrated in a broader framework of initiatives and tools from the global level to the community level)	A combination and integration of environmental impact assessment with supplementary social and other appraisals, which should: • cover all significant social, economic and environmental issues; • be applied to all new projects; • include early consultation with relevant community to identify local concerns; • be designed to address full set of sustainability issues and local concerns even if beyond legislated requirements; • be an inclusive, dynamic, ongoing process of integrating knowledge of impacts into decision making and practice; • be endorsed by community and government; • include independent monitoring of impacts; • be linked to development of a community sustainable development plan, integrated plan for closure, including efforts to sustainable benefits after closure.
North American working group of the Mining, Minerals and Sustainable Development project (MMSD-NA, 2002), sustainability assessment framework for mining undertakings	Seven questions to guide sustainability assessments of the full life-cycle of mining projects (complemented by further specification of objectives, indicators and metrics): • Are engagement processes in place and working effectively? • Will people's well-being be maintained or improved? • Is the integrity of the environment assured over the long term? • Is the economic viability of the project or operation assured, and will the economy of the community and beyond be better off as a result? • Are traditional and non-market activities in the community and surrounding area accounted for in a way that is acceptable to the local people? • Are rules, incentives, programmes and capacities in place to address project or operational consequences?

Source	Assessment approach characteristics
	• Does a full synthesis show that the net result will be positive or negative in the long term, and will there be periodic reassessments?
Global Ecovillage Network (undated) Community Sustainability Assessment, a comprehensive checklist for evaluating the sustainability of individual communities	Best judgement scoring of community status with a checklist of 148 multiple choice questions, each accompanied by numerically weighted possible answers: • questions organized in three equally important categories, each with seven topic areas:

- ecological checklist:
  - (a) sense of place (community location/scale, restoration/preservation of nature);
  - (b) food availability, production and distribution;
  - (c) physical infrastructure, buildings and transportation (materials, methods, designs);
  - (d) consumption patterns and solid water management;
  - (e) water (sources, quality and use patterns);
  - (f) waste water and water pollution management energy sources and uses;
  - (g) energy sources and uses;
- social checklist:
  - (a) openness, trust and safety; communal space;
  - (b) communication (flow of ideas and information);
  - (c) networking outreach and services;
  - (d) social sustainability (diversity and tolerance; decision making, conflict resolution);
  - (e) education;
  - (f) health care;
  - (g) sustainable economics (healthy local economy);
- spiritual checklist:
  - (a) cultural sustainability;
  - (b) arts and leisure;
  - (c) spiritual sustainability (opportunities for/ encouragement of spiritual practices);
  - (d) community glue (shared vision/principles, harmony/caring/support);
  - (e) community resilience (ability to respond to crises);
  - (f) holographic, circulatory world view (responsibility, caring, larger purpose);
  - (g) peace and global consciousness (harmony, community service, inner peace);

Source	Assessment approach characteristics
	• unusual spiritual emphasis (and absence of conventional economic category) indicative of diversity of possibilities in checklist rating system preferences; • not sustainability assessment as an approach to strategic or project decision making.
Hong Kong sustainability assessment system for integrated consideration of proposals (HKSDU, 2002)	Checklist-based system of pre-decision review of proposals for new strategic initiatives and major programmes, integrating attention to economic, social and biophysical factors: • initiated 2001; • meant to facilitate early identification of potentially significant, controversial and/or cross-sectoral issues, and negotiated resolution of conflicts; • eight guiding principles related to issue areas: economy, health and hygiene, natural resources, society and social infrastructure, biodiversity, leisure and cultural vibrancy, environmental quality and mobility; • 39 quantifiable indicators (included in computer-aided evaluation tool), plus expectation of evaluation of non-quantifiable factors; • process steps: set out proposal objectives/ assumptions; evaluate positive and negative implications through checklist application (plus non-quantifiable considerations); consider alternatives; prepare report on key findings; • emphasis on involvement of community groups and non-governmental organizations (NGOs); • guidance unit based in central administration bureau; • complemented by work of a Council for Sustainable Development, a Sustainable Development Fund for support of community initiatives that integrate consideration of sustainability issues.
Bradley et al (2002) use of sustainability criteria to evaluate onsite wastewater treatment technologies	Evaluation and decision making framework designed specifically for assessment of technology and management options for onsite wastewater treatment: • initial identification of general social, economic and environmental criteria for any wastewater treatment evaluation with consideration of quantifiability in long-term indicators/performance measures;

Source	Assessment approach characteristics
	• incorporation of site-specific factors by weighting of sustainability criteria according to values of relevant specific communities (social, economic and environmental) on a 1 to 10 scale; • comparative scoring/evaluation of conventional and alternative wastewater treatment and management options (no absolute score for sustainability); • identification of benefits and shortcomings; • identification of responses to shortcomings through alternative technologies and management approaches using same criteria; • consideration of costs and risks; • identification of barriers to improvement and possible responses; • recognition of links between site-specific option evaluation and larger issues (e.g. implications for housing density, availability of management support).
Stockholm Environment Institute (Maltais et al, 2002) sustainability assessment of World Trade Organization negotiations in the food crops sector	An applied sustainability assessment of food-sector trade liberalization options/effects using case studies of eight selected countries and focusing on two major crops (wheat and edible oils): • initial review of economic, social and environmental considerations and key sustainability issues in sector for each case; • assessment of changes in structure of economic incentives and opportunities, production system characteristics and sustainability aspects; • comparisons of baseline, liberalization and intermediate scenarios; • evaluation of potential policy responses and their implications; • consideration of positive, negative and ambiguous effects; • key sustainability effects include changes in water quality/quantity, land conversion, soil degradation, national income, employment, rural poverty/livelihoods and equality; • identification of key sustainability issues: budgetary expenditure, consumer prices, rural livelihoods and equity, rural landscape and biodiversity, water quality and soil degradation;

Source	Assessment approach characteristics
	• identification of key trade-off issues, including broadly distributed benefits competing with more focused adjustment costs; • identification of analytical problems, including aggregation of findings when sustainability conditions and impacts are diverse and context specific, and when aggregation obscures important details such as significant positive or negative effects on particular groups (e.g. the very poor).

Equator Principles (2003) for decision making on major project financing, prepared and adopted by a voluntary association of major financial institutions for assessment of environmental and social risk of proposed projects expected to cost over US$50 million	Financial institution commitment to specified information requirements covering a range of ecological and social matters as a complement to traditional financial considerations:
	
	• Where risk is potentially significant, the borrower must have completed an assessment report addressing:
	  – assessment of the baseline environmental and social conditions;
	  – requirements under host country laws and regulations, applicable international treaties and agreements;
	  – sustainable development and use of renewable natural resources;
	  – protection of human health, cultural properties and biodiversity, including endangered species and sensitive ecosystems;
	  – use of dangerous substances;
	  – major hazards;
	  – occupational health and safety;
	  – fire prevention and life safety;
	  – socio-economic impacts;
	  – land acquisition and land use;
	  – involuntary resettlement;
	  – impacts on indigenous peoples and communities;
	  – cumulative impacts of existing projects, the proposed project and anticipated future projects;
	  – participation of affected parties in the design, review and implementation of the project;
	  – consideration of feasible environmentally and socially preferable alternatives;
	  – efficient production, delivery and use of energy;

Source	Assessment approach characteristics

       – pollution prevention and waste minimization, pollution controls (liquid effluents and air emissions) and solid and chemical waste management.
- No indication of overall objectives or process for consideration of trade-offs.

Comprehensive sustainability assessment framework proposed by Jenkins et al (2003) to the Western Australia State Sustainability Assessment Working Group, created in response to an anticipated sustainability assessment commitment in the 2002 State Sustainability Strategy Consultation Draft	A comprehensive approach to strategic and project-level assessment and decision making:

- designed to fit in the context of a broader framework for sustainability-oriented governance, including regular status of sustainability reporting, a state sustainability strategy, regional sustainability strategies and action plans, agency sustainability action plans, sustainability performance auditing;
- regime to be built on expansion of existing environmental impact assessment regime, with insights also from integrated regional planning;
- concurrent environmental, social and economic impact assessments to be completed by proponents and reviewed by government bodies, with opportunity for public comment;
- reviews to be completed and submitted separately as advice to the political level (through a sustainability coordinator in the cabinet office) where integration and trade-offs are to be addressed;
- proposals to be assessed in light of sustainability criteria identified in the development of regional sustainability strategies (an expansion of regional land use planning);
- assessment results to feed back into revisions/ adaptations of regional strategies and action plans;
- assessment decisions to include approval conditions for proponents and action requirements for non-proponents (e.g. government agencies);
- appears to assume application to already initiated proposals;
- no discussion of approach to alternatives;
- dedication to political level control over trade-offs may limit effective integration of consideration in planning and proposal development by proponent.

Source	Assessment approach characteristics
Strategic environmental assessment for sustainability appraisal of Ghana's Poverty Reduction Strategy (Nelson et al, 2004)	Concurrent two-level strategic environmental assessment process, broadly scoped to address sustainability issues, applied to over 400 national-level sectoral policies/programmes and over 210 district development plans:

- driven by concerns about inadequate attention to environmental factors;
- initiated during completion of planning process;
- focus on links between poverty and the environment (key considerations: livelihoods, health, vulnerability);
- broad conception of 'environment' (biophysical, social, cultural, micro-economic and institutional);
- national-level basic process elements: understanding context, determining objectives and targets, defining baseline conditions, evaluating the existing policy/ programme/plan, developing indicators, considering alternatives, considering scope for mitigation, monitoring and evaluation;
- additional considerations: links between problem recognition and pursuit of suitable responses, (in)consistency and (in)compatibility between policies;
- criteria grouped under livelihoods, vulnerability, institutional context, social and cultural and local economic conditions;
- district-level application of sustainability appraisals with standard contents: overview of appraisal, baseline conditions, summary of relevant policies/programmes/ plans, key areas of concern for poverty reduction, performance of individual policies/programmes/plans (judged in light of a 'sustainability test'), measures taken to improve performance, measures for improving future policies, programmes and plans;
- work largely done by government officials, with some broader participation in later stages (constrained by short time scale);
- implementation accompanied by institutional capacity-building for strategic-level sustainability assessment at national and district levels;
- aims: appropriate modification of initial programmes/ plans; better integration of national policy and district-level practical delivery; and establishment of a base for earlier and more direct integration of broadly environmental factors in next rounds of programme/ plan development/revision.

Source	Assessment approach characteristics
Forest Stewardship Council (FSC) certification principles, criteria, standards and process for forestry operations and wood products (FSC, 2004b)	A global set of ten principles, elaborated in 56 criteria, for application by third-party certifiers accredited by the FSC: • principles and criteria apply generally to tropical, temperate and boreal forests, and to replanted and plantation forests; • more detailed standards for particular jurisdictions and forest-types prepared at the national or local level; supplement the generic objectives and criteria with local indicators and verifiers, and additional criteria; • principles and criteria set by FSC membership divided into three 'chambers' – environmental, social and economic – including representatives from environmental and social organizations, forestry and timber bodies and corporations, community forestry groups, indigenous people's organizations and forest product certification bodies; • FSC-accredited national and sub-national standards set by similarly representative multi-stakeholder bodies with a consultative process; • individual certifications are transparent, subject to peer review and follow-up audits; • supply train verification for wood products; • standard setting, certification and labelling accompanied by educational efforts focused on 'improving forest management, incorporating the full cost of management and production into the price of forest products, promoting the highest and best use of forest resources, reducing damage and waste, and avoiding over-consumption and over-harvesting'.

Regional Municipality of Waterloo terms of reference for assessment of a rapid transit initiative (RMW, 2005)	A set of six goals expanded to 15 criteria for assessing alternatives:
	
	 • Enhance our environment:
	   – relative amount of land consumed;
	   – relative impact on air quality;
	   – relative impact of emissions generated that contribute to climate change.
	 • Build vibrant urban places:
	   – relative contribution to region re-urbanization objectives;
	   – relative contribution to innovative urban design;
	   – relative contribution to public health.

Source	Assessment approach characteristics

	• Provide greater transportation choice:
	  – relative contribution to increased transportation choice;
	  – relative contribution to increased region transit ridership;
	  – relative affordability of personal transportation cost;
	  – relative flexibility to changes in operation.
	• Protect our countryside:
	  – relative contribution to the region's countryside protection goal.
	• Foster a strong economy:
	  – relative contribution to downtown revitalization;
	  – relative capital cost to the region.
	• Ensure overall coordination and cooperation:
	  – degree of compatibility with other regional plans and strategies;
	  – degree of compatibility with provincial and federal plans and strategies.

The Basic Sustainability Assessment Decision Criteria

Socio-ecological system integrity

Build human–ecological relations that establish and maintain the long-term integrity of socio-biophysical systems and protect the irreplaceable life support functions upon which human as well as ecological well-being depends.

Livelihood sufficiency and opportunity

Ensure that everyone and every community has enough for a decent life and opportunities to seek improvements in ways that do not compromise future generations' possibilities for sufficiency and opportunity.

Intragenerational equity

Ensure that sufficiency and effective choices for all are pursued in ways that reduce dangerous gaps in sufficiency and opportunity (and health, security, social recognition, political influence, etc.) between the rich and the poor.

Intergenerational equity

Favour present options and actions that are most likely to preserve or enhance the opportunities and capabilities of future generations to live sustainably.

Resource maintenance and efficiency

Provide a larger base for ensuring sustainable livelihoods for all while reducing threats to the long-term integrity of socio-ecological systems by reducing extractive damage, avoiding waste and cutting overall material and energy use per unit of benefit.

Socio-ecological civility and democratic governance

Build the capacity, motivation and habitual inclination of individuals, communities and other collective decision making bodies to apply sustainability principles through more open and better informed deliberations, greater attention to fostering reciprocal awareness and collective responsibility, and more integrated use of administrative, market, customary, collective and personal decision making practices.

Precaution and adaptation

Respect uncertainty, avoid even poorly understood risks of serious or irreversible damage to the foundations for sustainability, plan to learn, design for surprise and manage for adaptation.

Immediate and long-term integration

Attempt to meet all requirements for sustainability together as a set of interdependent parts, seeking mutually supportive benefits.

The Basic Sustainability Assessment Trade-off Rules

Maximum net gains

Any acceptable trade-off or set of trade-offs must deliver net progress towards meeting the requirements for sustainability; it must seek mutually reinforcing, cumulative and lasting contributions; and must favour achievement of the most positive, feasible, overall result, while avoiding significant adverse effects.

Burden of argument on trade-off proponent

Trade-off compromises that involve acceptance of adverse effects in sustainability-related areas are undesirable unless proven (or reasonably established), otherwise the burden of justification falls on the proponent of the trade-off.

Avoidance of significant adverse effects

No trade-off that involves a significant adverse effect on any sustainability requirement area (for example, any effect that might undermine the integrity of a viable socio-ecological system) can be justified unless the alternative is acceptance of an even more significant adverse effect.

Generally, then, no compromise or trade-off is acceptable if it entails further decline or risk of decline in a major area of existing concern (for example, as set out in official international, national or other sustainability strategies or accords, or as identified in open public processes at the local level), or if it endangers prospects for resolving problems properly identified as global, national and/or local priorities.

Similarly, no trade-off is acceptable if it deepens problems in any requirement area (integrity, equity, etc.) where further decline in the existing situation may imperil the long-term viability of the whole, even if compensations of other kinds, or in other places are offered (for example, if inequities are already deep, there may be no ecological rehabilitation or efficiency compensation for introduction of significantly greater inequities).

No enhancement can be permitted as an acceptable trade-off against incomplete mitigation of significant adverse effects if stronger mitigation efforts are feasible.

Protection of the future

No displacement of a significant adverse effect from the present to the future can be justified unless the alternative is displacement of an even more significant negative effect from the present to the future.

Explicit justification

All trade-offs must be accompanied by an explicit justification based on openly identified, context specific priorities as well as the sustainability decision criteria and the general trade-off rules.

Justifications will be assisted by the presence of clarifying guides (sustainability policies, priority statements, plans based on analyses of existing stresses and desirable futures, guides to the evaluation of 'significance', etc.) that have been developed in processes as open and participative as those expected for sustainability assessments.

Open process

Proposed compromises and trade-offs must be addressed and justified through processes that include open and effective involvement of all stakeholders.

Relevant stakeholders include those representing sustainability-relevant positions (for example, community elders speaking for future generations) as well as those directly affected.

While application of specialized expertise and technical tools can be very helpful, the decisions to be made are essentially and unavoidably value laden and a public role is crucial.

Appendix 5

The Basic Design Components for Formal Sustainability Assessment Processes

The formal process components recommended in Chapter 7 are collected and presented here in the form of provisions of draft sustainability assessment legislation.

Purposes

1 The purposes of sustainability assessment are:
   - to improve decision making on all undertakings that may, individually or in combination, have a significant effect on progress towards sustainability;
   - to ensure comprehensive and integrated attention to all factors affecting long-term as well as immediate desirability and durability;
   - to provide the core framework (the main structure, criteria and process) for deliberations and decisions on significant undertakings (in contrast to environmental assessment's usual role as one among many contributions to a broader decision making process);
   - to encourage overall consistency and efficiency in decision making from policy and programme design to post-approval project implementation monitoring (through application of a common set of fundamental requirements), while also favouring flexibility and decentralization by respecting uncertainty and context, working iteratively with the relevant stakeholders, and adapting to different ecosystems and communities, new understandings, and emerging challenges and opportunities;
   - to encourage effective public engagement in the conception, planning, approval and implementation of undertakings that may have a significant effect on progress towards sustainability;
   - to foster and facilitate creative innovation as well as just transition to more sustainable practices.

Decision criteria

2   The evaluations, choices, trade-offs and other decisions made in the sustainability assessment process must:
  * focus on maximum gains for sustainability, aim for selection of the best
    option (rather than merely judge the 'acceptability' of proposed undertakings) and seek enhancement of multiple, reinforcing sustainability
    benefits in addition to avoidance or mitigation of significant negative
    effects;
  * apply the sustainability-based decision criteria (concerning socio-
    ecological system integrity, livelihood sufficiency and opportunity,
    intragenerational equity, intergenerational equity, efficiency, socio-
    ecological civility and democratic governance, precaution and adaptation,
    and immediate and long-term integration) and the trade-off rules (concerning net gains, burden of argument, avoidance of significant adverse
    effects, protection of the future, explicit justification and open process)
    set out in the regulations (as in Appendices 3 and 4, here);
  * also take into account any specification of these criteria and trade-off
    rules – and associated values, objectives and criteria – for particular
    undertakings in specific contexts, made through informed choices by
    the relevant parties (stakeholders);
  * maximize the transparency and accountability of the process and facilitate open engagement of interested and affected parties.

Application rules

3a Sustainability assessment requirements apply:
  * generally to all undertakings, including policies, programmes and plans
    as well as capital projects and physical activities, that might have significant effects on prospects for sustainability; and more specifically
  * to undertakings in all categories identified in regulations made under the
    law;
  * to significant policies, programmes and plans that require ministerial
    approval;
  * to cases where the need for strategic level initiatives has been identified
    in the course of a project level assessment and is recognized by the
    relevant authorities;
  * to any other cases where the government chooses to require an assessment in response to public concern or its own recognition of issues of
    significance for sustainability.
3b Requests for exemption from sustainability assessment requirements:
  * may be sought from the assessment authority;
  * must be accompanied by reasonable argument and evidence that the
    potential for sustainability effects has been carefully considered and no
    such effects are likely;
  * must be open for public review and comment before a decision is made.

Hierarchies and tiers

4 Strategic level policies, programmes and plans that have been approved after sustainability assessment:
- may be used to guide the substantive scope of and/or the process for consequential assessments at the more specific programme, plan or project levels;
- may, in particular, be used to focus the lower level assessment on a more limited range of options than would be required in the absence of the broader level assessment;
- may be reconsidered at the more specific programme, plan or project levels only where the parties seeking reconsideration can establish justification on the grounds of exceptional circumstances or recent changes in important factors.

Streams

5 Cases subject to sustainability assessment may be allocated to different, more or less demanding assessment streams, as set out in the law:
- to ensure detailed substantive evaluation and rigorous public and institutional review of the most significant and potentially worrisome undertakings;
- to permit more expeditious assessment review of less significant and worrisome undertakings;
- so long as in every case the assessment provisions:
  - apply the full set of sustainability criteria and trade-off rules;
  - address the full range of basic requirements (see the provisions under 'scope', below), except where a narrowing has been justified by a higher tier assessment (see provisions under 'hierarchies and tiers', above);
  - include timely opportunities for public notice and comment;
  - include a mechanism for open consideration of applications (from a proponent, or the public or any other interested party) to bump-up an exceptionally significant or controversial case to more intensive review or to bump-down an exceptionally benign or insignificant case to less intensive review;
- with schedules providing, to the extent possible, clear early guidance and procedures for determining more specifically the stream of assessment and review required in all categories of reasonable anticipated undertakings.

Scope

6a The scope of all assessments must cover:
- the full suite of considerations relevant to specifying and applying the decision criteria including social, economic and biophysical aspects recognized as components of complex and dynamic systems;

- the full life-cycle of the undertakings;
- all key openings for critical examination and innovation, including requirements in every case:
  - to establish the need(s) and/or justify the purpose(s) to be served;
  - to identify the reasonable alternatives, including different general approaches as well as different designs, for serving the purpose; and
  - to integrate consideration of related undertakings and of cumulative effects of existing, proposed, consequential and reasonably anticipated undertakings, except insofar as these matters have been addressed at least as thoroughly and openly in a broader strategic assessment whose conclusions have not been superceded by subsequent developments.

6b The particular scope of an assessment must be specified through public process in ways that:
- focus attention on the most significant alternatives, socio-ecological system components and effects;
- match the level of assessment effort to the significance of the case, with significance in all cases determined through application of the sustainability-based decision criteria.

Participation

7 Transparency, accountability and effective engagement of participants must be provided throughout the sustainability assessment process, in all streams:
- to mobilize public knowledge as well as specialized technical expertise;
- to encourage all participants to look beyond their particular interests, mandates and expertise to recognize broader implications where trade-offs or positive reinforcements may be involved;
- to ensure effective public as well as technical notification and consultation at key points throughout the proposal development and assessment process including:
  - the initial identification of need(s), purpose(s) and potential alternatives;
  - the scoping of an assessment, including the identification of valued system components;
  - the selection of the preferred alternative;
  - the application for approval; and
  - implementation monitoring and adaptation;
- with support, including resources, for important participants who would not otherwise be able to play an effective role in key steps through the process, including early deliberations and post-approval monitoring;
- with convenient and open access to assessment documentation;
- with arrangements for public hearings on cases of particular public interest and significance for sustainability.

Evaluations

8 Open application of sustainability-based decision criteria (as specified for case-particular context) is required throughout the entire process, including in evaluations and other decision making in:
- the selection of appropriate purposes and reasonable options for consideration in particular cases;
- the scoping of assessments including through the identification of valued system components by the stakeholders as well as relevant experts;
- means of enhancing positive effects as well as avoiding or mitigating negative effects;
- the nature and significance of uncertainties (about effect predictions, mitigation and enhancement effectiveness, etc.) and associated risks;
- the relative merits of the reasonable alternatives and the justification for selection of the preferred alternative as the proposed undertaking;
- means of clarifying and, where possible, resolving conflicts;
- the approval (or rejection) of a proposed undertaking and identification of appropriate conditions of approval;
- the design and implementation of post-decision follow-up, including monitoring, adjustment and, where relevant, closure and/or replacement;
- in tiered assessments, the elaboration of substantive and/or process guidance for subsequent undertakings.

Approvals and authority

9 Approval decisions must:
- be explicitly and openly justified in light of the process purposes including case specific elaborations of the decision criteria and trade-off rules;
- take the form of, or be integrated into, effectively enforceable obligations for implementation, based on assessment commitments and approval conditions, including obligations for monitoring, review, adaptation, correction and, where appropriate, replacement or closure;
- include requirements and provisions for comparison of actual effects with predicted effects (to allow adaptive management and enhance learning from experience) through the full life-cycle of the undertaking;
- in the case of strategic level assessments, provide clear substantive and process guidance for subsequent undertakings covered by the assessed policy, plan or programme.

Administration

10 Process administration must:
- be directed by an impartial authority that serves, but is at arm's length from, the centre of decision making;
- be responsible for ensuring fair process, including opportunity for effective public participation in, and critical review of, assessment work

and of the development of regulations, policies and other process guidance;
- place special emphasis on guidance for and insistence on full and fair application of all the core sustainability decision criteria and trade-off rules;
- be subject to independent auditing with public reporting.

Linkages beyond assessment

11   To strengthen the effectiveness and efficiency of the larger set of policy-making, planning, regulatory and reporting processes in which it operates, the sustainability assessment process must:
- make best use of credible broader sustainability initiatives (such as the development of national or regional sustainability strategies, indicator lists or monitoring protocols) where these can help clarify application of the sustainability decision criteria;
- encourage and facilitate cooperative application with other affected jurisdictions, following the principle of upward harmonization to ensure application of the highest standard of sustainability assessment;
- organize its decision making and reporting to facilitate subsequent regulatory deliberations;
- facilitate other initiatives to situate sustainability assessment in a larger system in which:
  - broad sustainability needs, goals and indicators are identified, in part for sustainability assessment application;
  - sustainability assessment findings, including monitoring results, are used in continuous review and adjustment of the identified needs, goals and indicators.

Efficiencies

12   Efficiencies in and beyond the sustainability assessment process must be facilitated by:
- legal language that is firm on the application of fundamental components (including application of the general decision criteria, attention to purposes and alternatives, etc.) but flexible in case elaboration, and accompanied by clear procedures for seeking exceptions;
- application, streaming and scoping provisions that match assessment effort with the significance of the cases and issues involved;
- tiered assessment provisions that allow use of strategic assessment results to streamline subsequent assessments;
- provisions that allow sustainability assessments and resulting approvals to replace less comprehensive and ill-coordinated existing process or permitting requirements, and to guide other, more specific, licensing processes;
- linkages between the sustainability assessment process and the larger system of sustainability analysis and initiative.

Appendix 6

Assessment Process Decisions that Should Involve Sustainability-based Evaluation

General process design decisions

- Setting legislated purposes.
- Establishing the basic decision criteria and making provisions for specifying the criteria for particular cases.
- Specifying process components, including:
  - general rules of application;
  - design of assessment streams (more and less demanding assessment requirements and procedures) and tiering arrangements;
  - scope of considerations (purposes, alternatives, all sustainability-related factors, full life-cycle, etc.);
  - public information and involvement;
  - open review of proposals and assessment documents;
  - approval components including potential contents of approval terms and conditions;
  - provisions for guidance (regulations, policies, guidelines, completed strategic level assessments, related plans, etc.);
  - provisions for monitoring and enforcement;
  - processes for regulation making and preparation of other guidance material;
  - linkages beyond the assessment process (to other policy-making, planning, regulatory and reporting activities).

Application decisions

- Making generic application decisions (e.g. through regulations), including:
  - lists of included and excluded types of undertakings;
  - generic allocation of defined types of undertakings to different assessment streams (class review/enhanced screening/comprehensive study/ public hearings);
  - design of case specific application processes and decision criteria (for project and strategic level undertakings).

- Making case specific decisions:
  - application to unanticipated (kinds of) undertakings;
  - exemption of otherwise included undertakings;
  - bumping unexpectedly significant cases up to a more rigorous stream;
  - bumping unexpectedly insignificant cases down to a less rigorous stream.

Assessment decisions in particular case planning and proposal development

- Establishing consultation plans and practices.
- Determining case specific purposes and needs.
- Identifying potentially reasonable alternatives.
- Identifying related undertakings and other current or reasonably anticipated undertakings that might contribute to cumulative effects.
- Designing the assessment studies including identification of:
  - relevant context and related opportunities, expectations, needs and constraints;
  - potential concerns/effects and uncertainties;
  - appropriate scope (boundaries, foci);
  - suitable methodologies.
- Specifying the basic sustainability-based decision criteria for the particular case and context.
- Evaluating predicted effects (before and after mitigation or enhancement), including:
  - positive and negative effects;
  - direct and indirect individual effects, systemic effects and cumulative effects;
  - immediate and long-term effects;
  - reversible and irreversible effects;
  - uncertainties.
- Evaluating and comparing alternatives and selecting the preferred alternative:
  - integration and evaluation of effects predictions and uncertainties;
  - comparative evaluation of advantages and disadvantages, including trade-offs.
- Preparing detailed design of the preferred alternative with specific mitigation and enhancement measures.

Review, approval and implementation decisions

- Ensuring appropriate public and expert review.
- Judging overall desirability, including comparative desirability relative to other alternatives and design options, acceptability of trade-offs and adequacy of enhancement and mitigation measures.
- Setting approval terms and conditions including obligations to meet commitments specifying monitoring and adaptation requirements covering:

- – effects monitoring and priorities;
- – compliance monitoring;
- – adaptive management plans;
- – rehabilitation obligations.
- Proceeding with implementation including appropriate:
  - – response to unanticipated effects, problems and opportunities;
  - – continuous improvement;
  - – evaluation and documentation of lessons.
- Requiring suitable reporting to facilitate learning in and beyond the assessment regime.

Index

Page numbers in *italic* refer to Figures, Tables and Boxes.
Page numbers in **bold** refer to material in the Appendices.

The Atlas Series from
EARTHSCAN

Each book in the Atlas series includes:

- 50 full-colour global and regional maps
- essential facts and figures
- extensive graphics
- historical backgrounds
- expert accounts of key regions, issues and political relations
- world table of statistical reference

'The State of the World Atlas is something else – an occasion of wit and an act of subversion. These are the bad dreams of the modern world, given colour and shape and submitted to a grid that can be grasped instantaneously'
NEW YORK TIMES on *The State of the World Atlas*

Order online at
www.earthscan.co.uk